Performing Habakkuk

Performing Habakkuk

Faithful Re-enactment in the Midst of Crisis

JEANETTE MATHEWS

☙PICKWICK *Publications* • Eugene, Oregon

PERFORMING HABAKKUK
Faithful Re-enactment in the Midst of Crisis

Copyright © 2012 Jeanette Mathews. All rights reserved. Except for brief quotations in critical publications or reviews, no part of this book may be reproduced in any manner without prior written permission from the publisher. Write: Permissions, Wipf and Stock Publishers, 199 W. 8th Ave., Suite 3, Eugene, OR 97401.

Pickwick Publications
An Imprint of Wipf and Stock Publishers
199 W. 8th Ave., Suite 3
Eugene, OR 97401

www.wipfandstock.com

ISBN 13: 978-1-61097-573-5

Cataloguing-in-Publication data:

Mathews, Jeanette.

   Performing Habakkuk : faithful re-enactment in the midst of crisis / Jeanette Mathews.

   x + 252 pp. ; 23 cm. Includes bibliographical references.

   ISBN 13: 978-1-61097-573-5

   1. Bible. O.T. Habakkuk—Criticism, interpretation, etc. 2. Bible. O.T. Drama. 3. Religious drama—History and criticism. 4. Performance. I. Title.

BS1635.2 M40 2012

Manufactured in the U.S.A.

Contents

Acknowledgments · vii

List of Abbreviations · viii

Introduction · 1

one   The Prophetic Phenomenon in the Hebrew Bible · 5

two   An Introduction to Performance Studies · 23

three   Performance Criticism in Biblical Studies · 50

four   Preparing the 'Script' of Habakkuk · 73

five   A Performance Reading of Habakkuk 1 · 97

six   A Performance Reading of Habakkuk 2 · 118

seven   A Performance Reading of Habakkuk 3 · 142

eight   Reading Habakkuk through a Performance Lens · 164

Appendix 1: Glossary of Key Terms · 201

Appendix 2: Detailed Translation of Habakkuk · 204

Bibliography · 239

Acknowledgments

This study of the book of Habakkuk was undertaken with the assistance of two grants from Charles Sturt University: a scholarship from the Public and Contextual Theology Research Centre and a research award from the Centre for Research and Graduate Training. I am grateful for the opportunities that were offered and the positive environment of scholarship and worship that I have experienced at the School of Theology of CSU in Canberra.

I have received helpful comments on this text from colleagues who continue to inspire and critically examine my work. In particular, I acknowledge Matthew Anstey, Thorwald Lorenzen, and David Neville.

My thanks also go to my family for their unfailing love and encouragement: my husband John Clark and my sons Daniel, Benjamin and Joshua Mathews-Hunter.

This book is dedicated to the memory of David Hunter, with whom I began the journey of biblical scholarship.

Abbreviations

1QpHab	Qumran *pesher* of the Book of Habakkuk
8HevXIIgr	Nahal Hever Greek scroll of the Minor Prophets
ABD	David Noel Freedman, editor. *The Anchor Bible Dictionary*. New York: Doubleday, 1992
ASV	American Standard Version
Barb	Barberini Codex
BCE	Before the Common Era (= BC)
BDB	Francis Brown et al. *The New Brown-Driver-Briggs-Gesenius Hebrew and English Lexicon*. 1906. Reprinted, Peabody, MA: Hendrickson, 1979
BHS	Biblia Hebraica Stuttgartensia
CE	Common Era (= AD)
CEV	Contemporary English Version
cp	Common plural
cs	Common singular
EJ	Fred Skolnik et al. *Encyclopaedia Judaica*. 2nd ed. Farmington Hills: Thomson Gale, 2007
ER	Mircea Eliade, editor. *The Encyclopaedia of Religion*. New York: Macmillan, 1987
ESV	English Standard Version
fp	Feminine plural
fs	Feminine singular
G	Göttingen edition of Septuagint (Greek)
GKC	E. Kautsch. *Gesenius' Hebrew Grammar* 2nd ed. Translated by A. E. Cowley. Oxford: Oxford University Press, 1910
GNT	Good News Translation

HALOT	Ludwig Koehler and Walter Baumgartner. *The Hebrew and Aramaic Lexicon of the Old Testament*. Leiden: Brill, 2001
IBHS	Bruce K. Waltke and M. O'Connor. *Introduction to Biblical Hebrew Syntax*. Winona Lake, IN: Eisenbrauns, 1990
JB	Jerusalem Bible
JM	P. Joüon and T. Muraoka. *A Grammar of Biblical Hebrew*. Rome: Editrice Pontificio Istituto Biblico, 2003
KJV	King James Version
LXX	Septuagint
mp	Masculine plural
ms	Masculine singular
MT	Masoretic Text
MurXII	Wadi Murabba'at texts
NEB	New English Bible
NIB	Leander E. Keck, editor. *The New Interpreter's Bible: A Commentary in Twelve Volumes*. Nashville: Abingdon, 1994–
NIDOTTE	Willem A. Van Gemeren, editor. *New International Dictionary of Old Testament Theology and Exegesis*. Grand Rapids: Zondervan, 1997
NIrV	New International Reader's Version
NIV	New International Version
NJPS	*Tanakh: The New JPS translation of the Holy Scriptures according to the Traditional Hebrew text*
NRSV	New Revised Standard Version
OG	Old Greek
p(p).	page(s)
Q	Qumran text
RSV	Revised Standard Version
S	Syriac (Peshitta)

T	Targum (Aramaic)
TDOT	Johannes G. Botterweck and Helmer Ringgren, editors. *Theological Dictionary of the Old Testament*. Grand Rapids: Eerdmans, 1974–
The Message	Eugene H. Petersen. *The Message: The Bible in contemporary language*. Colorado Springs: NavPress, 2002.
TLOT	Ernst Jenni and Claus Westermann, editors. *Theological Lexicon of the Old Testament*. Translated by Mark E. Biddle. Peabody, MA: Hendrickson, 1997
V	Vulgate (Latin)
v(v).	verse(s)

Abbreviations for Biblical books follow Patrick H. Alexander et al., *The SBL Handbook of Style*. Peabody, MA: Hendrickson, 1999.

NOTES

1. While acknowledging sensitivity to use of the Tetragrammaton, my performance reading of Habakkuk has given rise to using the proper name 'Yahweh' when translating the Hebrew word יהוה.

2. Principles guiding my translation of the book of Habakkuk include a decision to translate as literally as possible from the MT, including attentiveness to pronouns, articles and verbal forms even when these are awkward in English translation. In this performance reading of Habakkuk, therefore, Yahweh will be portrayed as masculine. As will be implied below in discussions of performance as re-enactment and improvisation, this does not preclude other interpretive trajectories that might present other versions of characterisation (see, for example, Cook, "Habakkuk 3, Gender, and War," who proposes a female voice behind Habakkuk 3).

3. Biblical references are given as they are found in the MT, which sometimes means a discrepancy with English versions. This is most notable in the book of Psalms where the proscriptions of the psalms are often treated as the first verse, meaning that versification is altered throughout the psalm. Fortunately, no discrepancy exists between the MT and English translations of the book of Habakkuk.

Introduction

THIS STUDY IS MORE than just a new commentary on the ancient Hebrew book of the prophet Habakkuk. It has been read as a performance. I suggest that a great deal more can be gained when one goes beyond a mere silent individualistic reading of the book of Habakkuk. Part of the rediscovery of the oral culture as the natural home for Scripture is the recognition that in the ancient world reading was rarely an isolated pursuit. Texts that became Scripture were systematically read aloud to worshipping communities in a participatory manner. The holistic and communal nature of performance, difficult to capture in mere words, encourages a focus not just on *what* is being said but *how* it is being said, attending to sounds and silence, visual images, the physical senses, appeal to the emotion, intellect, and experience.

Reading Scripture as a performance, therefore, is consistent with the way it was originally communicated. The *Oxford English Dictionary*'s first definition of performance is "the accomplishment or carrying out of something commanded or undertaken; the doing of an action or operation." The performance of Scripture could be defined as carrying out or doing the words and traditions that have been preserved, embodying them in the reader. This definition of performance also emphasizes its active and continuing nature: the 'process' that is inherent in performing. The creation of the performance piece is as relevant as its presentation. Defining performance in this way forms a contrast with the concept of *theater* that derives from a root meaning "a place for viewing"[1] and thus concentrates on the actual presentation, dividing performer from spectator. While a performance is distinguished from other forms of communication by being "framed in a special way,"[2] the focus in performance studies is never only on the spectacular qualities

---

1. Jackson, *Professing Performance*, 13.
2. Bauman, "Performance," 262.

of a performance. Many performances aim to impact audience *and* performer as well as transforming the social spaces they inhabit.

The aim of transformation is seen especially when performance becomes protest, such as the Sebastian Acevedo Movement against Torture during the Pinochet regime in Chile. Members performed public ritual acts portraying the practice and effects of torture, exposing the clandestine practices of the state.[3] Examples of public protest expressed through embodied presence can be found universally, ranging from small groups such as the Black Sash movement in South Africa or Mothers of the Disappeared in Argentina to large public gatherings such as Gandhi's symbolic marches or hunger-striking students in Tiananmen Square. Such actions aim for media exposure and education of the public as well as transformation of political or social agendas, believing that dramatic action can achieve such aims more effectively than speech alone.

The canon of Judeo-Christian Scripture as the founding texts for faith-based communities also functioned to shape identity and practice, aiming to transform the listeners and their world. Hence, as Habakkuk is read through the lens of performance, I am not primarily interested in seeing Habakkuk acted out as a piece of theater, or asking whether it was ever presented in that way. Instead, attention will be paid to the aesthetic dimensions of the prophet's message and to the way in which those aspects present the message in order to motivate the audience to action. This 'performance reading' aims to examine the processes that gave rise to the message of Habakkuk in the midst of a crisis situation and that invite re-enactment to allow it to have relevance to new crises in new generations.

This study begins with a discussion of the book of Habakkuk as a prophetic book in relation to the Hebrew Bible as a whole. This enables us to better understand its historical and literary background. Chapter 1 also examines the current state of prophetic studies to show which interpretive influences are important in understanding the book and its message.

To do justice to reading Habakkuk from the perspective of performance studies I have sought to avoid a common problem articulated by Davis as a "lack of two-way interaction between adherents of performance studies and academics in other disciplines who claim performative territory, making use of the power of 'performance' as an explanatory

---

3. Wells, "The Drama of Liturgy," 179–80.

metaphor without regard for the implications of such claims."⁴ Thus, chapter 2 examines literature from the multi-disciplinary field of performance studies to elicit common themes and features that may be sought in the book of Habakkuk. The survey in chapter 3 of Biblical scholarship identifying performance criticism as a methodological tool shows that this type of investigation has not been systematically attempted. Where 'performance' has been utilized, it has frequently been at the level of metaphorical application, warranting the critique of Davis. This study attempts a deeper conversation with performance studies by analyzing an entire Biblical book as a performance. Chapter 4 discusses compositional and interpretive issues in relation to Habakkuk and establishes the 'script' of Habakkuk to be analyzed.⁵ Chapters 5–7 examine the text as a performance by way of the themes and features isolated earlier.

Arguably, Scripture is especially open to the aims and emphases of performance studies. In performance studies knowledge is transmitted in holistic, embodied form and involves the researcher in the subject matter. There is a recognized 'co-investigative' dynamic in performance studies where both researcher and subject contribute to meaning.⁶ When interpreting Scripture, the investigator is very often not an impartial investigator but a faithful reader convinced that the texts are imbued with the spirit of a living God and have the potential for transforming knowledge and praxis in the investigator, the faithful community, and the wider world. Reading Scripture as performance suggests that the biblical books are scripts to be enacted rather than deposits of propositional truth. There will be and should be a dynamic interaction between the script and those researching it, and the results should bring about change in the interpreter and their ideas and actions in their own lived experience. Such an approach to Scripture contributes to addressing the long acknowledged gap between the world of the text and the world of the reader. An admitted paradox in performance studies is that the ephemeral nature and particularity of embodiment is emphasized despite the ubiquitous nature of performance in culture. This paradox is expressed well by Kershaw, "how might knowledge created by the

---

4. Davis, *Cambridge Companion to Performance Studies*, 1.

5. The original Hebrew script (MT) and my translation are found in the Appendix, along with text-critical and translation notes.

6. Davis, *Cambridge Companion to Performance Studies*, 2.

liveness of performance be transmitted in its documentary traces?"[7] Kershaw goes on to claim that new 'truth' is discovered by a process of reflexivity when contradictory universes are yoked together.[8] In similar fashion, when performative features of Scripture are enhanced, the world of the text is brought to life to interact with the present-day performer. Viewing Scripture as script is a reminder that drama itself is polyphonic. The Word of God is dialogical—in conversation with words of prophets, kings, priests, believers, and unbelievers.[9] Since no two performances can ever be the same, the documentary nature of Scripture is subordinated to its renewed re-enactment in new 'live' situations, but its 'truth' is maintained in the dynamic interaction between the text's world and the world of the faithful reader. The insights gained from reading Habakkuk as a performance along with any interpretive implications for reading Scripture from the perspective of performance studies will be the focus of the final chapter in this book.

---

7. Kershaw, "Performance as Research," 26.
8. Ibid., 27.
9. Vanhoozer, *The Drama of Doctrine*, 272.

ONE

The Prophetic Phenomenon in the Hebrew Bible

UNDERSTANDING THE BOOK OF Habakkuk in its own milieu is a necessary preliminary step prior to approaching the book via a methodology of performance studies. Who were the prophets in ancient Israelite society? What was their role? How did the prophetic literature develop alongside the phenomenon of prophecy? Is there any significance in the fact that Habakkuk is the eighth book in the Book of the Twelve Prophets?

The most commonly understood meaning of the word 'prophet' is a predictor of the future. Hebrew Bible scholars have long stated that this is not the best description for the characters known as prophets in the Bible, arguing that the speeches and writings of the prophetic books are primarily concerned with analysis and interpretation of their own historical times. Despite this affirmation, not only has the popular meaning persisted in the understanding of the general community, it was clearly the common view of early Christian writers of New Testament documents who understood the prophets as forerunners of Jesus Christ whose messages were directly related to the events of Jesus' life, death, and resurrection.[1] Such an understanding is encouraged by the arrangement of books in the Christian canon, where the prophetic books come at the end of the Old Testament, in contrast to the Hebrew Tanakh where the prophetic books follow on immediately after the Pentateuch and precede the Writings.

1. See amongst others Matt 1:23/Isa 7:14; Matt 2:15/Hos 11:1; Matt 3:3/Isa 40:3–5; Matt 9:13/Hos 6:6; Matt 21:5/ Zech 9:9; Mark 11:17/Jer 7:11; Mark 14:27/Zech 13:7; Mark 15:28/Isa 53:12; Luke 4:18–19/Isa 61:1–2; John 12:38/Isa 53:1; Acts 8:32–33/Isa 53:7–8; Rom 11:26–27/Isa 59:20–21; 1 Cor 15:55/Hos 13:14; 1 Pet 2:24/Isa 53:5.

By applying the message of Hebrew prophetic literature to interpreting the life and teaching of Jesus Christ, Christian interpreters have 'updated' their Scriptural heritage and engaged in a process of what I would call 'improvisation,' an example of 'faithful re-enactment' of Habakkuk by reading communities whose reading has been shaped by their history and experience, including the advent of Jesus Christ. Nonetheless, the starting point for this study is the book of Habakkuk as found in the Hebrew Bible and the phenomenon of prophecy developed within the community of Jerusalem in the period stretching from the monarchic era to the second temple community in the Persian era.

The first part of this chapter will introduce three major issues in prophetic studies: first, the concept of the 'prophet' as an individual; second, the development of 'prophetic literature'; and third, recent developments in studies of the Book of the Twelve. It will demonstrate how an understanding of the shaping of prophetic traditions in the Yehud community of the Persian period has influenced research and how a variety of literary approaches to Biblical material have challenged old assumptions in historical-critical studies. The second part of this chapter will position the book of Habakkuk amongst the prophetic traditions of the Hebrew Bible. Finally, some preliminary comments will be made as to how a performance approach can be helpful in the study of prophetic literature.

PROPHETS AND PROPHETIC LITERATURE

The Hebrew words most commonly used to refer to prophetic figures are חזה (*seer*); ראה (*diviner*); איש האלהים (*the man of God*); and נביא (*prophet*) (with its feminine counterpart נביאה [*prophetess*]).[2] The last term became the established term for prophet as indicated by the frequency of its use across traditions, although there is no firm consensus about its root meaning. The common element in these terms is that they refer to individuals who functioned as intermediaries between the human and divine worlds.

These four terms are used throughout the Hebrew Bible, but inconsistently in the books identified as prophetic literature. Thus there is a discrepancy between the individuals identified as prophets in the

---

2. Gafney's book, *Daughters of Miriam*, is a corrective to the predominantly androcentric bias in prophetic literature scholarship that has largely ignored the presence of women prophets in ancient Israel.

various traditions and the fact that whole literary books are ascribed to an individual prophet in fifteen instances (Isaiah, Jeremiah, Ezekiel, and the twelve individual books that make up the Book of the Twelve, often referred to as the Minor Prophets). This observation has led to the development of what Ben Zvi has identified as two main foci in prophetic literature research: first, the historical characters identified as prophets, and second, the corpus of prophetic books, all of which were edited and finalized not earlier than the Persian period (538–332 BCE).[3] There is, of course, some overlap in these categories as it is those prophets whose oracles are preserved in written form who are considered by many to be the 'classical' prophets.

The Prophets as Historical Figures

Critical research tended initially to concentrate on the first of the foci mentioned above, that is, the historical characters themselves. These investigations took at least three directions: the psychological characteristics of a prophet, the relationship of the prophet to the cult and the oral nature of prophecy.

In a lengthy discussion, "What manner of man is the prophet?," Heschel identifies over a dozen characteristics of the prophet including sensitivity to God, loneliness, compassion, sensitivity to evil, and iconoclasm.[4] Focus on such characteristics led several major scholars to view the 'classical' prophets as essentially solitary figures who were isolated from the cult. For example, although very influential in the way he made links between the prophets and Israelite traditions, von Rad referred to the classical prophets as "members of a radical wing which increasingly declared its independence from the operation of the official cult"; and he states that their call accounts "[make] it quite clear that they felt very much cut off from the religious capital on which the majority of the

---

3. Ben Zvi, "Introduction," 24. These two foci are amongst the seven areas of research in recent studies in prophetic literature outlined by Tiemeyer, "Recent Currents in Research." The seven areas are continued interest in ancient near-eastern comparative studies; sociological approaches; the editorial shape of the prophetic books; the way in which prophetic words become prophetic literature; the literary presentation of the prophetic persona; newer literary approaches such as rhetorical studies and studies that bring prophetic books into dialogue with current issues such as feminist or environmental concerns.

4. Heschel, *The Prophets*, 3–26.

people lived, and dependent instead on their own resources."[5] Barton, likewise, refers to the prophets as "non-establishment figures."[6]

According to Koch, however, the fact that their words were transmitted suggests that they were not as isolated as the picture given in biblical narratives might suggest.[7] Furthermore, biblical references to 'false prophets' indicate that community discernment was needed to establish which individuals were accepted as authoritative. Most scholars concede that the prophetic phenomena were diverse, such that some individuals played an independent destabilizing role, but other active prophets were integrated into the institutional cult and their teaching was transmitted through those institutions. Comparative studies in the light of ancient near-eastern documents and artifacts have raised questions about the social location of prophets and their relationship to the cult.[8] Lines of demarcation between prophets, priests, and sages have become somewhat blurred, as have the divisions between central and peripheral prophets.

The third line of inquiry put particular emphasis on the words of the prophets. Given that very little biographical information about the prophets is available in the Biblical literature, the message of the figures and the impact on their society became the focus of attention. Prophets were recognized as oral speakers who delivered short, well-defined messages that were subsequently collected and compiled in writing. The study of these forms became a dominant method introduced in the early twentieth century and is still influential nearly a century later. The prophetic books were thus thought to be secondary compilations that needed to be examined via redaction criticism to uncover the *ipsissima verba* of the prophet so as to understand the meaning of the message in its historical context. Mowinckel supported this search for the original words but recognized the difficulty in isolating the original voice when he cautioned, "Sometimes the voice of the prophet sounds like a powerful leading melody, at other times like a deep undertone in the chorus of the tradition, and at others more subdued, flooded by the multi-stringed accompaniment of tradition."[9] More recent redactional studies have

5. von Rad, *The Message of the Prophets*, 32–35.

6. Barton, *Oracles of God*, 112.

7. Koch, *The Prophets*, 168.

8. For example, Mowinckel, *The Spirit and the Word*, 100; Nissinen, *Prophets and Prophecy*, 5–8.

9. Mowinckel, *The Spirit and the Word*, 80.

moved away from a search for original words to uncovering the text in its earliest written form, as will be discussed below.

Given the belief that the source material in prophetic literature is predominantly oral, the examination of the prophets as individuals has naturally been of interest in orality studies. Traditions that have been transmitted orally tend to follow common forms, themes and patterns. Oral studies have shown how traditions from ancient near-eastern literature, such as lamentations and curses, and from socio-cultural traditions, such as legal forms and creation themes, have influenced the prophets. Despite the variety of prophetic literature, such common forms and motifs are found across the literature. An interesting question arises as to how constrained by the traditions were the prophets and how much innovation can be attributed to the prophets? Hayes claims that the Biblical prophetic books "are often seen as conveying innovative messages for Israel, messages depending primarily not on interpretations of past traditions but on a direct insight from God that reveals a new view of past events."[10] Related to this is the question of whether the prophets had cultic or moral concerns primarily in mind. There has been a tendency to view the pre-exilic prophets as moral agitators, while the post-exilic figures have been considered to be more closely associated with the cult and priestly influences. This view resulted in an assumption that the period of the classical prophets was the 'high point' of the Hebrew Bible.[11] Prophets were seen to have matured from the earlier bands of cult prophets and were not yet eclipsed by the formal, legalistic and ritualistic approach of the Second Temple period with its priestly domination. Of course, such views can be challenged by the recognition that all prophetic literature was shaped in the Second Temple period and by studies that convincingly argue for theological concerns in all canonical books. The book of Habakkuk in fact is an example of a prophetic book influenced by the full gamut of theological, social, moral, and cultic issues.

Prophetic Literature and Its Social Setting

Over recent decades much more attention has been given to the second issue in prophetic studies, that of the corpus of books that make up

---

10. Hayes, *The Earth Mourns*, 228.
11. See, for example, Blenkinsopp, *A History of Prophecy*, 17.

the prophetic literature. A number of factors have influenced this shift in focus. These include recognition of the difficulty in separating the so-called original words of the prophets from their surrounding framework, the rise of canonical criticism that places primary emphasis on the final form of the book, and the explosion of diverse text-prominent methods including narrative, rhetorical and structural approaches, and reader-prominent methods such as reader-response and ideological approaches.

The observations both of redaction critics and scholars of the related field of intertextuality studies, that examine the use of earlier prophetic sayings and traditions in the prophetic books, has shifted the focus from the individual prophet to the compiler of the prophetic book. The highly influential view proposed by Scandinavian scholars Engnell and Mowinckel[12] that the prophets' followers or disciples compiled and transmitted their oracles has been challenged by lack of evidence for such a model: "The whole notion of prophetic disciples is an entirely speculative one, born of a purely theoretical necessity, about which we have no direct information whatsoever. In fact, in the only extensive description that we have of how a prophet's oracles came to be written down (i.e. Jer 36 . . .) no transmission through a group of prophetic disciples is involved; and in the few portrayals that we have of prophetic groups there is no indication that these 'sons of the prophets' were engaged in the preservation or transmission of their leader's pronouncements."[13]

Floyd, along with others,[14] assumes that the prophetic books are products of scribes and were not fully compiled and edited until at least the Persian period. There are, however, some variations in these scholars' approaches. For example, Floyd argues that in some cases one level of the written tradition can be traced back to the original prophets. He uses Habakkuk 2:1–5 as evidence for a written oracle as part of the original dissemination of the prophetic word.[15] Person, Culley, and Doan and Giles speak of the scribes as 'performers' who enabled the prophetic traditions to be maintained and made relevant to a new situation. The

---

12. Engnell, *A Rigid Scrutiny*; and Mowinckel, *The Spirit and the Word*.

13. Floyd, "Prophecy and Writing in Habakkuk," 467.

14. For example, Person, "The Ancient Israelite Scribe"; Ben Zvi, "Introduction"; Culley, "Orality and Writtenness"; Davies, "Pot of Iron"; Doan and Giles, *Prophets, Performance, and Power*.

15. Floyd, "Prophecy and Writing in Habakkuk," 462–81.

relationship between orality and literacy is seen to be on a continuum, with a long period of interplay between the two. Culley recognizes the dynamic interaction between orality and literacy when he states: "From a historical perspective, it may have been necessary, in order to be recognized as a genuine prophetic voice, to employ recognizable prophetic language . . . the persona of a 'prophet' was a given, even though a given capable of shifting and changing as old themes were explored and new themes were introduced. Whether a prophetic text reflects the words of a prophet or the words of a scribe, the language continues to function rhetorically."[16]

Several scholars concentrate on the scribal class as the exclusive means of transmission of prophetic traditions. Ben Zvi, for example, speaks of an elite literati class, arguing that written traditions were not widely distributed but transmitted orally by the literati.[17] Such a group would have held a high status in the largely illiterate community. Davies speaks of the phenomenon of prophecy as entirely literary.[18] He posits a model of transmission based in the archival activity of scribes, who collected and copied messages brought by intermediaries to the ruling classes, thus creating prophetic 'scrolls.' These would have been expanded over time via commentary and clarification and through the inclusion of later additions pertaining to new situations. He claims the prophetic scrolls were used for social critique, wherein the attribution of the message to a figure of the past allowed for a 'safe' method of critique, allowing the present author some anonymity. Thus both Davies and Ben Zvi speak of the importance of examining the social setting of the scribal class. Davies states: "To understand 'biblical prophecy' as an expression of social critique, we need to address less the functions of intermediaries, be they 'central' or 'peripheral,' and consider the social and ideological climate of the scribal class in Second Temple Jerusalem. How did they relate to the ruling class—Persian administrators, Judean aristocracy, priestly families?"[19]

Davies' question highlights an important issue in recent prophetic research. Attention has long been given to the role of society in shaping the prophetic literature, but whereas focus on the eighth and seventh

16. Culley, "Orality and Writtenness," 63.
17. Ben Zvi, "Introduction," 1–29.
18. Davies, "Pot of Iron," 65–66.
19. Davies, "Pot of Iron," 79.

centuries of the divided monarchies of Israel and Judah were once of special interest as the assumed background to the historical prophets, the focus is now moving to the society in the Second Temple period from the fifth century. If one assumes that the literature produced in that period reflects the issues and debates within the community that produced them, then the relationship between the various levels of Jewish society and the Persian Empire will naturally be of heightened interest. Indeed, O'Brien insists that "Persian-period texts cannot be read apart from the ideological and material dimensions of the empire in which they were created."[20] As an example of debates expressed through the writing and redaction of prophetic literature, Sweeney points to the difference between Isaiah 2:2–4 (and its parallel Mic 2:2–4) and Joel 4:9–10, whereby the former evinces a positive attitude towards the Persian Empire and the latter an ironic reversal of the tradition.[21]

These issues are of particular interest in the approach I am taking to Habakkuk. In performance studies the process of transmission is highlighted as important in itself, with less emphasis on the final literary product. The tendency towards re-enactment of the performance suggests that the social setting of those receiving the text will affect interpretation and re-presentation. A performance reading does not seek to identify precise historical details of the original book of Habakkuk, but instead stresses its ambiguous and open-ended character that allows for ongoing inspiration amongst communities of faith in times of crisis.

Studies of the Book of the Twelve

A third major issue of relevance is the relatively recent consideration of the phenomenon of the Book of the Twelve as a deliberate literary structure. Earlier scholarly works treated the prophets individually in relation to their assumed historical background. Much was made of the fact that the prophetic books do not explicitly refer to each other even though some were clearly active during the same period and intertextual references indicate the compilers of the books were aware of other prophetic writings. Until relatively recently, the prophetic books that comprise the Book of the Twelve were slotted into their appropriate

---

20. O'Brien, "From Exile to Empire," 214.
21. Sweeney, *The Prophetic Literature*, 172–73.

historical setting and usually discussed in isolation from the remaining books in the collection.

Several factors suggest that the Book of the Twelve was intended to be read as a single literary entity: mention of 'the bones of the Twelve Prophets' in the text of Sirach 49:10; several Qumran scrolls in which the twelve books are combined on a single scroll; and the evidence of MurXII and 8HevXIIgr all indicate that at least by the first century, and probably earlier, these books were viewed together. Masoretic practice was to separate Biblical books by four lines but the books in the Twelve Prophets are separated by three lines only, and Micah 3:12 is treated as the 'halfway point' for the Twelve Prophets as a whole in parallel to the halfway point indicated for each other Biblical book. If it is true that the arrangement of the Minor Prophets was not accidental, then the books should be analyzed not only separately, but also in their role as part of a larger literary work.

Much recent scholarship has concentrated on how the books were brought into relationship with each other, examining catchwords and thematic associations.[22] There have also been attempts to connect the books through an overarching theme, such as theodicy,[23] or theological organization, such as House's suggestion of a threefold 'plot' of sin-punishment-restoration underlying the order of the Twelve, linking Hosea to Micah inclusively with sin; Nahum, Habakkuk, and Zephaniah with punishment; and Haggai, Zechariah, and Malachi with restoration.[24]

An intentional chronological ordering of the Book of the Twelve is suggested by historically specific superscriptions in several of the books. The introductions to Hosea, Amos, and Micah all recall kings and

22. See, for example, Nogalski, *Redactional Processes*; Nogalski, *Literary Precursors*; Watts and House, *Forming Prophetic Literature*; Ben Zvi and Floyd, *Writings and Speech*; Nogalski and Sweeney, *Reading and Hearing the Book of the Twelve*; Petersen, *The Prophetic Literature*; Redditt and Schart, *Thematic Threads*; Sweeney, *The Prophetic Literature*; Seitz, *Prophecy and Hermeneutics*; and Redditt, *Introduction to the Prophets*. Not all contemporary scholars of the Book of the Twelve, however, agree that the collection was deliberately edited to be read as a unity. Ben Zvi, "Twelve Prophetic Books," 152–54, suggests that proponents of this view engage in circular arguments whereby evidence is found because of the assumption of unity. He points out a number of text markers suggesting the individual books were intended to be read on their own. These include titles and incipits that do not refer to any prophet other than the subject of the book in question, highly particular conclusions and the 'individual flavor' of books seen in quotations from other sources modified to fit with the book's theme.

23. Everson, "The Canonical Location of Habakkuk," 169–70.

24. House, *The Unity of the Twelve*, 63–109.

events from the eighth century BCE, the period of Assyrian domination. Nahum, Habakkuk, and Zephaniah refer to the fall of the Assyrian empire, the prominence and subsequent decline of Babylon and the judgment of Jerusalem, respectively. The books of Haggai and Zechariah mention the post-exilic Persian emperor Darius. Difficulties arise, however, when recognizing that there is different ordering of the books in the various traditions, especially the MT and LXX.

Challenges arise for any interpreter of this collection of prophetic books who must both do justice to the specific historical background of the individual witnesses and, at the same time, understand its role as part of a unified collection. The focus for this particular study is to read the individual witness (Habakkuk) as a distinctive performance, capable of re-enactment across time. Nonetheless, its placement in the Book of the Twelve is undoubtedly significant both chronologically and theologically. As will be discussed in Chapter 2, performance is characterized by self-reflexivity, universality, embodiment, process, and re-enactment. One cannot help but reflect upon process, re-enactment, and universality given that twelve compositions have been brought into correlation with each other and continue to interact with each other and with the reader in the light of new knowledge and different historical circumstances, a process aptly described by Seitz as 'affiliated witnessing.'[25]

THE BIBLICAL PICTURE OF PROPHECY IN ISRAEL AND JUDAH

The poem of the prophetess Deborah (Judg 5), widely considered amongst the earliest sources of the Hebrew Bible, supports the view that early forms of prophecy were connected to military and social crises.[26] Comparison with reports from other ancient near-eastern societies suggests they were connected to sanctuaries, functioning as intermediaries between the ruler and the deity and pronouncing curses on foreign enemies. While there appear to be definite phases in the development of prophecy in the Hebrew Bible period (1 Sam 3:1), the prophets of

---

25. Seitz, *Prophecy and Hermeneutics*, 119.

26. Spronk, "Deborah," argues that the historical reality behind the story of Deborah is that she was a cultic intermediary who practiced necromancy, and only in later redactions did the text attribute the term 'prophetess' to her due to Yahwistic influences. Such an interpretation, however, still attests to the tradition of intermediaries being consulted at times of military conflict.

the monarchic period understood themselves as heirs of a prophetic tradition.[27]

Stories of Samuel and Saul attest to the presence of bands of ecstatic prophets in Israel (1 Sam 10:5–7; 1 Sam 19:20, 24). These traditions are also connected with warfare against the Philistines. With the establishment of the united monarchy under David, court prophets were introduced, with Nathan being the most prominent example (2 Sam 7; 2 Sam 12).

During the period of the divided kingdom, between Solomon's death and the fall of Samaria in 722 BCE, prophetic references are most common in relation to the Northern Kingdom (Israel). The Elijah and Elisha cycles found in 2 Kings include much biographical material, although in the genre of hagiography rather than reliable historiography.[28] These prophets are portrayed as part of a prophetic community of ascetics who separated themselves from normal society (2 Kgs 2:7). Again in this period there is an association between prophets and warfare, but the role of the prophet as charismatic wonder-worker is also prominent. Although these individuals stand in the tradition of cult prophets, by virtue of their connection to large bands of prophets and their role as consultants to the kings, the traditions present them as powerful individuals with influence in the political arena.

This period raises the notion of a difference between 'professional prophets' and independent figures working in isolation from official structures. Amos claimed not to be a professional נביא (Amos 7:14) and although the term is used in the biographical *legendum* of Isaiah 36–39, it is not used elsewhere in Isaiah to refer to him. The characterization of the prophet in those chapters as a functionary in the monarchy is at odds with the sayings in the first thirty-five chapters of the book. Hosea identifies himself with the prophetic tradition (Hos 12:10), but was also aware of negative views against prophets in the community (Hos 9:7–9). Hosea, Amos, and Micah were active in the Northern Kingdom and Isaiah in the Southern Kingdom (Judah) and all were critical of the state cult and officials. There seemed to be a clear demarcation between professional prophets as functionaries, supportive of official policy, and independent prophets who were critical of it. On the other hand, the fact that oracles were delivered in public areas, often the temple, and the

---

27. Blenkinsopp, *A History of Prophecy*, 49.
28. Shemesh, "The Elisha Stories as Saints' Legends," 2.

messages were recorded and preserved and reworked for future generations implies a degree of toleration and acceptance even of independent prophetic figures.

The understanding of prophecy presented in the so-called Deuteronomic History had an important influence on views of prophecy in the Hebrew Bible. Deuteronomy's legislation regarding the role of prophets (Deut 18:9–22) reflects an attitude of segregation bordering on xenophobia, so that prophets were to be native Israelites speaking only in the name of Yahweh and were not to practice foreign modes of mediation. Yet the book of Deuteronomy does have a strong leaning towards social justice based on egalitarian principles, reflecting the interests of the 'people of the land'—a category that is often in contradistinction to the ruling elite. The 'test' for true prophecy in Deuteronomy 18:22, that the prophetic word spoken in the name of Yahweh must come to pass, subsequently gave rise to theological problems that are reflected in the book of Jonah where the announcement of doom for Nineveh by the prophet was averted by the response of his audience.

The book of Zephaniah is attributed to the period of the seventh century by its superscription identifying the context as 'the days of King Josiah' (640–609 BCE). Despite an ostensibly royal genealogy for the prophet identified as Zephaniah, the writings reflect the perspective of the 'people of the land' with its critique of the actions of priests, prophets, judges and officials in the royal court being contrasted with the 'humble of the land' who seek righteousness and humility (Zeph 1:2—2:3; 3:2–4). There are parallels with the book of Micah suggesting that Micah was edited and brought up to date during the time of Zephaniah's activity. Such re-editing of traditional material, as has been noted earlier, is a characteristic feature of the prophetic literature.

The books of Nahum and Habakkuk also belong to this period in their subject matter despite the fact they were in all likelihood edited in the Persian period. Both have foreign nations as their primary focus, Assyria and Babylon respectively. The nucleus of Nahum is usually dated to the early decades of Josiah's reign although it has clearly been adjusted to fit later scenarios. The dating of Habakkuk is less reliable but the majority of scholars date at least its first two chapters to the period of the rise of the Neo-Babylonian Empire in the early sixth century BCE. Both books pronounce oracles against foreign nations, both use hymnic and psalm-like material, and both use the mythological language of theophany that appears to have been common in cultic worship. Whereas other pre-exilic prophetic books use the word נביא in accusatory oracles against official functionaries, Habakkuk is identified as נביא in the title. The combination of unusual forms and the lack of certainty in identifying those to whom the book refers suggest it is not a book that is easily located in a specific historical time and place, an issue that will be discussed further.

The major prophet of this period, Jeremiah, stands out as an exceptional character. Jeremiah is presented as a person, not just a role. In particular, there is an increase in mimetic and symbolic actions when compared with earlier prophets.[29] Rather than the person disappearing behind the message, in the book of Jeremiah the prophet himself *becomes* the message. His life is identified with his mission and the suffering and rejection he experienced (recorded in the so-called 'confessions') indicate that his message of judgment was all-encompassing. This observation has important ramifications for the performance concept of embodiment discussed below.

According to the Biblical record, Jeremiah's forty-year mission spanned the period of Jerusalem's fall and the early period of the exile. The formerly common view that prophecy came to an end with the exile and was replaced by the ritualism and formalism of the priestly-led Second Temple community is now largely rejected. Nonetheless, prophecy underwent profound transformation in this time. A major change was the increase of written traditions under the influence of Babylonian scribal contact, such that the written word was favored over oral delivery and the wisdom of the past was viewed as more authoritative than inspiration in the present.[30] Thus prophetic books from the early post-exilic period already refer to the authority of 'former prophets' (Zech 1:1–6; 7:7). In this period it appears the Persian authorities supported the leaders of the Jerusalem cult, who were priests and temple functionaries in the absence of monarchic leaders, so the old alliance between monarchy and prophecy no longer existed. Individual and public dissent charac-

---

29. The marriage of Hosea to Gomer and the symbolic naming of their children (Hos 1–3), along with the names Isaiah of Jerusalem and his wife (the prophetess) gave their children (Isa 7:3; 8:3–4), are clearly important symbolic actions of earlier prophets. However, these represent a single symbolic action whereas there are many examples in the book of Jeremiah (and Ezekiel after him) that suggest a new appropriation of action as part of the prophetic message.

30. As proposed by Blenkinsopp, *A History of Prophecy*, 154.

terized by some of the former prophets would have been discouraged by both Persian authorities and Jerusalem leaders. The dominance of the priestly ideology can be seen both in the traditions favoring the returning exiles over the 'people of the land' who had stayed behind following the deportations (for example, Jer 24:1–10; Hag 2:10–14) and in the priestly recasting of existing narrative traditions. Examples include the reference to the priest Aaron as 'prophet' (Exod 7:1) and the conferring of prophetic charisma through the laying on of hands, a priestly function, rather than the direct inspiration of the Spirit (Deut 34:9).

The priestly influence in later prophetic literature can be seen in Ezekiel and the post-exilic books of Joel, Haggai, Zechariah, and Malachi as each of the prophetic *personae* of these individual books seem to have had a role closely associated with the temple and the official cult. The books of Chronicles, also post-exilic, emphasize the concerns of the Chronicler's own time and place, including the role of the priest, the temple, and its services.[31] According to Amit, the Chronicler had a particular view of prophecy that influenced his portrayal of history. Prophecy was the verbalization of God's will and so in Chronicles technical terms for prophecy such as "the spirit came upon . . ." and "man of God" are attributed to the Davidic kings (2 Chr 8:14) and to several other individuals holding official positions, such as army captains (1 Chr 12:19), temple musicians (1 Chr 25:1–9), Levites (2 Chr 20:14), and priests (2 Chr 24:20), as well as to named prophets, some of whom are not known in other traditions.[32]

The picture of prophecy that survives in the Second Temple period of a restored Jerusalem, as noted above, is filtered through scribal activity and shows ambivalence towards prophetic traditions. Ezra and Nehemiah, the biblical books that describe the Second Temple period, pay very little attention to prophetic activities of the time. Apart from references to Haggai and Zechariah, figures whose roles were closely associated with the temple and the official cult, prophets are referred to as figures of the past in Ezra and Nehemiah.[33] Zechariah 13:1–6 presents a

---

31. Kalimi, "Was the Chronicler a Historian?" 88.

32. Amit, "The Role of Prophecy and Prophets," 85–86.

33. The one exception, Nehemiah's reference to "Noadiah and the rest of the prophets" (Neh 6:14), associates the prophetess with Tobiah and Sanballat, the non-Israelite enemies of Nehemiah.

negative view of prophecy, implying that the canonizing of earlier prophetic traditions removed the need for new prophetic voices.[34]

A PERFORMANCE APPROACH
TO THE PROPHETIC TRADITIONS

Some preliminary comments as to how a performance approach has relevance to the field of prophetic studies are warranted here. Subsequent chapters that describe performance theory (Chapter 2) and its use in biblical studies (Chapter 3) will flesh out these issues comprehensively.

Prophecy concerns mediation and in the biblical witness mediation occurs through both individual mediators (the prophets) and a literary corpus (the prophetic writings). There is a danger, however, in viewing the prophets or the prophetic literature as mere channels for mediation. When Brueggemann states, "Because they [the prophets] are channels of communication, theological interest focuses much more on their utterances than on their personalities,"[35] he draws attention away from the important issue of embodiment. While it has been shown to be a difficult exercise to uncover the original historical figure behind a prophetic writing, in the work of redactors and compilers a prophetic *persona* is presented who is integral to the message. In a monograph devoted to Jeremiah, Polk expresses the essential link between the *persona* presented in the text and the text itself: "the text's intention—what through its grammar, syntax, tone, thematic structure, etc. it aims to do—is the delineation of a prophet who in circumstances of extreme conflict enacts in his speech the meaning of his life and message."[36] This link between person and message is especially shown in the symbolic actions found in the prophetic tradition where deeds rather than the words were designed to communicate the message. Indeed, Brueggemann speaks of the narrative of Jeremiah buying a field in Anathoth (Jer 32:1–15) as a key act of hope performed by the prophet despite his announcement of Jerusalem's destruction.[37] Symbolic acts notwithstanding, performance theory emphasizes embodiment in all modes of prophetic communica-

---

34. Petersen, *Zechariah 9-12*, 127–28.
35. Brueggemann, *Theology*, 623.
36. Polk, *The Prophetic Persona*, 165.
37. Brueggemann, *Like Fire in the Bones*, 183.

tion by drawing attention to the whole communication event, not just the words.

Attention to embodiment will prevent a discussion of prophecy becoming purely theoretical. Scholars have observed that prophetic figures spoke in particular times and circumstances and prophetic literature was shaped in response to concrete events and experiences. Performance theory pays attention to the liminal moments—times of crisis or flux—where old orders are overturned and new possibilities emerge. This is reflected in the fact that the prophetic witness was strongest at times of crisis for Israel, concentrated around the political upheavals of the eighth to fifth centuries BCE. Brueggemann has paid particular attention to the 'power of imagination' that is unleashed in such crisis moments. For him, prophets are not primarily political agents or social activists, even though their activity arises in response to public crises. Despite acknowledgement that "for the prophets, talk of God always carries with it socioeconomic-political talk,"[38] Brueggemann characterizes the prophets as 'utterers' who "speak most often with all of the elusiveness and imaginative power of poetry . . . they speak in images and metaphors that aim to disrupt, destabilize and invite to alternative perceptions of reality."[39] For Brueggemann, not only are prophetic utterances spoken at liminoid moments, they can be described as 'limit expressions' in that they push the limits of imagination.[40]

Embodying messages on liminal occasions requires enactment. Matthews refers to prophets as "masters of both the silent and sounded arts" including "the ancient and universal art of gesture . . . theater without script."[41] Not just the words, but prophetic acts could be catalysts for social change. This emphasis on enactment may seem irrelevant when speaking of prophetic *literature*, yet the very process of reworking traditions for new settings, that become authoritative for a community, can also be construed as enactment.

Furthermore, the preservation and reapplication of existing traditions constitutes a process, another key performance concept. Nissinen states that prophecy is "not just words from the mouth of a prophet but

---

38. Ibid., 199.
39. Brueggemann, *Theology*, 625.
40. Ibid.
41. Matthews, *Social World of the Hebrew Prophets*, 32–33.

a process, all components of which are relevant . . . A prophecy means nothing unless it is understood, interpreted and applied in a specific socio-religious and linguistic environment."[42]

These performative characteristics of prophecy point to the necessity of an audience for a prophet. As Nissinen states, "a prophecy makes no sense if it does not meet with any response from the audience."[43] Doan and Giles also emphasize the importance of the audience.[44] For them, the acknowledgement of an audience's participation in the prophetic communicative event is what moves analysis of prophetic traditions from rhetorical criticism to performance criticism. This dynamic is also important in my performance reading of Habakkuk.

Floyd applies performance language to the issue of understanding the development of prophecy into prophetic literature. Rather than viewing the prophets as orators whose words were subsequently written down, he argues for a new concept of understanding the oral–written process by applying the aspects of composition, transmission and performance to biblical documents.[45] Each category can be an oral or a written phenomenon. Floyd points out that the modern novel is a type of literature that is entirely written, while drama is performed orally but usually composed and transmitted in writing. As noted above, prophets themselves may have used writing as an integral part of communicating their messages, and scribes very probably communicated the written traditions via oral performance. Doan and Giles verbalize this concept when they speak of the scribes as performers who are using the prophetic traditions as scripts.[46] Their study examines the process of prophetic performance being transformed into written documents and looks at the nuanced relationship of performance and power that operate between oral and written deliveries. For them, the scribes take the prophetic message and capture, rearrange and even usurp it by committing it to writing. They argue that the authoritative embodied aspect of prophecy is transformed by the creation of the prophetic character in the script, in other words, by the creation of the 'prophetic drama.'[47] This idea will be further discussed in Chapter 3.

42. Nissinen, "What is Prophecy?" 29.
43. Ibid.
44. Doan and Giles, *Prophets, Performance, and Power*, 105.
45. Floyd, "Write the Revelation!" 123.
46. Doan and Giles, *Prophets, Performance, and Power*, 21.
47. Ibid., 29.

A final aspect of the discussion of prophets and prophetic literature that could be construed as a feature of performance is that of the re-use of older traditions in new settings. The terms 'intertextuality' and 'inner-biblical exegesis' are commonly used to describe this phenomenon of 'rewriting.'[48] In scholarship on the Book of the Twelve, Steck and his students have been influential in tracing the interpretation and actualization that contributed to the shaping of prophetic books in the process of their transmission.[49] Such a process provides a precedent for later faith communities seeking to make Scripture relevant for their day. If this process of intertextuality (or inner-Biblical exegesis) is understood as re-use of material in a new setting, it can be likened to the performance concept of improvisation. In performance terms, improvisation depends on knowledge of a set of formulas and themes, meaning that a connection to the past is maintained despite the new setting. It has long been noted in prophetic studies that there is borrowing and re-use of oracles and motifs by later prophets. Examining such a phenomenon in the book of Habakkuk by way of the concept of improvisation may shed light on the community that produced this ancient text.

In my view, those issues of special interest to the scholars of prophetic literature today—the transformation of prophetic witness to prophetic literature, the second temple context for the final redaction of the literature, the particular shape and editorial activity in the Book of the Twelve, and the ongoing role and place of the prophet in keeping the traditions relevant to new settings—will be elucidated substantially by approaching the text via performance criticism. It is through performance that the Word of God remains active and relevant over many generations. As Boda and Floyd have stated: "The Word of God which once spoke in living tones through the great prophets of Israel's history did not fall silent and inactive when the era of the written word began to replace the living voice of prophecy. As men collected the words of these prophets, and pondered the Word which had spoken through them, it proved to have continuing vitality and relevance to address them as they were challenged, judged and stirred by it to hope and faithfulness in successive generations and widely differing circumstances."[50]

---

48. See Miller, "Intertextuality in Old Testament Research," for a survey of scholarship on intertextuality.

49. See Steck, *The Prophetic Books*, 127–90.

50. Boda and Floyd, *Bringing out the Treasure*, 208.

TWO

An Introduction to Performance Studies

This chapter seeks to provide a thematic overview of the field of performance studies as it exists across a range of disciplines. Features pertinent to an examination of an ancient text through a performance lens will be isolated and described as a prelude to revisiting them in chapters 5–7 in the examination of the book of Habakkuk.

A decision needs to be made with regard to how to organize the material: chronologically, via particular theorists, or thematically. My approach has been a mixture of the latter two options, with a greater emphasis on pertinent themes. Performance criticism is used not just in the analysis of theater, but in a broad range of disciplines, including the arts, literature, linguistics, and social sciences. It is useful to examine the work of theorists who have applied performance studies to non-theater situations. Despite the breadth of disciplines that make use of performance theory, there are some themes that emerge as common to such an approach. The five themes that I have drawn out are *self-reflexivity* (where the performer is aware of the separation between self and role); *universality* (recognizing that performance is a holistic means of communication and therefore relevant to a broad range of experiences); *embodiment* (in that knowledge is participatory rather than abstract); *process* (the actual activity of the performance is as important as the completed event); and *re-enactment* (all performance is based on a pre-existing model). Each of these themes will be elaborated below and in subsequent chapters I intend to examine whether they can also be found when reading the book of Habakkuk.

Features that are important in enacted performance must also be considered when addressing Habakkuk as a 'performance.' In applying the features of author and script, actor, audience, setting, and improvisation to the book of Habakkuk, I believe we can draw out new insights and emphases. This chapter will give a general introduction to performance studies and then discuss the themes and features that have been identified as common to a performance approach.

OVERVIEW OF PERFORMANCE STUDIES

The genesis of performance studies has been attributed to many different sources, leading Sullivan to state "performance theory resides in a series of cross-fertilizing questions posed by scholars in some disciplines to investigators in others: linguistics, cultural anthropology, sociology, performing arts, ethno-medicine, comparative law, social psychology, and ethnomusicology."[1] In recent times 'performance' has also been taken up by theologians and biblical scholars as a method of analysis.

Along with the breadth of interest is a corresponding lack of clarity in definition. Carlson answers the question "What is performance studies?" by claiming that it is "an essentially contested concept."[2] Schechner, in his introductory text to performance studies, states, "The one overriding and underlying assumption of performance studies is that the field is open. There is no finality to performance studies, either theoretically or operationally. There are many voices, themes, opinions, methods, and subjects."[3] It is possible to state in broad terms, however, what proponents of performance studies are seeking to do. Walker notes that, against the trend of modernism towards the 'textualization' of culture, performance reclaims the material body in official cultural discourse with an emphasis on "*actors acting* upon the world."[4] It could be said that the concept that the world is 'a book' is being replaced with the idiom 'all the world is a stage.'[5]

In some fields performance has long been central, such as anthropology and cultural studies, but in others it has only recently emerged as a significant concept. For example, the field of linguistics was for a time dominated by Chomsky's theory of 'generative grammar,' where the formal structure of language with its abstract idealized rules was the

---

1. Sullivan, "Sound and Senses," 5.
2. Carlson, *Performance*, 1.
3. Schechner, *Performance Studies*, 1.
4. Walker, "Why Performance?" 149, author's italics.
5. Bial, *The Performance Studies Reader*, 57.

focus of linguists, while the performance of language, 'natural speech,' was considered deviant and imperfect, marked by grammatically irrelevant features. Yet anthropologists[6] and functional-cognitive linguists[7] have emphasized that performance is as important for communicative competence as grammar. Likewise, departments of literature and philosophy that once taught oratory and elocution came to relegate such performative skills as inferior to text criticism. Walker views the division between the study of literature and the study of theater and the separate development of professional institutions and departments in universities as the origin of the historical split between 'text' and 'performance.' She celebrates the return of performance as a dominant trope in the late-twentieth century, since print based scholarship excludes a whole realm of communication marked by vocal (and bodily) signification.[8]

Nonetheless, the reclaiming of performance as a metaphor still necessitates for many a separation from classic theater. Hence the term 'performative' is invoked by those who wish to describe a performance without the connotation of artificiality or superficiality that usually accompanies the term 'theatrical.' The term is also used linguistically to refer to words that perform an action (performative) rather than state something (constative), an idea attributed to Austin.[9] Goffman applied the concept of performance to everyday behavior, claiming that performing happens all the time as a person takes on a role, tells a story, or enacts a strip of restored behavior.[10] Turner similarly uses the language of drama to describe social interactions and social change[11] and in their introduction to *Social Performance*, Alexander and Mast claim that action in the present, or re-enactment of past performances in the present, constitutes a tenet of performance studies.[12] In recognition of this, another basic tenet is that performances are never static but always changing.[13]

6. For example, Hymes as referred to by Bauman, "Performance," 263.

7. For example, Langacker, *The Cognitive Basis of Grammar*; Tomasello, *Constructing a Language*.

8. Walker, "Why Performance?" 149.

9. Austin, *How to Do Things with Words*, 1–11.

10. Goffman, *The Presentation of Self*, 15-16.

11. Turner, "Universals of Performance," 8–18.

12. Alexander and Mast, "Introduction," 15.

13. Bial, *The Performance Studies Reader*, 215.

The rise of interest in performance methods across disciplines has arguably been closely connected to the interests of a postmodern culture. An emphasis on multi-faceted experience fits with the multiple perspective view of postmodernism and its suspicion of the hegemony of imposed meta-narratives. Hassan, an early postmodern theorist, cautiously characterized postmodernism in terms that could equally be applied to 'performative' activity: "open, playful, optative, disjunctive, displaced, or indeterminate forms, a discourse of fragments, an ideology of fracture, a will to unmaking, an invocation of silences."[14] Hassan contrasts the attitudes of the movements by speaking of modernism's 'work-in-itself' (finished, complete and unchanging) with postmodernism's 'work-in-progress' (incomplete, undetermined and fluid).

Conquergood, professor of performance studies at Northwestern University prior to his death in 2004, summarized the breadth of intention and influence of the field of performance studies in helpfully alliterated points: artistry, analysis, activism, or, creativity, critique, civic engagement. In his words: "We can think through performance along three crisscrossing lines of activity and analysis. We can think of performance (1) as a work of *imagination*, as an object of study; (2) as a pragmatics of *inquiry* (both model and method), as an optic and operator of research; (3) as a tactics of *intervention*, an alternative space of struggle."[15]

Such a threefold approach aims to overcome the entrenched division between scholars/researchers and artists/practitioners, retaining an imaginative-creative dimension of scholarship alongside a critical-intellectual component of artistic work. It also emphasizes the importance of scholarship's contribution to the life of the community. My examination of the book of Habakkuk adopts such a three-dimensional structure. The *artistry* of the book will be demonstrated through its translation, an *analysis* will be achieved through a performative reading and its potential for *activism* will be the focus of Chapter 8, exploring the effect such a book can have.

---

14. Hassan, "The Question of Postmodernism," 125.
15. Conquergood, "Performance Studies," 318, author's italics.

PERFORMANCE THEMES

Self-reflexivity

Bauman describes how performances reflect cultural expression, not in the simple sense of a mirror's reflection, but in the sense of making culture conscious to both the performer and the viewer. He deliberately avoids the still oft-used term 'reflective' that suggests that 'art follows life,' and instead uses the term 'reflexivity' in order to highlight the way performance has a formative impact on culture itself.[16]

Performance self-consciously uses formal features of communication in order to transmit meaning. These include movement in dance, language, and gesture demanded by script, tone in music, and so on. A social-psychological sense of reflexivity is at work whereby the performer takes the role or perspective of another while still being aware of his/her own separated self. Osipovich distinguishes performance from every other social occasion by highlighting the concept of 'pretence'—a pretence on the part of the performer that the interaction is somehow other than it actually is and an awareness on the part of the observer that pretence is occurring.[17] As will be further discussed below, some performance artists challenge the boundaries between pretence and real life, between performers and audience. A sense of self-consciousness and separateness, however, is critical to a definition of performance.

All the arts include a degree of self-reflexivity, where the creator is aware of creating from within him/herself, but in the theatrical performing arts, above all, people become an audience to themselves. As Levy puts it: "It is the nature of the actor's art to be and not to be in the role at one and the same time. Actors are 'vice-existers,' often in a typically theatrical heightened psychological state of self-referentiality, because they use their own bodies, voices and feelings to portray the characters of others."[18] Levy notes that some artists and artworks are especially self-reflexive, examples being autobiographies, self-portraits, and theatrical devices that heighten the nature of a play such as addresses to the audience.[19] Ironically, perhaps, such devices that place greater emphasis on the creator also demand greater involvement by the spectator, listener or

16. Bauman, "Performance," 266.
17. Osipovich, "Theatrical Performance," 468.
18. Levy, "The Performance of Creation," 197.
19. Ibid., 194.

audience who are 'invited' into the creative process. Carlson argues that while many cultural activities are performative, 'theatrical' performance in particular can be a powerful tool for cultural analysis and self-reflection since both performer and audience "regard the experience as made up of material to be interpreted, to be reflected upon, to be engaged in."[20] Nonetheless, the fact that 'performance' can indeed cover many cultural activities is the crux of the next theme.

Universality

Having earlier identified performance studies within postmodern culture, a word of explanation is needed to explain the way the term 'universality' is being used here. I am using the term in the sense of 'ubiquitous' rather than as a totalizing meta-narrative that applies to all situations. Because performance studies focuses on holistic features of communication rather than text alone, it is seen as a more universal method of analysis, applicable to many social, cultural, and artistic phenomena. Performance studies takes note of extralinguistic features of communication such as tone, cadence, vocal and gestured nuances. Conquergood gives the example of Negro spirituals and laments that communicate the experience of slavery far more effectively than reading accounts of slavery.[21] The turn from 'informative' to 'performative' analysis allows for a methodology that addresses a much more universal experience. There is also an acknowledgement of the co-investigative nature of performance studies that involves the practitioner through participation, observation and reflection on the topic of study.

The universal nature of performance has support from the field of neuroscience. Iacoboni describes the discovery of 'mirror neurons' that 'hardwire' human beings to imitate others, thus predisposing them to empathy and co-operation. A second neural system, the 'default state network' also connects people to each other as they constantly define themselves in terms of their relationships. According to neuroscience, therefore, the way others perform affects one's own performance neurologically. "While mirror neurons deal with the physical aspects of self and others . . . the default state network deals with more abstract aspects of the relationship between self and other—their roles in the society/

---

20. Carlson, *Performance*, 216.
21. Conquergood, "Performance Studies," 314–15.

community they belong to."[22] Iacoboni refers to this phenomenon as 'embodied cognition' in that "our mental processes are shaped by our bodies and by the types of perceptual and motor experiences that are the product of their movement through and interaction with the surrounding world."[23]

These neurological insights have been expressed philosophically by the term *mimesis* championed by theorists such as Auerbach and Girard. The recognition that humans are mimetic creatures, whose desires and ideas are based on the desires and ideas of others, carries the positive potential for empathy and the negative potential for conflict and violence. Auerbach traces the way literature represents the reality of everyday life across a wide span of literature from the Bible and ancient Greek writings through to twentieth century novels.[24] Mimetic desire is the foundation of Girard's understanding of human individual and social behavior, where the desire to acquire the object that another desires can lead to violent conflict and scapegoating. Girard observes that in children "imitation precedes consciousness and language,"[25] a fact that supports his mimetic theory. Like Iacoboni's insights mentioned above, Girard's writing shows he believes mimesis can be a force for good: "It is the structure and dynamic enabling human beings to open themselves to the world and engage in loving relationships."[26]

Many theorists have focused on ritual as a performance-like feature of human life.[27] Anthropological and ethnographic studies have shown that all cultures use ritual. Whether consciously or not, these rituals serve to exemplify and reinforce the values and beliefs of the group that perform them. Alexander speaks of ritual as a 'successful' performance whereby cultural meaning is transferred from actor to audience who 'believe' in the role the actor is playing. He suggests that as societies grow larger and more complex, ritual becomes less central and less convincing. But Alexander argues that the goal of modern secular performance,

---

22. Iacoboni, *Mirroring People*, 257–58.
23. Ibid., 92.
24. Auerbach, *Mimesis*.
25. Girard, *The Girard Reader*, 277.
26. Ibid., 290–91.
27. For example, Goffman, *The Presentation of Self*; Grimes, "Ritual Studies"; Schechner and Appel, *By Means of Performance*; Turner, *From Ritual to Theatre*; Turner, "Universals of Performance."

"whether on stage or in society, remains the same as the ambition of sacred ritual. They stand or fall on their ability to produce psychological identification and cultural extension. The aim is to create, via skillful and affecting performance, the emotional connection of audience with actor and text and thereby to create the conditions for projecting cultural meaning from performance to audience."[28] He speaks of this as achieving 'fusion' whereby the performance is authentic and persuasive.

Grimes shows that there is a significant overlap between ritual studies and performance studies when he points out that the field of ritual studies has moved away from traditional religious studies by focusing on performance and action rather than analyzing texts and social contexts.[29]

Performance theorists highlight the presence of performance in everyday life, including political gatherings, sporting events, religious gatherings, communication, and play. Linguistic studies and semiotics have pointed to the performative nature of much communication, where the success of the communication is understood not as conveying 'truth' but in achieving action. Such discussions range from the classic example of a celebrant stating "I now pronounce you husband and wife" (a 'perlocutionary act') to utterances that may have a certain force such as ordering and warning ('illocutionary acts'), terms developed by Austin.[30] Performance terminology is appropriate for such analysis because drama is interactive rather than descriptive. Psychological studies also find the language of performance helpful in describing behavior, recognizing that all social behavior is 'performed' to some extent and social relationships can be seen as 'roles.' As noted already, Goffman was one of the first theorists to apply performance to everyday life ('social drama'), but unlike the more common tendency to focus predominantly on the performer, Goffman stresses the effect of performance on an audience.[31] The relationship between actor and audience will be discussed further below.

---

28. Alexander, "Cultural Pragmatics," 54–55.
29. Grimes, "Ritual Studies," 422.
30. Austin, *How to Do Things with Words*, 94–108.
31. Goffman, *The Presentation of Self*, 1–16.

Embodiment

An important feature in performance studies is the celebration of embodiment, especially in a culture where much communication is remote, as noted by Kirshenblatt-Gimblett: "At a time when media—and, in particular, digital technologies—have altered our relationship to the material world, including our very own bodies, Performance Studies has much to offer to an understanding of materiality, embodiment, sensory experience, liveness, presence, and personhood as they bear on being-in-the-world and as they are mediated by technologies old and new."[32]

For Conquergood, the central value of performance theory is its emphasis on embodiment. As he compares 'map' and 'story' as 'different ways of knowing' he refers to the first as propositional knowledge (the view from above) and the second as participatory knowledge (the view from a body). He adds that both ways of knowing must interact for effective knowing: "Performance studies struggles to open the space between analysis and action, and to pull the pin on the binary opposition between theory and practice. . . . Performance studies brings this rare hybridity into the academy, a commingling of analytical and artistic ways of knowing."[33]

This aspect of embodiment, according to Weber, is what defines theater amongst the arts: "A certain assemblage of bodies: whether of actors, puppets, musicians, or spectators, *all sharing the same space*, has always set theatre apart from the other arts, such as painting, sculpture, literature, architecture, and music, which could be performed before isolated audiences and in which the mimetic medium did not require the simultaneous presence of actor and audience."[34]

Performance art, growing as it did out of the visual arts, has placed a great deal of emphasis on embodiment. The performer is the artist, deliberately pursuing the idea of embodiment, wanting to focus on the present body rather than an absent text. Academic discussions of such performances have been inspired and challenged by poststructuralist theorists such as Derrida, in whose writings presence and absence are in interplay rather than in opposition.[35] The question of whether spoken language is privileged over written language and the implications for

---

32. Kirshenblatt-Gimblett, "Performance Studies," 49–50.
33. Conquergood, "Peformance Studies," 311–12, 318.
34. Weber, *Theatricality as Medium*, 297, author's italics.
35. Derrida, *Writing and Difference*, 108.

the role of the script in performance will be discussed below. Derrida argues against the notion that presence can be immediate, claiming that all performance conforms to an iterable model.[36] Nonetheless, whether immediate or repeated, performance is 'enactment'—dependent upon the process as well as the interaction between 'actor' and 'audience' as will be further explored below.

Process

The term 'performance' harbors some ambiguity, since the use of the noun can suggest accomplishment or execution of a specific action or the enactment of a script or score. Performance studies, however, emphasizes the actual activity of the artist or actor, not just the completion of an event or action. As Bial notes, "One of the basic tenets of performance studies is that a performance is not a static finished product. Performances are always in-process, changing, growing, and moving through time."[37] This emphasis on process is particularly reflected in the growing sub-discipline of performance studies emerging from the University of Sydney known as 'Rehearsal studies.'[38]

Because the focus in performance is acting in/upon the world and the dynamic relationships between social, political and cultural spheres can be effectively spoken of in performance language, many historians and anthropologists describe culture in terms of performance. As noted above, the rituals and traditions of particular cultures can be seen as a community's performances, but these performances can also shape and define the values and beliefs of cultures.

The emphasis in performance studies upon action in the world reflects the last of Marx's widely circulated *Theses on Feuerbach*, published by Engels, namely: "The philosophers have *interpreted* the world in various ways; the point however is to *change* it."[39] As noted earlier, in linguistic terms 'performative utterances' are not just descriptive but capable of constituting social reality. A broader view of performance beyond mere entertainment raises ethical questions in relation to the

---

36. Ibid., 247–49. This claim was challenged by experiments such as Artaud's 'Theatre of Cruelty' that aimed for immediate audience reaction and will be further discussed below in the section on 'audience.'

37. Bial, *The Performance Studies Reader*, 215.

38. McAuley, "State of the Art," 5–6.

39. Engels, *Ludwig Feuerbach*, 84, author's italics.

effect of the performance. Nonetheless, even those engaged in 'mere entertainment' will characteristically aim to give a performance that challenges, changes, or moves their audience. The existence of censorship in entertainment is a reminder that performance can adversely affect those observing and is often thought to require careful monitoring. With regard to media violence, Iacoboni's discussion of mirror neurons raises the potential for imitative violence alongside the positive 'force for good' recognized in mimetic behavior.[40] Alexander and Mast point out that in many real-life performances such as peace marches, political protest and the like, societal change is the desired outcome.[41] As Zarrilli observes: "Performance as a mode of cultural action is not a simple reflection of some essentialized, fixed attributes of a static monolithic culture but an arena for the constant process of renegotiating experiences and meanings that constitute culture."[42]

Schechner describes political street protest as 'direct theater,' in the mode of carnival. In an article analyzing the 'theater' of street protest he notes that some street action brings change, such as Eastern Europe in 1989, but others end with the old order restored, such as Tiananmen Square in the same year. He states: "When oppressed or angry people sense a weakening official power, they take to the streets. Their carnival can last only so long; every Mardi Gras meets its Ash Wednesday. Whether that Wednesday will see a new order or the return of the old cannot be known in advance."[43]

Re-enactment

There is widespread agreement that performances are based upon pre-existing models, scripts or patterns. Therefore performance is seen as the presentation of rehearsed behavior—'restored behavior' in Schechner's terms[44] or 'pre-formance' according to MacAloon.[45] Carlson writes "all performance involves a consciousness of doubleness, according to which the actual execution of an action is placed in mental comparison with

---

40. See Iacoboni, *Mirroring People*, 208–9.
41. Alexander and Mast, "Introduction," 15.
42. Zarrilli, "For Whom Is the King a King?" 16.
43. Schechner, "Invasions Friendly and Unfriendly," 98.
44. Schechner, *Performance Studies*, 34–36.
45. MacAloon, *Rite, Drama, Festival, Spectacle*, 9.

a potential, an ideal, or a remembered original model of that action."[46] Nonetheless, these theorists acknowledge that there is not mere repetition at work. Accordingly, the concept of 're-enactment' becomes important. Past performances are re-enacted in the present, albeit with small revisions of familiar scripts and always with the knowledge that change will come about in the re-enactment. These 'small revisions' that serve to alter or undermine tradition are spoken of in different ways. Turner's influential terms 'liminal' and 'liminoid' refer to sites in cultural performance that are open to negotiation: the 'in-between' places where rules may be ignored.[47] As an anthropologist he refers to initiation rituals as a prime example of such liminal experiences. Bakhtin similarly refers to the global tradition of carnival as marking "moments of crisis, of breaking points in the cycle of nature or in the life of society."[48] During such events new laws reign, social roles are suspended or inverted (often through use of costumes and masks) and new ideas are tested. Bakhtin's terms 'carnivalization' or 'carnivalesque' capture this idea. The question of how much revision is possible, or preferable, in relation to the original 'script' is open for discussion, with the issue of authority in the foreground. In the field of biblical narrative studies Alter has spoken of the 'narrative art' in a biblical text in which there is a balance between convention (established tradition) and innovation. He speaks of this as 'necessary' in a literary creation, "the necessity to use established forms in order to be able to communicate coherently and the necessity to break and remake those forms because they are arbitrary restrictions and because what is merely repeated automatically no longer conveys a message."[49] Whether in relation to retelling a narrative or any other form of performance, change is inevitable in the light of new experience and it may therefore be argued that change allows a tradition to live on in a new context.

This theme of re-enactment raises the issue of interpretation. Since re-enactment is not mere repetition, the choices made by the director and performer, the messages conveyed through setting, and the knowledge and experience of the audience will combine to provide a unique experience in each performance. Some argue that an interpretation must

46. Carlson, *Performance*, 5.
47. Turner, "Universals of Performance," 11, 14.
48. Bakhtin, *Rabelais and His World*, 9.
49. Alter, *The Art of Biblical Narrative*, 62.

not significantly depart from the author's original intention,[50] while others allow more freedom to the interpreter.[51] This is an important issue in the interpretation of a script that is in fact Scripture. While the canonical text remains normative in a Christian interpretive endeavor, there is an equally important place for faithful interpretation by the community. Where 'correct' interpretation is made problematic by a lack of clarity in the author's intention, several different interpretations each may be 'faithful performances.'[52]

PERFORMANCE FEATURES

The above survey of performance studies shows that the rubric of performance has been used as an analytical tool more broadly than in relation to theater alone. When performance is viewed from a more traditionally theatrical stance, however, many pay homage to Greek theater as foundational and continue to use the terminology and features of these Greek origins. Around 600 BCE followers of the Dionysian cult moved beyond ritual to perform creative myths about the gods, using a chorus and an independent character (the so-called first 'actor') and following a plot line entailing exposition, complication and denouement. The basic Greek categories of epic, lyric, and drama, with the latter divided into tragedy and comedy, still form the basis of many dramatic analyses of literature including biblical literature. Drama inherently involves a multiplicity of characters and voices that allows for multiple perspectives and opens itself to alternating movement of stories and experience.

Burke's development of a dramatistic 'pentad,' although primarily developed for analyzing human motivation, has been influential in performance studies. His five key terms are "what was done (act), when or where was it done (scene), who did it (agent), how he did it (agency), and why (purpose)."[53] These are further developed by Pelias in his text *Performance studies: The interpretation of aesthetic texts*, a study that also seeks to apply insights from performance studies to aesthetic texts in-

---

50. For example, Friedman, "In Defense of Authenticity."

51. For example, Barthes, "The Death of the Author."

52. For example, the translation of an obscure Hebrew word may affect interpretation. In Habakkuk, the terms "Shigionoth" (Hab 3:1) and "Niginoth" (Hab 3:19b) are obscure, yet their meaning may be important for understanding how the script is to be performed. See discussion in Chapter 7.

53. Burke, *A Grammar of Motives*, xv.

cluding biblical poetry. Pelias describes four distinct speakers amongst the 'Agent' category as Creator, *Persona*, Performer, and Audience.[54]

Although performance criticism, as has been seen, can be used outside of theater studies, the language of theatrical performance remains relevant and useful. Drawing partially from Burke and taking note of Pelias' refinement of his categories, the five theatrical features of author and script, actor, audience, setting, and improvisation are able to provide a framework through which to interpret other phenomena. Author and script corresponds to Burke's 'act' and Pelias' 'Creator.' I am using the term actor in a similar way to Burke's 'agent' and, as will be seen below, to cover both '*Persona*' and 'Performer' as used by Pelias. Audience is a category ignored by Burke[55] but, as will be seen, essential to any concept of performance. Setting corresponds to Burke's 'scene' and improvisation is a category that relates to the 'how' of Burke's pentad. As was noted in the above discussion of re-enactment, performance relies on pre-existing models but is never mere repetition. A degree of improvisation is thus implied in every re-enactment. While utilizing these conventional features of theatrical performance in my analysis of Habakkuk, it will be evident that application to a new context may involve re-imagining their traditionally understood properties.

Author and Script

Although these categories could be considered separately, similar issues arise in any discussion of the role of the author, or the role of the script for a performance. Departments of theater studies have traditionally placed a greater emphasis on the foundational text than its performance, analyzing and critiquing plays from their scripts and considered performances of those plays an 'interpretation' of the text. Indeed, Conquergood comments "scholarship is so skewed toward texts that even when researchers do attend to extralinguistic human action and embodied events they construe them as texts to be read."[56] Given that theater studies grew out of schools of literature it is not surprising that until recently literature has dominated analysis: a traditional division

---

54. Pelias, *Performance Studies*, 52.

55. Unless it could be construed as "purpose," a correspondence that would be logical when one considers that "audience transformation" is a common intent in performance (see discussion of "audience" below).

56. Conquergood, "Performance Studies," 313.

of literature into epic, lyric, and drama (and their counterparts prose, poetry, and drama) all assume a foundational text.

In oral cultures performers were the presenters and carriers of the culture, a point well made by Rhoads in relation to the Second Testament period, particularly in his discussion of the probable scenario in the delivery of Paul's letters to different churches.[57] In traditional theater, however, Pelias makes the point that performers do not have the same responsibility as writers for maintaining cultural continuity. For example, an actor may be dealing with a religious or political subject but is not seen to be the authority on that subject.[58] In print culture a clear separation can be discerned between the creative acts of writing and performing whereby performers have come to depend on writers more than vice versa. Interestingly, a recent article by playwright Williamson undermines this assertion when he describes writing specifically for actors, commenting: "Playwrights were named playwrights in Elizabethan times because, like shipwrights, it was a very hands-on profession. Always tinkering. Always listening to the actors and trying to make it a little better."[59] One could also see this in relation to creating poetry or music, and one may even view the redactional process behind biblical texts in a similar fashion. It was noted above that a key characteristic of performance theory was that of 'process' but in relation to a script it is when the script is acted out that the dynamic process can be seen since the script itself is often considered a completed work.

And yet, the rise of performance art with its close relationship to the visual arts and non-text contexts such as circus, sideshow, and parade, has brought an acknowledgement that performance does not have to be wedded to literature. Supra-literary aspects including plasticity, looks and gestures, music, and variables in film all play a part in understanding a performance. Conquergood claims that print-based scholarship excludes a whole realm of communication, partly in reference to the non-literary features outlined above and partly as a social class phenomenon. Literacy has always been a middle-class to upper-class privilege, with academia being dominated by these social strata, while performance can be identified in all societies at all social levels. This

---

57. Rhoads, "Performance Criticism—Part 1," 128.
58. Pelias, *Performance Studies*, 30.
59. Williamson, "Retire? Just a Mitty Fantasy," 19.

observation underlies Conquergood's appeal for the necessity of a hybridity of text and performance in any approach to performance studies.

Another issue related to the text is that of authority, discussed by Worthen. Does the authority lie with the author, the text itself, or the performance of it? Noticing a "surprisingly romantic sentimentality" in theater studies that opposes "'performance' (transgressive, multiform, revisionary) to the (dominant, repressive, conventional, and canonical) domain of the 'text,'"[60] Worthen suggests the prejudice against 'texts' stems from an implicit understanding of them as vessels of authority. Rather, he argues, texts should be thought of in three interwoven ways: "(1) as a canonical vehicle of authorial intention; (2) as an intertext, the field of textuality; (3) as a material object, the text in hand."[61] He suggests the first two categories are similar to Barthes' distinction between 'works' and 'texts,' where the former represent authorial intention that must be interpreted and therefore could be described as "authoritarian, closed, fixed, single, consumed" and the latter represent an open field that is free to be interpreted separately to the author's original intention, therefore "liberating, open, variable, traced by intertexts, performed."[62] Sherwood also uses Barthes' work when she contrasts 'readerly' (lisible) texts and 'writerly' (scriptable) texts: "The readerly text is a classic text: it does not disturb the reader but reinforces her expectations and gratifies the desire for a unified meaning and narrative closure. The writerly text . . . enlists the reader 'no longer [as] a consumer' but as a 'producer,' or co-writer, of the text."[63] Sherwood's analysis would support Worthen's statement: "Barthes' sense of the *text* is self-consciously performative."[64]

When the text is a script that is intended to be performed, the issue of authority is especially relevant. Is a performance to be a faithful rendition of a text, or does a text only reach its essential meaning in the circumstances for which it was originally intended, that is, a stage performance? Moreover, given that every performance is unique, a question is raised as to whether one rendition of an original script is more 'authoritative' or 'faithful' than another.

---

60. Worthen, "Disciplines of the Text," 11.
61. Ibid., 11.
62. Ibid., 12; compare Barthes, "The Death of the Author," 155–64.
63. Sherwood, *The Prostitute and the Prophet*, 84.
64. Worthen, "Disciplines of the Text," 12, author's italics.

According to Friedman: "Authorial intentions do not entirely restrict the meaning of a work. Any playtext signifies far more than its author consciously incorporates into its composition, and the same collection of dialogue and stage directions may convey completely different ideas, unforeseen by the author, when encountered by audiences in later times and places."[65] Nonetheless, against a tendency to deny the author's voice, he claims that any text has a range of meaning that can be identified and authentic performances are "*enactment[s] that express one version of the significance of a text that demonstrably falls within that text's range of meaning.*"[66] He spells this criterion out by means of examples from Shakespeare's plays, concluding that a production approaches authenticity "to the degree that it abides by what the text demands or encourages and avoids what the text discourages or forbids."[67] Osipovich goes further in countering the view of theatrical performance as an interpretation of a literary work by noting that not all performances are script based, and, further, as all performances are unique they are also "essentially un-scriptable."[68] He emphasizes the characteristic of embodiment in performance when he argues that while interpretation of a script is a crucial component of performance, the critical factor is the live encounter of actor and audience. These categories are the focus of the next two sections.

Actor

Clearly there is a close relationship between actor and the other aspects of performance. In traditional theater the actor presents the work of the author/creator, adopting the *persona* at the focus of the work. Various dramatic techniques have explored the relationship between actor and *persona*,[69] opening up the question of 'pretence' in performance.

---

65. Friedman, "In Defense of Authenticity," 36.
66. Ibid., 38, author's italics.
67. Ibid., 50.
68. Osipovich, "Theatrical Performance," 462.

69. A well known example is 'Method Acting' popularized in the 1930s, where actors try to replicate real life emotional conditions under which the *persona* operates. This method was influenced by the Russian actor and director Stanislavski, whose 'system' focused on developing artistic truth on stage by teaching actors to 'live the part' during performance. At the other end of the spectrum is Brecht's 'Epic Theatre' movement, which intends that the audience is always aware it is watching a play, so that techniques are utilized that distance the audience from the play. It should be clear to

Performance theory has been critiqued at this point, especially when used as a metaphor in everyday life. Where is the place of integrity if 'performers' are 'putting on an act' or 'hiding behind a mask'? This is a particular objection encountered in literature that deals with issues of religious belief under a performative rubric and may be one of the reasons that the early church was suspicious of theater. The use of the theater for persecution and its connection with loose morality added to that view.

Pelias explores the relationship between actor and *persona* when he claims all communication is performative. He states there is always a separation between the actor and the *persona*, since being able to stand outside of the *persona* and make judgments about one's performance is essential to a good performance (as was seen in the discussion of self-reflexivity above). Nonetheless, he also states performing is not a means of hiding one's real self, but "a process in which individuals display and create themselves through the roles they elect to portray."[70] Pelias claims performance is such a central part of how humans communicate that "we might best classify humankind not as *homo sapiens*, the intelligent species, but as *homo histrio*, the performing species . . . Through the act of performing, people make their lives meaningful and define themselves."[71] Goffman also claims that people constantly 'play a part,' whether unconsciously or consciously (in his words: convincingly or cynically) and he approvingly quotes Park who states: "It is probably no mere historical accident that the word person, in its first meaning, is a mask. It is rather a recognition of the fact that everyone is always and everywhere, more or less consciously, playing a role . . . It is in these roles that we know each other; it is in these roles that we know ourselves."[72]

In the narrower realm of stage performance, one question facing actors is the amount of freedom and responsibility allowed to them in relation to a script. As Bruno states in relation to musical performances in particular: "When we listen to a performance of a work, we are in part

---

the audience that the actors are not actually the characters they are portraying, so they speak directly to the audience, refer to the choices they have made, self-consciously exaggerate gestures, etc. See Brecht, "Short Description of a New Technique," 93–104; and Stanislavski, "Intonations and Pauses," 386–91, for descriptions of their techniques.

70. Pelias, *Performance Studies*, 6.

71. Ibid.

72. Park, *Race and Culture*, 249; quoted in Goffman, *The Presentation of Self*, 19.

interested in 'hearing the work,' but we are also interested in *how* the performance realizes the work, what its performers do with the musical material, and even in qualities of the performance that are independent of the work at hand, such as level of instrumental virtuosity, or sheer beauty of timbre."[73] Thus actors/performers have a key role in a successful performance. Indeed, Glavin claims "in so far as they are skilled at what they do, those actors must of course be producing affect. Masters of perlocution, they are stirring, rousing, thrilling, exciting, irritating, angering, appeasing—the list goes on—the audience. Affect, we may well claim, is the intended effect of all their telling."[74]

As noted already, the relationship between actor/performer and *persona* is an interesting one that has been explored in a variety of ways. Pelias relies on a traditional view of theater in which performers portray 'characters' unrelated to them and scripted by others when he describes the characteristics of the *persona* as being presented through a literary frame while a performer acts through a theatrical frame. In much performance art, however, there is a blurring of the distinction since performers frequently perform as themselves; conveying aspects of their own personalities.

The role of the director is another important aspect of performance with a close relationship to the actor. Directors as artistic visionaries, making decisions on the interpretation of the text and its staging in a performance, are a relatively late addition to the theatrical world, as are dramaturges—those responsible for helping the director to make sense of the script both for the players and for the audience. Dramaturges take responsibility for researching the script and preparing the text for performance, often 'translating' it for a new context. Wilson speaks of the roles of the dramaturge and director in aiding an audience's interpretation of the performance: "Contextualization, adaptation, historicization, and period transfer are simply frames upon which the director and dramaturge hang the canvas of the text."[75]

Directors and dramaturges assist actors in creating successful performances, but, as mentioned above, the more recent phenomenon of performance art has challenged these traditional roles by blurring the

---

73. Bruno, "Representation and the Work–Performance Relation," 361, author's italics.

74. Glavin, *After Dickens*, 31.

75. Wilson, "Literary Theory and Dramaturgy," 13.

divisions between creator, actor, director, and work. Throughout history popular forms of performance, such as jugglers, minstrels, and animal shows, have been looked upon with suspicion, at times being outlawed by the rulers of the land. Such non-scripted activities have a close relationship to contemporary performance art. It is not until the 1960s or 1970s that performance art can be readily identified, but the alternative theater movements of the early twentieth century provide a link back to a similar critique of conventional theater. In both cases there was a striving for reality, where role-playing and mimesis would be removed from performance, or at least recognized for its artificiality.

Performance artists often used their own bodies and everyday experiences in their 'acts'—an oft-quoted example being that of Chris Burden's *Shoot*, in which a friend literally shot him in the arm with a handgun, removing all elements of pretence and make-believe from the event.[76] Such acts understandably have a fascination for media and audiences. Performance artists have been quoted as being amazed at how accepting audiences will be of very provocative acts and how willing to engage themselves in such acts. Sherwood claims that sensation is integral to performance art and she has explored the relationship between performance art and the Israelite prophets as she finds a similar intention on the part of prophets to shock their audience.[77] Having an impact on the audience, however, is not limited to performance art. In a concluding coda to his book, entitled "An apologia for theater," Carlson describes theater as an opportunity for a community's self-reflection, functioning as a mirror but also an aid to shape cultural perceptions in community. He states: "This makes 'theatrical' performance, whether it takes the form of 'traditional' theater or of performance art, a special (if not unique) laboratory for cultural negotiations, a function of paramount importance in the plurivocal and rapidly changing contemporary world."[78]

Audience

An audience is essential in any discussion of performance. The nuances of the role of an audience may be debated but, as Wollheim puts

---

76. The event took place in 1971 and is described in Carlson, *Performance*, 113.
77. Sherwood, "Editorial to Prophetic Performance Art," 1.1.
78. Carlson, *Performance*, 214.

it, "the value of art, as has been traditionally recognized, does not exist exclusively, or even primarily, for the artist. It is shared equally between the artist and his audience."[79] Bial's definition of performance relies on the presence of a 'spectator' when he says "the term 'performance' most commonly refers to a tangible, bounded event... [or] events that involve a performer (someone doing something) and a spectator (someone observing something)."[80] There is a growing interest, however, in overcoming the division between actor and audience. Some projects have made this an aim, such as Artaud's 'Theatre of Cruelty,' that attempts to engage with suffering through theater and to involve the audience so they are not just spectators.[81]

Osipovich claims the necessary conditions for theatrical performance are liveness and enactment: liveness entails actors and audience members sharing the same space at the same time and enactment means the pretense (and awareness of this) that the performance is somehow other than itself.[82] By contrast Boal describes audience ignorance as an essential component of 'Invisible Theatre,' a performance event in which actors create a scene within an ordinary community setting, such as a restaurant: "During the spectacle, these people must not have the slightest idea that it is a 'spectacle,' for this would make them 'spectators.'"[83] Generally, however, performance art and performance artists rely on audience participation and reaction as part of the 'performance.' Indeed, McAuley speaks of "the performance contract: for an activity to be seen as a performance there needs to be a certain intention on the part of the performer and a corresponding awareness on the part of the spectator, or *vice versa*."[84] From re-enactments of historical events with costumed performers acting out real life[85] to videotaping reactions of spectators at

---

79. Wollheim, *Art and its Objects*, 86.

80. Bial, *The Performance Studies Reader*, 57.

81. Artaud's aims have been interpreted more strongly than this: according to Arrandale he wanted to violate the "self-protective distance between stage and audience," to develop a theater that "wakes us up heart and nerves... overwhelm the spectator in such a way that he cannot be left intact... having the effect of shocking and transforming us." Arrandale, "Artaud and the Concept of Drama," 104–5.

82. Osipovich, "Theatrical Performance," 469.

83. Boal, "The Theatre as Discourse," 82.

84. McAuley, "State of the Art," 2.

85. Carlson, *Performance*, 109, notes that "by the mid 1980s there were over 650 living history homes and communities in the United States." In Australia an example

installations,[86] the interactions between performers and spectators are integral to the event. The inclusion of audience participation, however, is not a phenomenon restricted to performance art. Fiddes points out that in *The Tempest* Prospero turns to the audience at the end of the play, asking for prayer, forgiveness, and mercy: "The convention of asking the audience pardon for a faulty performance has merged with the need to live a life of forgiveness. The barriers between art and life are being broken down. We had thought that Prospero was safely locked away on the stage 'in a play,' but with a shock we find that he is drawing us into the reality of his own story . . . The drama has not finished after all, and we feel that it never will be."[87]

Even those who speak of audience in terms of spectators rather than participants still acknowledge the critical role of the audience in the performance event. Pelias speaks of the role of the audience as having three stages: first, they must become engaged by being empathic and receptive; second, they must show sensitivity combined with knowledge of theatrical and textual conventions; and last, they must reflect on the experience.[88] Audiences, for Pelias, must critically evaluate performances with aesthetic and ethical considerations in view. This active role, however, still falls short of the full engagement of audiences spoken of elsewhere.

Pelias' reference to ethics raises the question of whether audiences are expected to change in the light of performances. Glavin argues that this is an aim of modern theater, stating that theater has always aimed to move its audience, but it "always kept its audience moving more or less in place, passively stimulated, unchanged, indeed unchallenged, in feeling or belief."[89] In the new, modern theater, however, "not only do

---

would be the Sovereign Hill gold mining town at Ballarat, Victoria, where employees dress in period costume for the benefit of tourists.

86. A famous example of cultural performance art in the 1990s was a performance piece created by Guillermo Gomez-Pena and Coco Fusco titled *Undiscovered Amerindians* (see Carlson, *Performance*, 201–4). The display parodied the practice of exhibiting indigenous people in fairs, shows, and circuses, and had an unexpected reaction of viewers, over half of whom believed the fictitious identities were real. The cultural implications of the event and its reactions were analyzed in a 1993 documentary titled *The Couple in the Cage*.

87. Fiddes, "Story and Possibility," 30.

88. Pelias, *Performance Studies*, 144–45.

89. Glavin, *After Dickens*, 32.

the spectators become part of the work of performance but the key goal of that performance becomes the spectators' transformation . . . self-consciously modern theater set out to make things not only new but different, to make something happen, in the audience even more than on the stage."[90] Likewise, Doan and Giles comment: "One of the dynamics investigated by performance criticism is the interplay among spectator, actor, and character. A powerful outcome of the interaction among these three is the formation of a social identity or the propagation of a shared belief that becomes owned by a spectator. The power of a performance is often judged by its ability to move an audience, to enable the audience to think, believe, or act differently."[91]

Smith explores the use of audience response in undermining dominant societal structures as she examines Shakespeare's *The Taming of the Shrew*. The presence of an 'on-stage' audience by virtue of the 'play within a play' technique means that the reaction of the on-stage audience encourages the off-stage audience to react in certain ways. For example, the unfavorable labeling of Petruchio's actions and the laughter of the on-stage audience encourages those watching to conclude that his portrayal of dominant husbandly behavior should not be taken seriously.[92]

Iser's works on reading of texts provides a parallel emphasis on the 'reader' as the equivalent to the 'audience' in performance. He argues that the study of a literary work should include not only the actual text but "in equal measure, the actions involved in responding to that text"[93] because literature has two poles: the artistic (the author's text) and the aesthetic (the realization accomplished by the reader). The 'work' is between these poles, neither reducible to the text nor to its realization.[94] In a sense the reader cannot be separated from the text, as "literary texts take on their reality by being read, and this in turn means that texts must already contain certain conditions of actualization that will allow their

---

90. Ibid.
91. Doan and Giles, "The Song of Asaph," 35–36.
92. Smith, "Performing Marriage with a Difference," 306.
93. Iser, *The Act of Reading*, 21.
94. Clearly Iser does not share Barthes' view of the 'work' nor of the difference between author and reader. Barthes claims that classic criticism has not paid attention to the reader and thus "the birth of the reader must be at the cost of the death of the Author." See "The Death of the Author," 142–48. By contrast, Iser's model of reading gives equal weight to authorial intention and reader response.

meaning to be assembled in the responsive mind of the recipient."[95] Iser's model of an 'implied reader' is a functionalist model, emphasizing that if what is to be communicated is of any value it is not the 'meaning' that is important, but the 'effect,' thus echoing the expectation that audiences will be transformed.

Iser's discussion, though focused on literature, borrows from speech act theory and includes an emphasis on extra-textual aspects of communication. He states, "if all linguistic actions were explicit, then the only threat to communication would be acoustic. As what is meant can never be totally translated into what is said, the utterance is bound to contain implications, which in turn necessitate interpretation."[96] In performance, such extra-textual aspects are of even greater importance for the audience's interpretive and affective responses. Likewise, the setting or context of a piece of communication is essential.

Setting

Shusterman proposes that viewing art as performance is a way of bringing together two opposing ideas about art. The argument of naturalism is that art is deeply rooted in human nature and finds expression in virtually every culture. Natural human needs and drives, such as an inclination towards mimesis or aesthetic experience, gives rise to art forms. The historicist view suggests that art is a particular historical cultural institution produced by the Western project of modernity and it is this institutional setting that distinguishes art from the rest of life. Bringing these ideas together, Shusterman argues that to put something on stage is to put it in "a frame, a particular context or stage that sets the work apart from the ordinary stream of life and thus marks it as art."[97] The natural inclination towards aesthetic experience nonetheless needs institutions that create the social space for their staging: the *mise-en-scène* (literally: 'put in a frame'). McFague claims that "Art frames fragments of our world: paintings, poetry, novels, sculpture, dance, music help us look at colors, sounds, bodies, events, characters—whatever—with full attention. Something is lifted out of the world and put into a frame so that we can, perhaps for the first time, *see* it."[98]

---

95. Iser, *The Act of Reading*, 34.
96. Ibid., 59.
97. Shusterman, "Art as Dramatization," 367.
98. McFague, *Super, Natural Christians*, 29, author's italics.

Shusterman points out that framing allows also for heightened experience: "The scene of *mise-en-scène* is not a blandly neutral space, but the site where something important is happening. Even the very word 'scene' has come to connote this sense of intensity. In colloquial speech, the 'scene' denotes *not* just any random location, but . . . where the action is . . . a frame is not simply an isolating barrier of what it encloses. Framing focuses its object, action, or feeling more clearly and thus sharpens, highlights, enlivens."[99]

Any discussion of film or photography places a large emphasis on the framing decisions. Much information can be conveyed (or, conversely, hidden) by choice of distance, focus, angle, point of view and so on. The visual aspect of performance means that a scene can always be envisaged with or without verbal support. Monaco points out that in a filmed scene the viewer is told: "Where we are, why we are there, whom we are with, what is going on now, what has happened to get us there, who the other characters of the story are, and even suggests possible ways the story might develop—all effortlessly and quickly and without a spoken word! Paragraphs of prose are condensed into seconds of film time."[100]

Even performance art and other forms of theater that attempt to challenge the separation between art and life nonetheless rely on some sense of the frame to claim their artistic status. Framing has an additional important role, that of providing a protective environment in which disruptive passions and events can be contained, protecting both individual and society. Though an important concept, this is not a new idea, given that Aristotle spoke of the role of catharsis in theater in his *Poetics* in the fourth century BCE.

A discussion of setting must also consider the material context and the socio-historical circumstances of actors and audience in a given performance. The experiences and expectations of an audience will affect their response to the performance, so this also acts as a frame. It has been noted that a key characteristic of performance is re-enactment, and every new presentation will be affected by changes in location and circumstance. It is this fluidity created by re-enactment that is the concern of the next area of discussion.

---

99. Shusterman, "Art as Dramatization," 368–69, author's italics.
100. Monaco, *How to Read a Film*, 178.

Improvisation

The earliest written records of performance of singers in Greek rituals give evidence that performers relied on formulas and themes when telling new stories. They maintained a connection to the past even when using a new setting. This link to the past is an important aspect of improvisation. The concept of improvisation is most commonly understood in musical contexts. Young speaks of the skills needed in musical improvisation: "In order to improvise effectively, the performer not only has to have technical competence, but also needs to understand musical theory, the rules of harmony and counterpoint, the accepted conventions of development, the stylistic character of the work within which the cadenza is to figure. She has to have a sensitivity to the actual score of that work, its form, its themes and subjects, and their 'generative' potential."[101]

Wells describes the process of improvisation, claiming the well trained improviser knows how to keep a story going and does so by accepting an offer by another actor rather than blocking it and bringing the story to a halt.[102] He also speaks of cherishing a tradition without being locked in the past. Improvisation respects and builds on a tradition but allows a new situation to create new possibilities. When discussing the process of an improvised performance he describes how the actors at first have a vast array of possibilities, but once a scenario is established they must retain dramatic coherence within the established frame, allowing for the changing of the frame as the actors work with each other.

Sawyer outlines five characteristics of improvisation that are helpful in understanding its role in performance.[103] First, there is an emphasis on the creative process rather than creative product, a characteristic shared with performance in general, as noted above. Second, these creative processes are problem-finding rather than problem-solving. Sawyer explains the differences between these approaches by contrasting medieval art with twentieth century art. In the middle ages artists were commissioned, so the content of the painting was determined in advance. In the abstract art of the twentieth century the subject was found through experimentation with the form. Third, conversational language is an example of improvisation, since those engaged in the conversations do not

---

101. Young, *The Art of Performance*, 160.
102. Wells, *Improvisation: The Drama of Christian Ethics*.
103. Sawyer, "Improvisation," 152–58.

speak from a script nor is it directed, yet the constraints of a framework of conversation topic, social relationships and physical environment impact on the direction and length of the conversation. Fourth, improvisation relies on collaboration, both between fellow actors and between actors and audience. In improvised performances, not only are the audience invited to be involved, the actors assume they share with the audience a large body of cultural knowledge and references. Fifth, Sawyer reiterates the role of the ready-made, or cliché, in improvised art. This term originates in linguistics where constructed discourse makes use of memorised clauses and clause-sequences that come 'ready-made,'[104] but is also used in jazz improvisation in reference to the store of 'licks' (a musician's own personally developed patterns) and in improvised theatrical performance when actors use short motifs or clichés already in their repertoire.[105]

Improvisation is an important concept not only in the arts, but also in social performance as Alexander and Mast note: "Performers in the present innovate, create, and struggle for social change through small but significant revisions of familiar scripts which are themselves carved from deeply rooted cultural texts—as actors in a production of Macbeth . . . mourning musicians and pallbearers in a New Orleans jazz funeral . . . or protesting mothers of Argentina's 'disappeared' children . . . the imagined past weighs heavily on the present, but actors are shown to be capable of lacing the coded past with significant, at times profoundly dramatic revisions."[106] As this quotation implies, improvisation is a form of re-enactment, which, as noted above, often occurs in liminal situations and is characterized by small changes.

The recognition that performance has the potential to provide a site for social and cultural resistance through improvisation is important when approaching Scripture by way of performance theory. Evidence of improvisation in a text or performance reflects choices made by script writers and actors in response to new circumstances including changed beliefs, settings, and audience reaction. The concept of improvisation in relation to Scripture in particular will be revisited in chapter 8.

104. Mackenzie, "Improvisation," 173.
105. Sawyer, "Improvisation," 157.
106. Alexander and Mast, "Introduction," 15.

THREE

Performance Criticism in Biblical Studies

THIS CHAPTER REVIEWS THE way in which performance theory has been used by biblical scholars in relation to biblical texts. In general biblical scholars have used performance criticism haphazardly and not necessarily with much connection to performance criticism theorists, although the interaction between the fields is strengthening. The importance of performance emerges in three fundamental ways: first, as a metaphor for the articulation of the presentation of Christian theology; second, through a focus on the phenomena of oral performance of the text both in the ancient world and the present context, and third, by considering the intrinsic performative aspects of a given text and their interpretive significance. Each of these approaches will be examined in more detail below. The last part of the chapter will suggest a way in which performance criticism can be considered a discipline for biblical research, setting out such a methodology in relation to the book of Habakkuk.[1]

---

1. It could be argued that ritual studies and linguistic studies using speech-act theory are fields of research that engage with performance studies. Both fields use similar 'performance' language but are highly specialised: the former focusing on ritual acts rather than texts and the latter using the term 'performative' in its narrow linguistic sense of the use of words to perform an action. Neither field will be considered here but an interested reader might consult Grimes, "Ritual Studies," for a description of ritual studies and Briggs, "The Use of Speech-Act Theory in Biblical Interpretation," for an overview of the use of speech-act theory in biblical interpretation.

PERFORMANCE AND BIBLICAL INTERPRETATION

Performance as Metaphor

One broad approach has been to use the language of performance as a formative metaphor in Christian theology. Von Balthasar in his five-volume *Theo-Drama* uses the metaphor of drama for Christian faith, describing how God has acted decisively through Jesus and how the believer can choose to act in response to this. Von Balthasar was concerned to articulate a method that involved the theologian, which meant opposing an 'epic' approach in which the narrator is detached from the events. On the other hand, he was not willing to dissolve the freedom of God implied in a 'lyric' approach in which the author is identified with the subject. Von Balthasar found a balance in the notion of drama, particularly due to the key aspects of linearity and sociality in drama. Von Balthasar argued that the drama of Christian faith has a story line including God's action in the death and resurrection of Jesus Christ that will be brought to its finale in the events of the Parousia. Unlike novels that come to a conclusion, there is an open-endedness in drama that encourages imagination. Unlike poetry, drama has a communitarian focus with an emphasis on dialogue and multiple viewpoints. This many-voiced nature of drama is seen in the Christian witness that is made up from many perspectives and enacted in many missions.[2]

Several authors use a musical analogy to describe the task of biblical interpretation and praxis. The points of comparison can be seen in that the central act of interpretation in music is in the performance, when the score is enacted in a place and time. Moreover, it is an act that requires an audience as well as the musicians, so is essentially a communal experience. Lash speaks of the focal expression in this performative interpretation in the celebration of the Eucharist.[3] Young uses the metaphor of improvisation when she likens the interpretation of the ancient text of Scripture today to 'cadenzas' in concertos. When an artist performs a cadenza there is the need for faithfulness to the style and themes of the concerto, but also virtuosity and inspiration in developing these in ways fitting both to the music and to the occasion. For Young this 'cadenza' occurs in the act of preaching—the means by which the

---

2. Von Balthasar's monumental five-volume work has been summarized in a very accessible "guide" by Nichols titled *No Bloodless Myth*.

3. Lash, *Theology on the Way to Emmaus*, 45.

score is interpreted for a new situation.[4] These authors perhaps reflect their own denominational traditions with a central emphasis on either liturgy or preaching. Another metaphor that is sometimes used is to view the Bible as a libretto (the text for a musical performance).[5] Page, for example, describes the faithful 'disciple' taking their lead from the text and seeking to 'live' the text in "a visceral and full-bodied process that engages all of the senses."[6]

Craigo-Snell suggests that the language of theater is useful for understanding the Christian experience: like the theater the church uses sets, costumes, lighting, and music to allow for an embodied response in a carefully chosen and adorned space; the church relies on Scripture in the same way that the theater relies on a script; both a church community and a theater company are groups focused on a common goal; Christians 'perform' Scripture when they re-enact scenes from Jesus' life, obey commandments and allow words and actions to be shaped by Scripture. For Craigo-Snell, the embodiment of the script is essential: "One can study a script as a piece of literature, but to do so is, to some degree, to miss the point. It is meant to become an event."[7] She focuses particularly on the rehearsal process as the metaphor for the Christian experience, through which one aims to 'become' the role one is playing.

Building on the idea of salvation history as a drama whereby history is divided into five 'acts',[8] Vanhoozer picks up the performative nature of drama in a thorough analysis of Christian doctrine viewed from the perspective of theater.[9] He speaks of the Bible as 'script', the cultural, social, and intellectual context the church moves in as 'setting', God as the 'actor', Holy Spirit as 'director' and pastor as 'assistant director', believers as an 'engaged audience', theologians as 'dramaturges', and so on. He speaks of the church as 'amateur, interactive theatre': performing 'for the love of it', aiming to draw outsiders in, improvising in response to new settings. Vanhoozer's engaging study moves logically from 'drama' (the story to be communicated) through 'script' and 'interpretation' to

---

4. Young, *The Art of Performance*, 162.

5. Nichols, *No Bloodless Myth*, 7; Page, "Performance as Interpretive Metaphor—Prolegomenon," 21.

6. Page, "Performance as Interpretive Metaphor—Prolegomenon," 22.

7. Craigo-Snell, "Command Performance," 481.

8. See, for example, Wright, "How can the Bible be Authoritative?" 11.

9. Vanhoozer, *The Drama of Doctrine*.

'performance.' He deals with a potential critique that such a metaphor leads only to 'play-acting' by stressing the aim of good theater for an actor to 'become the role,' and acknowledging that under a broad doctrine of election the Christian does not choose a role but responds to the 'divine casting-call.'

Wells, like Young, focuses on the performative concept of improvisation, but uses this as a metaphor for Christian ethics.[10] Like Young's 'cadenza,' he speaks of the need for connecting the past to the present by drawing on habits of character learned in worship that inform decisions to be made in new situations. In his view the church's role is to keep the drama going while relying on God to ensure that the church's performance will be properly enacted.

This approach of using performance as a metaphor has been applied more often in theological studies than in biblical studies, although, as has been seen, there has been a special focus on the interpretation of Scripture. The main drawback of this approach is that it is difficult to find an exact match between the entities of theater and church. While there are useful comparisons to be made, the application can only be in very general terms before the metaphor becomes labored. The critique that opened this chapter, that biblical scholars have not engaged with performance theorists seriously, is echoed in a 'cautionary note' offered by Khovacs based on his own experience that combines theological studies and formal training in the dramatic arts. He is concerned that Christian scholars "merely [exploit] the drama to enrich the language of theology" without "a real commitment to a theological-theatrical exchange."[11] While he values attempts by scholars such as Vanhoozer and Craigo-Snell to engage theology with the language of performance interpretation, he feels there are large areas of potential exchange that have been neglected. Moreover, despite the broad identification of performance beyond the theater, these metaphors have focused on recent manifestations of theater as director-driven interpretation of scripts. My own research has shown that, until recently, few theological or biblical scholars have engaged deeply with the scholars of performance studies and often the terms are used indiscriminately with little scholarly analysis.

---

10. Wells, *Improvisation: The Drama of Christian Ethics*.
11. Khovacs, "A Cautionary Note," 33.

Performance of *Biblical Traditions*

Important work is being done in the area of orality studies, recognizing the underlying oral nature of the transmission of most biblical traditions. By regarding the Bible as a witness to living traditions, a number of scholars have sought to examine biblical traditions from the point of view of their original existence in a largely non-literate culture. These scholars are interested in the performance *of* the material, either in its original setting or in a contemporary setting.

For a long period biblical studies was dominated by exegetical techniques that were focused on the written, fixed text, but more attention is now being given to the oral world behind the written texts of the Bible. Most work in this area has been done in New Testament studies,[12] but the work of Niditch has been of key significance in Hebrew Bible studies. She asserts that "literacy in ancient Israel must be understood in terms of its continuity and interaction with the oral world."[13] Orality studies offer an important reminder that many written traditions from the ancient world were originally transmitted and received orally. From a New Testament perspective, Rhoads claims "the overwhelming majority of first century Christians (perhaps 95 percent) experienced their traditions—including gospels, letters, and apocalypses—only in some form of oral performance."[14]

Niditch examines the interaction between oral and written cultures, claiming that they co-existed and influenced each other so that even in a society where writing and reading was common the oral culture was still highly influential. She therefore attempts to uncover the features of an 'oral register' showing oral influence in the Hebrew Bible, including repetition, formulas, and patterns of content. She proposes various models related to the type of composition explaining how oral material became written. For example, oral performances of prophets may have been recorded and preserved by the prophet's own followers or supporters and longer narratives may have been performed to audiences with the aid of written notes and shaped in response to the audience reaction and later written down: "a process whereby oral becomes written but also a

---

12. See Iverson's survey of recent research ("Orality and the Gospels") and Maxey's work on the implications for performance criticism for translation of biblical texts ("Performance Criticism—Parts 1 and 2").

13. Niditch, *Oral World and Written Word*, 1.

14. Rhoads, "Performance Criticism—Part 1," 118.

process whereby the written becomes oral and then that oral production is eventually recreated in fuller written form."[15]

Attention to the performed delivery of biblical material beyond the oral-aural mode of communication means a heightened awareness of the dynamics of performer, audience, physical location, and socio-historical circumstances of the event. Rhoads offers insights from his own memorizing and performing of New Testament books to show what has been 'missing' in biblical studies that have focused only on written texts. He speaks of his imagination being enlivened as he hears and sees the scenes in his mind: "By taking on the persona/voice of the narrator or speaker in a text, I enter the world of the text, grasp it as a whole, reveal this world progressively in a temporal sequence, attend to every detail, and gain an immediate experience of its rhetoric as a performer seeking to have an impact on an audience."[16]

An oral performance 'fills in' what is missing from a text through sounds, gestures, facial expressions, glances, pauses, pitch, volume, movement, posture, body language, and so on. While some of these elements may be explicit or implicit in the text, the performer will often have to interpret a text, and indeed should interpret a text for a new situation. When characterizing oral cultures, Rhoads claims that performers were the tradents of culture and as such were "faithful to the past (retentive) as a means to preserve group identity and fluid in the retelling (inventive) in order to make traditions relevant."[17]

Doan and Giles, professors of theater and theology respectively, have collaborated to explore the concept of performance in biblical studies in several publications. In their book *Prophets, Performance and Power*, they focus on the performance of the prophets of the Hebrew Bible. The book examines the interplay between oral and written (scribal) performance, introducing the concept of power in the dynamics of performance—how a performer such as a prophet is granted social power, how that power operates on an audience, and how it is transformed and transferred by scribal performance into a written text. Contrary to Niditch's insistence that the dynamic interplay between oral and written media persisted throughout the Hebrew Bible period,[18] Doan and

15. Niditch, *Oral World and Written Word*, 120.
16. Rhoads, "Performance Criticism—Part 1," 120.
17. Ibid., 121.
18. Niditch, *Oral World and Written Word*, 134.

Giles assume that 'ownership' of the performance is transferred from an oral audience to a much smaller group of 'literati.' Nevertheless, they envisage the process as a "continuity of performance, preserved through orality, repetition of the tradition, and the creation of the text, or script, through which the pattern of prophetic performance is preserved."[19]

Doan and Giles build on orality studies but apply further insights from performance analysis. They reject the once commonly held view of a school of prophets or disciples who preserved the oral words of the prophet in written form and instead explore the relationship between prophet and scribe with the aid of performance language. They speak of the relationship as akin to performer and script where the prophet is a performer who exercises social power through the immediacy of the performance. For the tradition to be preserved, however, the words must be recorded in a script, at which point the power of the prophet is curtailed and usurped. A script is a limitation on the performance because it controls the message. This observation is spoken of in terms of actor and character: "The scribes create prophetic *characters* out of the prophets themselves (prophetic *actors*), [characters that continue] long after the actor has left the scene."[20] The character becomes the locus of authority. The written text cannot replicate the actual experience of a prophet engaging an audience so instead creates an illusion of the prophetic experience, which Doan and Giles call "the prophetic drama."[21] In this way the message can continue to be transmitted, not only for a reading audience but also for a non-literate audience, and yet the message has been shaped by the scribe in the transmission. Doan and Giles argue this moves the power "from performer to playwright."[22]

Using the theories of orality to shed light on text critical studies, Person argues that the oral mind-set can be seen to lie behind text variants in the Hebrew Bible.[23] Since even literate scribes were members of a primarily oral society, they might have preserved texts for the ongoing life of the community in the manner of performers of oral epics rather than slavishly copying word for word. Thus, even in written form, the

---

19. Doan and Giles, *Prophets, Performance and Power*, 17.
20. Ibid., 23, authors' italics.
21. Ibid., 29.
22. Ibid.
23. Person, "The Ancient Israelite Scribe," 609.

tradition being transmitted might include unconscious changes based on personal knowledge or a tendency in the social environment.

The focus on orality in biblical studies quite correctly challenges the text-centric mindset of modern scholarship and highlights the missing non-literate aspects of communication that might well influence the reception and meaning of a tradition. It suggests a different starting point in that rather than finding the 'original tradition,' the range of variants may be viewed as evidence of a lively and ongoing tradition.

Performance in *Biblical Traditions*

Of particular interest to me are those scholars who are finding the methods of performance criticism helpful in uncovering intrinsic performative aspects in the texts as they stand. These approaches of finding performance *in* biblical traditions can be divided into: (1) those who focus on particular aspects of performance theory and apply them to a text; (2) those who see the traditions themselves as having been deliberately composed as dramas; and (3) those who illuminate the intrinsic performative qualities in the text. This book will continue in the third trajectory, furthering and deepening this approach by using the insights and methods of performance criticism in relation to the text of Habakkuk.

Applying Aspects of Performance Theory in Biblical Studies

Bakhtin is a Russian theorist whose perspectives on literature have been applied in performance studies and are being used more and more frequently by biblical scholars. In particular, his notions of the carnivalesque and dialogism, the latter sometimes referred to as heteroglossia (diversity of voices), have been utilized by both Hebrew Bible and New Testament scholars to understand the dynamics of biblical narratives.[24] The concept of carnivalization, in which normal laws are suspended, social hierarchies inverted, and misalliances of lofty with low and sacred with profane are allowed, have effectively been applied to interpretations

---

24. See Green, *Mikhail Bakhtin and Biblical Scholarship*; Bakhtin, *The Dialogic Imagination*; Bakhtin, *Rabelais and his World*.

of the stories of Ruth,[25] Esther,[26] and Ahab[27] in the Hebrew Bible and to Acts[28] and the passion narrative in Luke[29] in New Testament studies.

Newsom[30] and Stordalen[31] apply Bakhtin's concept of dialogism to the book of Job—a book that lends itself to such an analysis with its extensive use of dialogue. Tull claims that the historical source for studies of intertextuality in the Hebrew Scriptures is Bakhtin's concept of dialogism.[32] In her review article she points out that dialogism is not just searching for allusions between literary works, but draws on "all manner of language existing in the environment."[33] Doan and Giles also have a specifically performance-oriented view of intertextuality, whereby not only the words of an earlier tradition are appropriated, but also the social place and influence (performative power) of the original.[34]

Bakhtin's categories are taken from literature and easily applied to narrative, but the concept of performance art in the form of protest or provocation has also been connected to biblical texts, focusing especially on the prophetic literature. The prophets Hosea, Jeremiah, and Ezekiel have come under particular scrutiny, because of the identifiably dramatic form of their prophetic action. Hornsby, for example, refers to Ezekiel 'off-Broadway' when she speaks of the prophet's tendency to take ordinary objects and actions into the public space for display, thus disrupting societal norms.[35]

Sherwood points out that performance art differs from conventional drama "in which the author-director transmits a message through a straightforward act"[36] by blurring the distinction between actor and spectator. She speaks of the deliberate use of sensation at the heart of pro-

25. Aschkenasy, *Reading Ruth through a Bakhtinian Lens.*
26. LaCocque, *Esther Regina: A Bakhtinian Reading.*
27. Garcia-Treto, "The Fall of the House."
28. Thomas, "The World Turned Upside-down."
29. Brawley, "Resistance to the Carnivalization of Jesus."
30. Newsom, "The Book of Job as Polyphonic Text."
31. Stordalen, "Dialogue and Dialogism in the Book of Job."
32. Tull, "Intertextuality and the Hebrew Scriptures," 68.
33. Ibid., 69.
34. Their example of the re-use of Psalms 96, 105, and 106 in 1 Chronicles 16 as set out in "The Song of Asaph," 31, is further elaborated in *Twice Used Songs.*
35. Hornsby, "Ezekiel Off-Broadway."
36. Sherwood, "Editorial to Prophetic Performance Art," 1.3.

phetic language and performance: "Prophetic performers and speakers seem particularly, indeed peculiarly, dedicated to provocation and the ideal of turning the prophet and the audience inside out."[37] In the same journal of essays Brummitt shows how several incidents in Jeremiah, conventionally understood as individual symbolic acts, may be interpreted differently if viewed as performance pieces, since "performance is a complex art in which gesture can either uphold or subvert text or script—a phenomenon explored, if not exploited, by twentieth-century dramatists such as Bertolt Brecht—and such ideas of a simple univocality prove inadequate for the narratives as they now stand."[38] In one incident (Jer 19) the audience is unavoidably involved in the performance so that they are no longer merely spectators; in a second (Jer 18:1–12) the acting out of the creation of a pot from clay would undermine a simple explanation of justice that understands Israel to be at fault and deserving of punishment, since it is the potter whose actions determine the outcome of the pot. In a third example (Jer 13:1–11) the text gives no record of an audience, rendering the prophet's 'symbolic' actions nonsensical.

Stacey's study, *Prophetic Drama in the Old Testament*, also questions the way symbolic acts have been interpreted. He examines a variety of cultic actions, including processions, sacrifice, dance, and cultic drama, to see if prophetic drama can be similarly viewed as part of the cult. He claims that prophetic actions are different from other forms of action in the cult because they are single actions, unlike ritual that is repeated many times by different people. He states: "Prophetic actions must, therefore, be seen as a class by themselves. They were specific actions with a specific purpose, carried out by a peculiar kind of person, who believed himself to be, and was generally acknowledged to be, called by God, perhaps even from the womb (Jer 1:5), to this special service."[39] Stacey rejects the view that prophetic action was merely illustrating the word, or even heightening the word. Instead, he speaks of the word and the drama as two inseparable parts of the dynamic package that is the divine will.

Page also presents the idea of prophets as performers when he speaks of the prophets as "akin to present day *performance artists* and

37. Ibid., 1.1.
38. Brummitt, "Of Broken Pots and Dirty Laundry," 3.2.
39. Stacey, *Prophetic Drama*, 62.

public intellectuals for whom preaching was an all consuming passion."[40] He points out that despite the diversity of traditions the common factors between them are 'logocentricity' and 'artistry.' He does not amplify his view of them as performance artists other than a reference to being "totally absorbed by their vocation and even a bit *eccentric*,"[41] but speaks of the poetic nature of their performances. Page is concerned to encourage a closer affinity between Christian theology and the arts, a motivation that underlies his discussion of Christian performance.

The power of performance as communal protest has also been examined by several biblical scholars: for example, Lischer describes the performative intent of Martin Luther King Jr's reading of Scripture, "in order to form people who would be capable of creating a new spiritual and political climate in America";[42] and Ackermann relates the *Black Sash* movement of apartheid South Africa to biblical lament.[43]

There are many studies of the use of the Bible in the arts, such as in film, visual art, opera, and oratorio.[44] These studies tend to focus on the way the narratives and traditions have been portrayed, rather than using theories of performance analysis to shed light on the biblical stories. Thus technical issues such as framing, painting technique, use of light and shadow, use of color, portrayal of characters, and so on, have been the focus of such studies. Such studies draw attention to the non-verbal aspects of communication that are of importance in performance analysis and pave the way for a more thorough analysis of the way in which performance theory might enhance biblical studies.

Biblical Books as 'Dramas'

Some scholars argue that particular biblical books were originally intended to be performed as dramas. It is difficult to find evidence for the use of theater amongst the community that gave rise to the Hebrew Bible.[45] As outlined above, it is highly probable that most of the material

---

40. Page, "Performance as Interpretive Metaphor," 49, author's italics.
41. Ibid., author's italics.
42. Lischer, "Martin Luther King, Jr: 'Performing' the Scriptures," 167.
43. Ackermann, "Lamenting Tragedy from 'the Other Side.'"
44. See Davies, "Oratorio as Exegesis," 477, for several citations.
45. The earliest evidence for Jewish drama in antiquity is a Greek-style tragedy entitled *Exagoge* ("The Exodus") by Jewish writer Ezekiel, 'the writer of tragedies.' The date of composition is assumed to be between the second century BCE (due to its dependence upon the Septuagint) and mid-first century CE when it is mentioned

that has come to form the Hebrew Bible canon was initially transmitted orally and there was clearly interplay between oral and written culture. Some have stressed the theatrical nature of ritual that might lie behind the use of cultic psalms (e.g., Mowinckel, who refers to particular psalms as "the text for a dramatically performed procession" comprising "different acts and scenes"),[46] but a few scholars suggest that some biblical books were deliberately shaped under the influence of dramatic structure[47] or in order to be performed as a drama.[48]

Several commentators have applied a dramatic framework to the book of Isaiah, particularly Deutero-Isaiah, arguing that the book has been intended for the stage or cult. Eaton proposed a direct link between Deutero-Isaiah and an annual New Year Enthronement festival,[49] Watts claims the whole book of Isaiah was a straightforward drama,[50] and Baltzer refers to Deutero-Isaiah as a "liturgical drama."[51] The commentaries vary in the way they imagine the dramatic portrayal: Watts envisages a huge cast while Baltzer claims just a small number of actors could be used with a range of visual props.

Wilks's evaluation of these proposals is rather devastating.[52] Despite acknowledging the possibility of staged drama in Israel in the post-exilic period due to spread of Greek culture throughout the ancient world, Wilks argues that Eaton's views are undermined by a growing lack of support for New Year festivals in Israel and that neither Watts nor Baltzer explain how the drama was logistically produced.[53] Wilks finds confusion between poetic imagery and dramatic stage sets: "My primary concern with Baltzer's proposal is that he has misinterpreted the visual imagery so typical of a *poem* as a series of stage directions for a *drama*.

---

by Alexander Polyhistor. The plural epithet suggests that this author may have written other dramas on biblical themes according to Hurwitz, "Ezekiel the Poet,"649.

46. Mowinckel, *The Psalms in Israel's Worship*, 5–6.

47. House, *Zephaniah: A Prophetic Drama*; Brant, *Dialogue and Drama: Elements of Greek Tragedy in the Fourth Gospel*.

48. Watts *Isaiah 1–33*; Watts, *Isaiah 34–66*; Baltzer, *Deutero-Isaiah*; Shelton, "Making a Drama out of a Crisis?"

49. Eaton, *Festal Drama in Deutero-Isaiah*.

50. Watts *Isaiah 1–33*; Watts, *Isaiah 34–66*.

51. Baltzer, *Deutero-Isaiah*.

52. Wilks, "The Prophet as Incompetent Dramatist."

53. Ibid., 531–32.

He goes to the absurd length of presuming that virtually any image generated in the text must have been visually presented in some way."[54]

In a more nuanced study that brings the world of the theater together with the Hebrew Bible, Sherwood applies the insights of drama theory and semiotics to the prophetic book of Hosea rather than merely treating the book as a drama.[55] She argues that because the prophetic texts are rich in signs there is a connection to the world of the theater that uses semiotization, in which objects and bodies defined within the stage are bestowed with signifying power. By drawing on the theatrical qualities in the prophetic book of Hosea, Sherwood creatively re-examines the characters portrayed and the message of the book.

In another prophetic study, subtitled *A Prophetic Drama*, House finds the genre of drama the most fitting for understanding the message of Zephaniah. He proposes a dramatic framework for the prophetic book but overcomes the obvious historical objections of how, where, or if such a drama was staged by referring to the book as 'closet drama.' He states, "Closet drama . . . is composed in dramatic style, but is written without the play ever meant to be staged. The author is thereby able to concentrate on poetry and content without worrying about how the play will affect an audience . . . The importance of closet drama for biblical studies is that its existence proves a literary piece need not be staged to be drama . . . Its presence leaves open the possibility of exploring literature that has dramatic characteristics, plot, character, dialogue, etc., as drama."[56] House goes on to analyze Zephaniah in relation to plot and characterization, suggesting that the speeches mark divisions between acts and scenes. He applies the characteristics of classical drama to the book, concluding that he can "firmly establish that within a classical framework Zephaniah takes a dramatic form."[57] The book, however, cannot easily be characterized as tragedy or comedy, the two traditional sub-genres of drama. He argues the book is a mix of comic mode and "prophetic mode," the latter being a particular mix of ideas, themes, and characteristics shared between a number of biblical books.

House's characterization of Zephaniah is similar to the assessment of "tragedy and comedy in the latter prophets" made by Gottwald in an

---

54. Ibid., 539, author's italics.
55. Sherwood, *The Prostitute and the Prophet*.
56. House, *Zephaniah: A Prophetic Drama*, 50.
57. Ibid., 105.

earlier essay. Gottwald argues that in the overall shape of the prophetic books "there can be little doubt that it is the comic voice that subtends the tragic,"[58] despite the fact that the route to the comic conclusion may encompass suffering and catastrophe. He suggests that the mixtures of genres, written over long periods that make up the prophetic books, mean they cannot necessarily be read as coherent narratives, but are nevertheless open to being analyzed under the headings of plot, theme, hero or protagonist, and social context. In the ensuing discussion Gottwald concedes that prophecy may be more like forms of tragicomedy where a double plot of both tragedy and comedy are offered. In general, Israel's leaders who have brought ruin on the community are subject to the "inverted U-shaped tragedy plotline" while the community as a whole benefit from the "U-shaped comedy plotline."

The book of Job is one that has been open to dramatic readings by virtue of its framing plot of fortune's destruction and restoration. Habel's commentary on Job views the book as a carefully structured literary unit of three 'movements.'[59] Shelton builds on Habel's work and suggests the structure is dramatic, divided into three 'acts' that explore the conflict that is at the heart of drama. Where a traditional scholarly view is to see Job as an extended dialogue in an independent narrative framework, Shelton argues that the framework is integral to the drama as it sets up the conflict that is then explored and resolved in the second two parts. Using theatrical terminology she describes it as a play within a play: "In the book of Job, the framework play gives the *mise-en-scène*—the rules by which the drama will be played out."[60] Shelton believes it is plausible to see Job as drama, but given that does not fit either of the classical patterns of tragedy or comedy, and given the lack of knowledge about Semitic drama, she concludes that Job is an 'untheatrical drama'—a concept similar to House's 'closet drama.' She then brings the biblical book into dialogue with twentieth-century theatrical drama to draw out further meaning. Her study thus becomes an exercise in intertextual methodology rather than viewing dramatic qualities as intrinsic to the biblical book.

Classifying biblical books as 'closet drama' or 'untheatrical drama' may serve to highlight the dramatic qualities of a written text but, in my

---

58. Gottwald, "Tragedy and Comedy in the Latter Prophets," 84.
59. Habel, *The Book of Job*.
60. Shelton, "Making a Drama out of a Crisis?" 70.

view, ignores some important performance features, especially ignoring the presumption that all performance requires an audience. The next section describes approaches that seek to illuminate intrinsic performative qualities *in* the texts themselves that call for response by an audience.

Intrinsic Theatrical Qualities

Levy's book *The Bible as Theatre* exemplifies this approach as it provides a broad exploration of the Hebrew Bible, particularly the narrative traditions, from a purely theatrical perspective. Levy argues that despite their "equally dramatic Hebrew myths"[61] the post-exilic Jewish community did not present these myths in theatrical form, as was common amongst Greek culture, because of the sacred nature of the Scriptures for the Jewish people. He observes that the Hebrew word במה, usually translated *high place* and connected with idolatrous practice, translates as *stage* in modern Hebrew. This suggests that the sacred in Judaism "found its expression in traditional rituals, never on a secular stage."[62] It may also reveal reluctance on the part of orthodox Jews to allow the stage to 'create reality' rather than describe it. Although acknowledging that biblical books such as Esther and Ruth have often been dramatized in the Hebrew theater, Levy's aim is not to explore the influence of the Hebrew Bible on drama, but rather to seek to discover the influence drama might have on the stories of the Bible.

Levy engages with secular theorists such as Schechner and Carlson, playwrights Brecht and Ibsen and directors Grotowski and Brooks in order to throw new light on biblical stories. Characterization, dialogue, stage direction, scene design, and other theatrical concepts are used to analyze familiar texts. In many cases, he argues, the biblical 'stage-instructions' are 'built-in,' especially in regard to props, costuming, and gestures. Moreover, Levy believes these 'stage directions' can sometimes reveal hitherto unnoticed revolutionary attitudes, especially with regard to the role of women in the Hebrew Bible.

Levy maintains the role of the Bible as sacred Scripture where "the way the message is conveyed is less prominent than the message itself" by speaking of passages as "*potential* theatre,"[63] although he does suggest that *Song of Songs* may have been acted out in ancient times. As an

---

61. Levy, *The Bible as Theatre*, 3.
62. Ibid.
63. Ibid., 15, author's italics.

analytical framework, theater is three-dimensional and thus sensitive to words, gestures, the passing of time, and the significance of space. All of these aspects are explored by Levy in a variety of biblical passages.

Levy admits that some of the scenes and 'plays' from the biblical literature fall half way between the distinction of 'Dramatic Ritual' and 'Ritual Drama' as outlined by Turner.[64] He appropriately begins his discussion with the story of the calling of Samuel (1 Sam 3), an 'initiation ritual,' then examines biblical stories about women (the Levite's concubine, Deborah, Tamar, Ruth, Esther); relationships between men and women (Song of Songs, Proverbs); a number of prophets (Elisha, Jonah, Ezekiel, Daniel); and key biblical leaders (Moses, Jehu, David).

Levy's section on "prophets as performers" suggests that by the nature of their vocation prophets became performers. He contrasts theater's "willing suspension of disbelief" with the common theme in biblical prophecy of "attempts to impose belief on the unwilling" both on the part of the prophets and also the spectators to their symbolic acts.[65] Levy's treatment of the prophetic books also focuses strongly on the concept of performative speech, in which the words of the prophet combine with God's life-giving רוח (*spirit*), to achieve the prophet's vision.

Some of the helpful insights of Levy's studies include the distinction between 'on-stage' and 'off-stage' action, the role of silence in drama; the frequent use of a 'play within a play' technique; the dramatic form of dialogue that is so prevalent in biblical narratives; the importance in many stories of props, which are both real objects 'on stage' and metaphorically charged images; the dramatic characterization achieved through naming in biblical accounts and attention to the audience/spectator, especially in the section on prophets, which highlights the importance of this feature in a performance analysis of prophetic literature.

Boogaart is a biblical scholar who also argues for the inherent drama in the narratives of Scripture, particularly those of the Hebrew Bible. He claims, "The character of the Old Testament narratives clearly indicates that narratives are dramas. They are divided into scenes. Each scene contains an important encounter between the main characters . . . In each scene, third-person narration usually introduces and reinforces the dialogue. The scenes progress in dramatic fashion so that a conflict raised in the first scene develops in the middle scenes and is resolved in

---

64. Turner, *From Ritual to Theatre*, 89.
65. Levy, *The Bible as Theatre*, 10, 186.

the final scene . . . In short, narratives as they have come down to us are scripts of Israelite plays."[66]

Although Levy and Boogaart deal predominantly with narrative traditions, the same insights can be applied to non-narrative material such as the poetic prophetic books and wisdom literature. This can be seen in Anstey's study of Habakkuk that applies a similar "performative interpretation" to the book of Habakkuk, attempting to read the text dramatically.[67] Amongst other features, Anstey speaks of dramatic tension, plot twists, the significance of the settings and interjections. He particularly draws out the effect the text (as 'script') would have had on an audience and the expectation that the audience was being invited to a performance through identification with the prophet as well as shifting between third-person and second-person verbs that draws the listener in. Anstey concludes: "This is a script to be enacted thoughtfully, not mined for propositions. It provides direction for faithful re-enactments, without micromanaging the outcome."[68]

The original and fresh approach to the biblical literature as shown in the work of Levy, Boogaart, and Anstey is hampered by a lack of clarity in methodology. Anstey admits he has read the book of Habakkuk in a "relaxed style" to demonstrate the potential of a performative reading.[69] Boogaart's claim that the Hebrews "had a rich dramatic tradition" is based on an assertion that narratives can be read as drama but his comments about any ancient Israelite performance are based purely on "speculation."[70] While Levy provides a fuller study with many more examples, he analyses texts in a variety of ways, depending on the nature of the text, so that his book is more a creative exploration of interpretative possibilities than a systematic inquiry.

---

66. Boogaart, "Drama and the Sacred," 40–41. Boogaart's essay is the basis for "The Ancient Hebrew Drama Project" at Northwestern College, Iowa, directed by Professor Jeff Barker. A link to this project can be found on the website www.biblicalperformancecriticism.org.

67. Anstey, "Habakkuk the Faithful Dissident," 50.

68. Ibid., 55.

69. Ibid., 50.

70. Boogaart, "Drama and the Sacred," 39, 41.

PERFORMANCE CRITICISM: A DISCIPLINE FOR BIBLICAL RESEARCH?

Theorists such as Rhoads,[71] Giles and Doan,[72] Maxey,[73] and Wendland[74] are among those attempting to create a methodological discipline of performance criticism to be applied in biblical studies. Rhoads argues that such an approach addresses the neglect of performance as a central concept in the life of the early church while Maxey and Wendland are especially interested in the theory and practice of Bible translation.[75] Giles and Doan offer a framework for understanding a performance critical approach that will, in their view, take its place alongside other historical-critical methodologies to shed new light on the performative nature of certain portions of the Bible. Each of these scholars examines performance criticism as a broad category and gives guidelines for its application to biblical studies. They consider how it is possible to understand the significance of the history of material that was performed in a community, with various participants and with responses expected from the audience. Each has the oral culture that lies behind biblical texts firmly in mind and thus seeks to develop a methodology that draws out the remnant of oral performance to aid in interpretation. Rhoads writes, "the medium is part of the message, if not the message itself. Studying these texts in an exclusively written medium has shaped, limited and perhaps even distorted our understanding of them . . . Taking oral performance into account may enable us to be more precise in our historical re-constructions and more faithful in our interpretations."[76]

Such reconstructions, Wendland argues, are possible by being attentive to instances of intertextuality, where citations, echoes, allusions of other associated traditions would enhance the message of the text at hand.[77] The use of imagery is also important, as oral delivery enhances the visual imagination. The reactions of the audience may have altered or enhanced the transmission of the message also. Wendland concludes:

71. Rhoads, "Performance Criticism—Parts 1 and 2."
72. Giles and Doan, "Performance Criticism of the Hebrew Bible."
73. Maxey, "Performance Criticism—Parts 1 and 2."
74. Wendland, "Performance Criticism."
75. Maxey and Wendland have edited *Translating Scripture*, a forthcoming volume of essays devoted to performance criticism and Bible translation.
76. Rhoads, "Performance Criticism—Part 1," 126.
77. Wendland, "Performance Criticism," 3.

"Accordingly, PC [performance criticism] seeks to analyze *the entire hypothetical performance event*, including the complete oral composition in relation to performer and audience, their historical circumstances and social location, the physical locale and interpersonal setting, the audience's reactions, as well as the presumed rhetorical and transformative impact of the communication event as a whole."[78]

Giles and Doan interact with the insights of performance critical theorists to elicit five "core principles" that help give performance criticism its unique contribution.[79] These principles are (1) "medium transferability," recognizing that a performance is an event rather than a genre and the performative characteristics are retained when transferred to a new, written medium; (2) "act-scheme," the presentational structure of a performance that has a distinctive pattern and therefore is recognized by performers and spectators; (3) "audience formation" that occurs in the relationship between actor and audience as an event is presented and the audience responds to shared or conflicting values; (4) "iconic" and "dialectic" modes of presentation in which patterns of activity pertaining to either being (iconic) or becoming (dialectic) can be recognized and reused in future performances; and (5) "explicit" and "implicit" activities that refer to the performative patterns embedded in biblical texts such as prophesying, singing, debating, and the implicit questions arising from these activities, such as tone of voice, gestures accompanying the speech, and so forth. Such questions provide a way into the oral and performed world of the Bible and thus impact how the text might be understood. Giles and Doan are beginning to provide a methodology for examining the performative structures resident within biblical texts, thus building on Levy's approach of illuminating intrinsic theatrical qualities. As they themselves admit, the methodology is in its early stages but will become increasingly utilized in biblical studies.[80]

As has been seen from this survey, adherents of 'biblical performance criticism' are moving in either practical or theoretical directions. In both cases, the emphasis remains with the actual performance of the text: some analyze a text through the translation, preparation and performance of a text including interaction with the audience while others interact with other disciplines such as traditional historical-critical

---

78. Ibid., 4, my italics.
79. Giles and Doan, "Performance Criticism of the Hebrew Bible," 278–82.
80. Ibid., 284.

approaches as well as orality studies, ethnopoetics, rhetorical studies, and so forth, to reconstruct the probable performance parameters for the original presentations of the tradition. Both approaches are found on www.biblicalperformancecriticism.org, where links may be found to the Network of Biblical Storytellers and other similar lay networks as well as to scholarly publications.

Attempts to develop a method of biblical performance criticism in interaction with the insights of performance theorists in other disciplines reflect a more mature approach than simply borrowing the metaphor of performance and applying it to Christian theology or Scripture. While cross-disciplinary studies are susceptible to gaining only a limited understanding of each sub-discipline, valuable insights can be gained from viewing the biblical books through different lenses.

This study moves beyond the application of a performance 'concept' to a biblical book and rather asks whether it is valid to view an ancient text such as the book of Habakkuk in its entirety from the perspective of performance theory. Can performative features be found in it that will influence the interpretation of that text as a written text? Can the themes that have been identified as common to performance critical approaches be found in this ancient text also? Finally, is it a text open for re-enactment by communities of faith, not necessarily as a staged 'drama' (although that may be possible also) but as a 'script' that continues to be acted out in the life of today's faithful communities? Clearly the book has had a continuing impact in the Jewish and Christian faiths, but in what ways does a performance reading of it allow it to have a broader relevance in times of crisis beyond the Neo-Babylonian invasion of Judah in the seventh century BCE?

A PERFORMANCE CRITICAL METHODOLOGY TO APPLY TO HABAKKUK

The remaining chapters in this book will attempt to answer these questions in the affirmative by offering a 'performance reading' of Habakkuk. Chapter 4 establishes the 'script' via a new translation of the Masoretic Text (MT). I have chosen to use the MT as it has been the most influential text in Hebrew Bible studies over generations, being based on the oldest complete codex now extant.[81] The 'script' will be divided into

---

81. While recognizing the impact that the Qumran discoveries have had on textual criticism given that the Q texts are centuries older than the MT, the fact that Habakkuk

acts and scenes that will be established on the basis of changes in genre, actors, and content. In chapters 5–7 each 'scene' in the script will be analyzed according to the pertinent features highlighted in chapter 2, namely author and script, actor, audience, setting, and improvisation. Particular attention will be paid to any new insights that result from such an analysis. Each of chapters 5, 6, and 7 will conclude with a discussion of the way the themes that have been found to be common across the many disciplines that make use of performance criticism—self-reflexivity, universality, embodiment, process, and re-enactment—can be found in Habakkuk as well. I will also be examining the degree to which they are helpful in analyzing the message of Habakkuk.

PERFORMANCE DEFINITIONS

The performance themes of self-reflexivity, universality, embodiment, process, and re-enactment were described in Chapter 2 and don't need further explication, but it is important to define the way I understand the performance features of author/script, actor, audience, setting, and improvisation, since these terms are open to greater ambiguity when used outside of theatrical performance alone.

I have combined 'author' and 'script' as one category. This is indicative of a broadly 'canonical' or 'synchronic' approach to the Hebrew Bible, which understands the final text to be the major object of inquiry. This approach acknowledges that a text has emerged from a long process of composition and redaction, by more than one historical community and setting. Its final form, however, is the product that has been preserved as inspired scripture and is the starting point for ongoing reflection. The identification of the original 'author' is problematic. Even the historical circumstances giving rise to the text are partially lost in its transmission through later occasions and communities. As will be discussed in the next chapter, authorship of the book of Habakkuk undoubtedly lies with several hands across a long period, probably culminating with a final redactor in the Persian era. Nonetheless, from the point of view of a performance reading of the book of Habakkuk, I intend to represent this multi-layered process in terms of a single 'author' whose finished product, the 'script,' reflects compositional choices that transmit mean-

---

3 was not preserved has influenced my choice to base my translation on the MT in which a complete text is preserved.

ing. Performance of this script implies an openness of interpretation, inviting new meanings when read by new audiences in new settings.

I will use the term 'actor' to refer to the characters presented in the script of Habakkuk. Such terminology opens itself to the question of integrity since the script of Habakkuk is recognized as Scripture. Is the prophet only 'pretending' when expressing frustration or faith? Is Yahweh choosing to speak and act in a way that is contrary to his character? Does the enemy just 'play' the bad guy while the genuine person underneath is warm and affable? When actors perform a script, there is an implication that they have set lines that reduce their freedom as participants in the performance. This claim can be counteracted by attention to the non-verbal aspects of performance, recognizing that different meanings can be conveyed by tone of voice, posture, gesture, and expression. The same words may be conveyed in a number of different ways. The recognition of this script as Scripture does in fact affect the concept of actor I am using. Rather than performers portraying characters unrelated to themselves, the characters in this performance are acting a drama that is integral to their being. As such they could be characterized as performance artists, who use their own experiences and their own bodies in their art. Nonetheless, they act in such a way that the meaning of the script is faithfully conveyed.

When speaking of an 'audience' for this performance, I lean towards a participatory understanding such as might be described in performance art events as opposed to a view of audience as mere spectators. In other words, the performance of Habakkuk expects an audience, deliberately involves an audience and aims for transformation of its audience. This claim would be true of Scripture in general but the lens of performance highlights the need for engagement by an audience. This is seen, for example, in the direct address used at several points in the script. The term 'audience' in relation to the book of Habakkuk has multiple layers. There would have been an audience for an eighth century prophet, for the prophetic traditions as they were used and transmitted in subsequent generations, for the compilers of the canonical text in about the fifth century and for later Jewish and Christian faith communities who preserved and used the book as Scripture. Because of the privileged place Scripture holds in faith communities across generations, the identity of the audience cannot be limited to any one place and time, but continues through to the present day.

In chapter 2 the category of 'setting' was discussed in relation to *mise-en-scène* or 'putting in a frame.' Thus, when examining the setting of the book of Habakkuk, I am interested in the frame that has been used to present the message of the book. The overall historical setting of the kingdom of Judah at the time of the Neo-Babylonian empire can be inferred by the reference to the Chaldeans (Hab 1:6), but the physical, social, and cultural settings of the individual scenes are also important in conveying meaning. The discussions of setting thus gives attention to changes in grammar and vocabulary that allow division of the content of the book into scenes, as well as any physical or cultural clues that suggest a particular context such as the crisis of invasion or the cultic experience. Location and movement of the actors in the performance are also noted when attending to setting.

The term 'improvisation' has a definition that is broader than its common usage in jazz music in which a musician explores variations on a theme. It is also broader than improvised performance in the theater that usually refers to non-scripted performance. Here improvisation refers to the way in which established traditions are re-used and modified in order to convey new meanings. I use it in relation to the choices made by the 'author' of the book of Habakkuk in presenting the material and also in relation to the re-enactment of the Habakkuk material by later communities of faith that often demonstrate small revisions in the light of new situations. Similar terms I could have chosen include intertextuality, inner-biblical exegesis, innovation, and transposition, but the term 'improvisation' retains the emphasis on performance whereas each of these other expressions have been used primarily in reference to texts and musical scores.

FOUR

Preparing the 'Script' of Habakkuk

THIS CHAPTER SETS OUT some background discussion on the book of Habakkuk in relation to literary-critical issues before presenting a new translation of the book. Principles guiding this translation are given and the book is set out as a 'script' divided into acts and scenes. This script forms the foundation for the next three chapters in this book, which present a performance analysis of the three chapters of Habakkuk.

For interested readers, the second appendix to this book shows Habakkuk set in parallel columns with the Hebrew of the MT in the right hand column and my translation in the left. Each section (determined by division of the book into scenes) is followed by translation notes on pertinent exegetical issues arising from the translation.

LITERARY-CRITICAL ISSUES

Text

My translation is based upon the critical edition of the MT as it appears in *BHS*, taking into account variant readings when these are considered important. The principal ancient versions that have influenced this translation of Habakkuk include the *Habakkuk pesher* (1QpHab) from Qumran and the Greek Septuagint. 1QpHab was amongst the first of the discoveries of the Dead Sea Scrolls in 1947. On the basis of reference to contemporary events within the commentary it is assumed to have been written sometime in the latter half of the first century BCE.[1] There is some variation in word order and grammar but also several significant lexical changes, including the rendering of הכשדים (Chaldeans) as *Kittim* (*Westerners*), which apparently serves as a code for the Romans

---

1. Collins, "Dead Sea Scrolls," 90.

in the commentary. The Septuagint exists in several editions but the main Göttingen edition has been used and will be referred to as G in this analysis.

Other texts that have influenced this translation are 8HevXIIgr, a scroll of the Minor Prophets in Greek attributed to the first century CE, a second century CE Hebrew scroll of the Minor Prophets from Wadi Murabba'at (MurXII), the Vulgate (Latin), Targum (Aramaic), and Peshitta (Syriac) versions.

The many variant readings found in the ancient manuscripts and versions contribute to the text being regarded as 'problematic'.[2] Particularly notable are the significant number of *hapax legomena* spread through the three chapters (ten nouns[3] and five verbs[4]), which provides challenges for translation and interpretation.

'Habakkuk' as a Historical Figure

The book of Habakkuk begins with a reference to 'Habakkuk the prophet' but provides no information about his lineage or historical placement other than the reference to the Chaldeans in Habakkuk 1:6. None of the post-Biblical apocryphal traditions about the prophet are considered to have significance for historical identification. The name of the prophet is not explained in the book, but may be etymologically related to חבק (*to clasp* or *embrace*), so that Széles suggests the prophet's name may have meant "'embraced,' a person who is folded to another's heart," noting Luther's translation of the prophet's name as *Herzer* for its reference to the heart.[5] Others have suggested that the name is related to the Assyrian plant *hambakuku*.[6] Neither of these explanations for the origin of the prophet's name, however, aids in identifying him or the circumstances of the prophecy.

With no external evidence, literary assessment of the book alone underlies the theories of the dates of the prophet, his vocation, and the

---

2. Sweeney, "Habakkuk, Book of," 2.

3. מגמה (*eagerness*) (1:9); משחק (*object of derision*) (1:10); עבטיט (*heavy debts*) (2:6); כפיס (*rafter*) (2:11); מעור (*nakedness*) (2:15); קיקלון (*shameful shame*) (2:16); חביון (*hiding place*) (3:4); פרז (*warrior*); עליצות (*exultation*) (3:14); רפתים (*stalls*) (3:17).

4. עקל (*to be crooked*) (1:4); נוה (*to abide*) (2:5); עור (*to be laid bare*) (3:9); רום ([adv] *on high*) (3:10); חמר (*to heap up*) (3:15).

5. Széles, *Wrath and Mercy*, 5.

6. Ward, *A Critical and Exegetical Commentary*, 3; *HALOT*, 287.

relationship between his message and the historical events of the time. Differences in style throughout the book and connections to other literary traditions give the impression that the book of Habakkuk is made up of various genres that have been creatively edited by a redactor. Széles, while agreeing with this assessment, claims the writings are based on the prophecies of a historical figure who was a cultic prophet,stating: "It is indisputable that Habakkuk received his call in Jerusalem and that his whole period of service was connected with the temple. It was there, even as he performed his office, that he accepted the revelation and passed it on to the worshiping community (2:1–5)."[7] Other scholars have also assumed Habakkuk was a temple official: that is, a cult prophet, composer or singer.[8] Support for this view of the identity of the prophet include the terminology of complaint psalms in Habakkuk 1, the psalm-like character of Habakkuk 3, the ecstatic effects of the reception of the message on the prophet (Hab 3:16), and the mention of the place where the prophet watched for Yahweh's response in Habakkuk 2:1. Jeremias, for example, finds a parallel use of משמרת between Habakkuk's *watch* (2:1) and the offices of Levites in post-exilic writings (Neh 13:30; 2 Chr 7:6; 8:14; 35:2).[9] Although the majority of scholars agree with this view, some have specifically argued that Habakkuk was a visionary prophet without cultic connection.[10]

The messages in the book of Habakkuk function differently from those in other prophetic books: they are not couched in 'messenger speech' formulas and seem to represent the victim's point of view more readily than delivering the judgment of God. They are described as differing from liturgical prayers: "more personal than set forms . . . [with] spontaneity about them."[11] The words are closest to Jeremiah's confessions and indeed many think the two prophets were historical contemporaries given that similar themes and vocabulary are found in the books of Habakkuk and Jeremiah.[12]

7. Széles, *Wrath and Mercy*, 5–6.

8. Eaton, *Obadiah, Nahum, Habakkuk, Zephaniah*, 82; Jeremias, *Kultprophetie*, 103; Mowinckel, *The Psalms in Israel's Worship*, 61; Watts, *Books of Joel, Obadiah, Jonah, Nahum, Habakkuk and Zephaniah*, 122.

9. Jeremias, *Kultprophetie*, 103–7; also Sweeney, *The Twelve Prophets*, 454.

10. Keller, "Nahoum, Habacuc, Sophonie"; Rudolph, *Micha—Nahum—Habakkuk—Zephanja*; Jöcken, "War Habakuk ein Kultprophet?"

11. Andersen, *Habakkuk*, 93.

12. Széles, *Wrath and Mercy*, 6; Hiebert, "The Book of Habakkuk," 623; Andersen, *Habakkuk*, 92.

On the question of the prophet's historical identity, Roberts's view is convincing: "it is not clear that a firm answer to that question [of whether he had employment in the service of the cultic establishment], whether negative or positive, would contribute significantly to a better understanding of the prophet's message. A theological evaluation of the message can only be based on its content, not on the prophet's position inside or outside the establishment."[13]

Authorship

Even if one could know the identity and role of the prophet, the question of authorship would not necessarily be resolved. Few scholars attribute the entire text to the historical prophet[14] and even those who argue for a unified composition acknowledge that it might have been written in different periods and could well have drawn upon older material.[15]

For many, the content of the book implies a period of internal strife within Judean society, to which is added the crisis of the Babylonian invasion. Discussion revolves around whether the same author reacted to these different crises or whether the anti-Babylonian material was added by a redactor. In addition, material that suggests a cultic setting points to the possibility of expansion of the book in the post-exilic period when priestly influence was greater. Evidence from the manuscript found at Qumran that the third chapter of Habakkuk did not circulate with the first two chapters also raises the possibility of multiple authorship.

While it seems impossible to state definitively who wrote the book of Habakkuk, it is probable that the personal prayers of a historic figure who was recognized as a prophet were recorded in a situation of oppression by a foreign power. A series of woe oracles was incorporated as a response, and a psalm celebrating the sovereignty of Yahweh was added to form a unified whole. From the perspective of performance criticism,

---

13. Roberts, *Nahum, Habakkuk, and Zephaniah*, 85.

14. Exceptions include Lindblom, *Prophecy in Ancient Israel*, 254, who states: "the Book of Habakkuk is not the work of a secondary collector of prophetic revelations, but a composition by the prophet himself, who was certainly a cultic prophet at the temple of Jerusalem"; and Bruckner, *Jonah, Nahum, Habakkuk, Zephaniah*, 202–3. Recent commentators who argue for a single author for the entire composition, though not necessarily an historical prophet named Habakkuk, include Gowan, *The Triumph of Faith*, 68; Smith, *Micah—Malachi*, 115; Robertson, *The Books of Nahum, Habakkuk, and Zephaniah*, 214; and Haak, *Habakkuk*, 11–22.

15. For example, Watts, "Psalmody in Prophecy," 217–21.

however, historical identification of the original prophet or author is of less interest than the openness of the script to re-interpretation and re-enactment. This notion will be discussed further in Chapter 8.

The Setting of Habakkuk

A performance critical reading of a script does not necessarily rely on a determination of its original historical circumstances. Understanding the framework through which the message of the book of Habakkuk is presented, however, facilitates appropriate re-enactment of the message. Therefore a discussion of historical background is warranted. The rise and prominence of the Neo-Babylonian Empire is widely agreed to be the historical backdrop for the first two chapters of Habakkuk. The description of warfare tactics including the use of horses and horsemen (1:8), the mention of speed (1:8, 11) and fortresses (1:10) reflect what is known of ancient near-eastern warfare at the time of the Assyrian and Neo-Babylonian empires.[16] The term כשׂדים (*Chaldeans*), is used regularly in the Hebrew Bible to refer to the Neo-Babylonian Empire, which reached the zenith of power under Nebuchadrezzar (605–556 BCE). Although arguments have been made for identification of the invading forces as the Assyrians[17] or the Macedonians/Greeks,[18] the chronological ordering of Habakkuk in the Book of the Twelve, particularly its placement immediately following the description of the downfall of Assyria in Nahum, suggests that a setting in the Neo-Babylonian era would not be unexpected for the book.

The Neo-Babylonian dynasty was founded by Nabopolassar in 625 BCE in the wake of the Assyrian demise. Nabopolassar united Arameans, Chaldeans, Arabs, and Elamites and gradually gained supremacy in the ancient Near East. The new force impacted directly upon Judah after the battle against Egypt at Charchemish (605 BCE) was won by Nebuchadrezzar, Nabopolassar's son, who acceded the throne at the death of his father in the same year. In the years following the victory at Charchemish Nebuchadrezzar was unopposed in Syro-Palestine and received tribute from the kings in the region. His defeat of the Philistine

---

16. Hiebert, "The Book of Habakkuk," 635.
17. Shepherd, "Compositional Analysis of the Twelve," 188.
18. Duhm, *Das Buch Habakuk*, discussed in Wade, *The Book of the Prophet Habakkuk*, 158–59. See Andersen, *Habakkuk*, *Habakkuk*, 146–49, for a lengthy refutation of the suggestion that כשׂדים refers to any group other than the Chaldeans.

city of Ashkelon in 604–603 BCE probably prompted a change of loyalty on the part of the Judean king, Jehoiakim, who became a vassal to Nebuchadrezzar. Some speculate that it was this period that gave rise to Habakkuk's oracle on the growing power of the Chaldeans.[19] Under Jehoiakim and his son Jehoiachin, Judah fluctuated between allegiance to Egypt and Babylon (2 Kgs 24:1–12). During a period of rebellion against Babylon, Jerusalem was captured by Nebuchadrezzar in 597 BCE, its prominent citizens exiled to Babylon, Zedekiah installed as vassal king, and tribute enforced (2 Kgs 24:13–17). In 587 BCE Zedekiah rebelled, instigating a second invasion resulting in the thorough destruction of Jerusalem and the end of the kingdom of Judah (2 Kgs 24:18—25:7).

Some clue to the historical background can be found in the terminology of Hab 1:2–4. While the passage begins as an individual complaint (with verbs in the first person), terms such as שד וחמס (*devastation and violence*), ריב ומדון (*strife and contention*), משפט (*justice*), and especially תפוג תורה (*Torah is paralyzed*), point to a community in crisis. Whether this crisis is caused by the Neo-Babylonian invasion or internal injustice in the community is debatable, given the uncertain identification of רשע (*wicked*). As alluded to above, possible referents include the Assyrians in Hab 1:4 and the Chaldeans in Hab 1:13,[20] or the Chaldeans in both instances,[21] although such a view does not make sense, as the text stands, for Yahweh would hardly raise the Chaldeans in response to the problem of the wicked Chaldeans! In order to deal with this problem scholars such as Budde[22] and De Vries[23] rearrange the order of the passages, placing 1:5–11 after 2:2–5. A more common view is that רשע in Hab 1:4 refers to a group of Judaeans who are not upholding justice demanded by the law and the term in Hab 1:13 refers to the Chaldeans brought as punishment.[24] Theological difficulties arise, however, if the prophet's complaint of injustice is answered by a greater injustice. Suggestions that have been offered to resolve the difficulty include viewing the second

---

19. Holladay, "Plausible Circumstances," 124; Miller and Hayes, *History*, 466.
20. Smith, *The Book of the Twelve Prophets*, 119–24.
21. Ibid., 118–19.
22. Budde, "Habakuk," 139–47.
23. De Vries, "The Book of Habakkuk," 494–95.
24. Baker, *Nahum, Habakkuk and Zephaniah*, 45–46; Robertson, *The Books of Nahum, Habakkuk, and Zephaniah*, 34–38; Patterson, "Habakkuk," 127–29.

pericope as a 'flashback' reflecting on an earlier prophecy[25] or understanding both passages as referring to the effects of the Chaldeans—in the first passage the invasion of the foreign nation renders the Torah 'paralyzed' (Hab 1:4) and the second passage is a heightened form of the complaint.[26] Such suggestions are of interest to this study and will be examined further in chapter 5.

Whatever identification is made, the grounding of Habakkuk's complaint in the broader issues of the community prevents a purely individualistic reading, despite the prominence of the 'I' in the book. This is an 'I' in the context of a community in crisis.

The relationship of the five woe oracles in Hab 2:6–20 to the earlier complaints is also problematic. The Chaldeans are not mentioned by name in Habakkuk 2, although most understand the woes to be a description of the fate awaiting the greedy, cruel and idolatrous nation.[27] Such scholarship has influenced popular translations such as the NRSV *Harper Study Bible* (1991) so that the book is divided with section headings, identifying Hab 2:2–20 as "God's Second Answer: the Chaldeans will be punished also," with further sub-divisions entitled "Chaldea is greedy," "Chaldea is covetous," "Chaldea is cruel," and "Chaldea is idolatrous." The third and fourth woes are combined in this instance. Whether the oracles were originally composed in relation to the Chaldeans is debated by scholars. Budde believes that Assyria, not Chaldea, is the tyrant who is subject to the taunts.[28] Wade casts doubt on the claim that the Chaldeans were the subject of the last woe regarding idols (2:18–19), stating "the irreligion ascribed to them by Habakkuk (1:11, 16) renders it improbable that he would credit them with any trust in supernatural powers, real or imaginary."[29] Holladay contends that the first complaint of Habakkuk (1:2–4) and the woe oracles (2:6–20) in their original recension were directed against King Jehoiakim of Judah around 601

---

25. Cleaver-Bartholomew, "An Alternative Approach," 214–15, reiterating an idea suggested by Ward, *A Critical and Exegetical Commentary*, 5–6.

26. Johnson, "The Paralysis of Torah," 261.

27. For example, Driver, *The Minor Prophets*, 54; Széles, *Wrath and Mercy*, 36; Roberts, *Nahum, Habakkuk, and Zephaniah*, 83; Hiebert, "The Book of Habakkuk," 646; Andersen, *Habakkuk*, 233.

28. Budde, "Die Bücher Habakuk und Zephanja," cited in Smith, *The Book of the Twelve Prophets*, 125.

29. Wade, *The Book of the Prophet Habakkuk*, 192.

BCE.[30] Others also argue that 'the localized nature' of the crimes mentioned in the woe oracles suggests they were originally directed against internal Judean wrongdoers.[31] On the other hand, as Sweeney argues, it was not unusual for prophets to refer metaphorically to international events by speaking of localized crimes. Various statements in these oracles presuppose an international situation and could logically be applied to the Chaldeans as a continuation of the first chapter.[32] Whatever the original occasion that gave rise to the woe oracles, in their present form they should be understood in relation to the enemy that is threatening the prophet's community.

The historical setting for Habakkuk 3 is also much debated. As noted above, the fact that 1QpHab does not include the third chapter of Habakkuk has cast doubt on the original unity of the book, although it is notable that no commentaries on complete books have been found among the *pesharim* of Qumran.[33] In addition, Habakkuk 3 is present in the next earliest evidence (8HevXIIgr and MurXII).

Roberts suggests that the psalm in Habakkuk 3 is the content of the vision promised in Hab 2:2–3.[34] This idea is taken up by Holladay who supports the proposal with a plausible date for the composition by comparing texts in Jeremiah. He suggests that the drought described by Hab 3:17–18 is the same drought mentioned in Jer 14:1 and relates the public fast implied in Jer 14:12 to the one called during the reign of King Jehoiakim as recorded in Jer 36:9.[35]

Some consider Habakkuk 3 a separate composition on the basis of content and stylistic differences.[36] Ward points out that the allusions to Deuteronomy, Second Samuel, Isaiah, Jeremiah, Micah, and exilic Psalms found in Habakkuk 3 suggest a date of composition later than those works. On this basis he argues for a date in the fifth or fourth century BCE.[37] On the other hand, reference to a warrior theophany in the

---

30. Holladay, "Plausible Circumstances," 125–26.

31. Jeremias, *Kultprophetie*; Otto, "Die Stellung der Wehe-Worte"; Janzen, "Eschatological Symbol"; Peckham, "The Vision of Habakkuk"; all cited in Sweeney, "Structure, Genre, and Intent," 238.

32. Sweeney, "Structure, Genre, and Intent," 238–39.

33. Haak, *Habakkuk*, 7–8.

34. Roberts, *Nahum, Habakkuk, and Zephaniah*, 81.

35. Holladay, "Plausible Circumstances," 124.

36. For example, Avishur, *Studies in Hebrew and Ugaritic Psalms*, 122–24.

37. Ward, *A Critical and Exegetical Commentary*, 6, 24.

psalm suggests affinities with much earlier material such as the poems found in Exodus 15 and Judges 5, thought to be eighth century BCE, and leads to the suggestion that Habakkuk incorporated an ancient composition into his writing,[38] or at least the composition was "moulded on archaic models."[39]

Smith concludes that the musical notation in Habakkuk 3 found in the superscription and subscription as well as the thrice repeated *selah* (3:3, 3:6, 3:13) relates the chapter more closely to psalms in the period of the Second Temple than to prophetic literature.[40] It is notable that the third chapter of Habakkuk reappears almost in its entirety in the book of Odes,[41] appended to the Psalter in G. Hiebert argues that the psalm, including the musical notation, is ancient, noting that since the subscription is included in all the versions it should not be understood as a later addition when the psalm began to be used in communal worship.[42] At whatever point a psalm was incorporated with the other content of the book of Habakkuk, the use of the specific musical notation is unique to prophetic literature.

The relevance of these questions regarding the text's background (military invasion? drought? communal worship?) will become obvious as 'setting' is discussed in relation to reading the book of Habakkuk as a performance.

Genre

The superscription that introduces the book identifies Habakkuk as the recipient of the message and also contains three terms identified from other prophetic literature as having specific referents: משׂא (*revelation* or *oracle*), often understood as judgment against foreigners; a prophecy, either a warning of judgment or a promise of mercy; through the designation of Habakkuk as הנביא (*the prophet*); and the verb חזה (*to see*), a verb commonly associated with prophetic revelation. The fact that this statement is immediately followed by a prayer characterized

---

38. Andersen, *Habakkuk*, 24; Hiebert, "The Book of Habakkuk," 653.
39. Smith, *The Book of the Twelve Prophets*, 127.
40. Ibid., 126–28.
41. The words τοῦ προφήτου μετὰ ωδῆς (*of the prophet with a song*) are missing from the superscription in the Odes.
42. Hiebert, *God of my Victory*, 1, 141–42.

by lament terminology illustrates the unusual combination of genres present in the book.

Typical laments include an address to the deity, a petition, motivation clauses, description of one's situation, an expression of confidence or trust, a vow of praise anticipating Yahweh's intervention, and are often written with a characteristic *qina* meter. Despite combining an address to Yahweh with the typical phrase עד־אנה (*how long*), and a description of the problem experienced by the speaker, the lack of a confession of trust, petition or vow of praise suggests the term 'lament' does not fit the first prayer in the book of Habakkuk (Hab 1:2–4). The term 'complaint,' defined as a direct challenge or protest to Yahweh about the way he has acted or threatened to act, may be the best term for this prayer. Nonetheless, the macro-structure of the book could be classified as a lament: beginning with a description of the problem, followed by a confession of confidence in the intervention of Yahweh, and finally a vow of praise. This suggestion will be taken up more fully in Chapter 8.

The multiplicity of genres in the book of Habakkuk; including prayers, oracles, taunts and woes, theophany, victory hymn, and wisdom material; provides intertextual links with other parts of the Hebrew Bible. Its prayers are evocative of Jeremiah's confessions (Jer 12:1–2, 20:8) and its questions 'how long?' 'why?' 'until when?' remind the listener of Job's complaints (Job 19:1, 7) and complaint psalms (Ps 13). As already noted, the musical notation in Habakkuk 3 has affinity with the Psalter, while the theophanic poem evokes the Exodus tradition. The significance of these intertextual links will be considered in chapters 5–7.

Kelle observes that Biblical prophecy is presented as "a discourse whose goal is to persuade for decisions to be made about belief and action in particular situations."[43] He argues that the communicative, situational, argumentative public address of the prophets is analogous to Greek oration. In analyzing prophetic speech, attention needs to be paid to the external factors of audience, situation and the problem being addressed as well as internal factors of style, devices, and arrangements used.[44] As will be seen below, a performance critical reading of the prophetic book of Habakkuk fulfils these expectations.

---

43. Kelle, "Ancient Israelite Prophets," 62.
44. Ibid., 78.

Structure of the Book and Relationship between Sections

Although debate continues regarding literary unity of the book of Habakkuk,[45] most scholars agree that it presents a thematic unity. A variety of unifying themes that draw elements of the book together have been proposed, including theodicy,[46] faith and doubt in the face of injustice,[47] and the sovereignty of God.[48] Floyd's presentation of the intention of the prophetic book is couched in dramatic terms where he describes the book as a "script for a ritual dramatization of the prophet's reaction."[49] The prophet is held up as a model example of a change in attitude and behavior towards Yahweh in a difficult situation and readers are invited "to try on this attitude for themselves through vicarious dramatic impersonation of the prophetic character."[50] The subtitle of this study suggests a similar theme for the book when it encourages 'faithful re-enactment in the midst of crisis.'

Childs claims there is a 'consensus' among scholars regarding the structure of Habakkuk into three major sections that follow a superscription, namely: (1) a dialogue between the prophet and Yahweh, (2) a series of woe oracles, and (3) a concluding psalm that was added later.[51] Despite this claim, persistent problems regarding structure, genre, and theme remain.

Recognition that there are two superscriptions in the book (Hab 1:1 and 3:1) suggests a two-part demarcation. Széles and Sweeney divide the book into two distinct but interrelated sections: the Pronouncement (משא) of Habakkuk (Hab 1–2), and the Prayer (תפלה) of Habakkuk (Hab 3).[52] Andersen also suggests a two-part division, describing the first part as "Interchange between Habakkuk and Yahweh" and the second part

---

45. See Dangl, "Habakkuk in Recent Research," 135–39.

46. Gowan, *The Triumph of Faith*, 10; Smith, *Micah—Malachi*, 96; Thompson, "Prayer, Oracle and Theophany," 34–50; O'Brien, *Nahum, Habakkuk, Zephaniah, Haggai, Zechariah, Malachi*, 58.

47. Hiebert, "The Book of Habakkuk," 623; Andersen, *Habakkuk*, 11–14; Bruckner, *Jonah, Nahum, Habakkuk, Zephaniah*, 197.

48. Achtemeier, *Nahum—Malachi*, 31; Széles, *Wrath and Mercy*, 7; Robertson, *The Books of Nahum, Habakkuk, and Zephaniah*, 136; Sweeney, *The Twelve Prophets*, 453.

49. Floyd, *Minor Prophets Part 2*, 89.

50. Ibid.

51. Childs, *Introduction*, 448.

52. Széles, *Wrath and Mercy*, 7; and Sweeney, "Structure, Genre, and Intent," 226.

as "The Prayer-Hymn of Habakkuk."[53] I have adopted this suggested two-part division in my translation and presented the 'performance' of Habakkuk in two acts.

House points out that at its most fundamental level, "the framework of a drama is marked by scenes and acts, which are basically major movements of the story. Scenes build upon one another to form acts and the sum of these acts composes a play."[54] In this study the two major sections of Habakkuk, 1:1—2:20 (Act One) and 3:1–19 (Act Two), are further divided into five and three 'scenes' respectively, marked by changes in actor, location, and time. In Act One the scenes build upon the theme of 'crisis' and in Act Two on the theme of 'faith.' Downer refers to the scene as the basic unit of dramatic construction: "a portion of the total play in which the stage is occupied by an unchanging group of players."[55] In the performance of Habakkuk the scene changes are seen more subtly, especially as the prophet is probably present in every scene (see chapter 8). The first three scenes of Act One are two complaint speeches by the prophet (1:2–4 and 1:12–17) framing an announcement by Yahweh (1:5–11). These have been presented as three separate scenes because the speeches cannot be characterized as a conversation since the prophet's questions are not answered by Yahweh. The introduction to Scene Four (2:1) has the character of a soliloquy and is further separated from the previous scene by changes in time (a description of a period of waiting) and characterization (development in the prophet's character). Scene Four (2:2–5) re-introduces Yahweh but is distinguished from Scene Five (2:6–19) by the change in setting and actors where an on-stage audience is included in a public denunciation of the enemy. The unity of Scene Five (2:6–19) is determined by its content of five woe oracles, although v. 14 interrupts the flow of woe oracles and is characterized as an interjection. Act One is followed by an interlude at Habakkuk 2:20. This is a transition point in the drama with its change of setting from public square to temple, preparing for the new theme of faith and worship. In Act Two three scenes build upon this new theme, although each is centered on the prophet's experience. Thus Scene One (3:2) is a prayer, Scene Two (3:3–15) is a theophanic vision and Scene Three (3:16–19) is a reflective soliloquy.

53. Andersen, *Habakkuk*, 14.
54. House, *Zephaniah*, 94.
55. Downer, *The Art of the Play*, 170.

This basic framework of acts and scenes has been supplemented by preludes (1:1; 3:1), an interjection (2:14), an interlude (2:20), and a postlude (3:19b). These additions give a dramatic role to otherwise disparate elements of the text.

This dramatic division of the book of Habakkuk into acts and scenes is in fact similar to many literary divisions made by commentators.[56]

Dramatic Division of the Performance of Habakkuk

Prelude	1:1

Act One—Crisis

Scene One	1:2–4
Scene Two	1:5–11
Scene Three	1:12–17
Introduction to Scene Four	2:1
Scene Four	2:2–5
Scene Five, Part 1	2:6–13
Interjection	2:14
Scene Five, Part 2	2:15–19
Interlude	2:20

Act Two—Faith

Prelude	3:1
Scene One	3:2
Scene Two	3:3–15
Scene Three	3:16–19a
Postlude	3:19b

---

56. See, for example, Smith, *Micah—Malachi*, 97; Széles, *Wrath and Mercy*, 16, 44; Roberts, *Nahum, Habakkuk, and Zephaniah*, 82; Andersen, *Habakkuk*, 15; Sweeney, *The Twelve Prophets*, 457–58.

TRANSLATION OF HABAKKUK

Poetry in Habakkuk

This translation follows the MT in presenting the whole of Habakkuk as poetry, although the witness in G, in which the first two chapters are prose, illustrates the difficulty in determining what makes a Hebrew text poetic. In comparison to other examples of poetry there are few classic bicola in Habakkuk and the scansion is not regular. The poetic intention of the author of Habakkuk is evidenced, however, by several characteristics common in Hebrew poetry:[57] the sparse use of prose particles (articles, *nota accusitavi*, and relative pronouns) and particularly the lack of a definite article when one would normally expect it; the terse nature of the text, seen for example in missing objects for some verbs (e.g. Hab 1:2a where the verb שמע [*to hear*], has no object) or in ellipsis; the use of double-duty items (e.g., in the same verse where the question עד־אנה [*how long*], is to be understood as applying to the second part of the verse also, enabling both parts to be understood as questions); and irregular syntax. The most common feature of Hebrew poetry, parallelism, is not as prevalent in the book of Habakkuk, although Haak in his analysis of Hab 1:1—2:4 concludes that there are enough examples of semantic and grammatical parallelism in both near and distant contexts to warrant identification of the material as poetry.[58]

Appreciation of the text as poetry has implications for a performative reading. Several scholars of Biblical poetry have pointed out that it is only in the hearing that rhythm (and, indeed, other features such as assonance) can be properly detected.[59] Alter claims that prophetic poetry differs from other forms of Biblical poetry by being presented as divine speech, thus lifting the utterances to a "second power of signification."[60] This gives the document originally addressed to a specific historical

---

57. See Kugel, *The Idea of Biblical Poetry*, 94; Miller, "The Theological Significance of Biblical Poetry," 210–25, Berlin, "Introduction to Hebrew Poetry," 308–9; Niccacci, "Analysing Biblical Hebrew Poetry," 77–78.

58. Haak, "'Poetry' in Habakkuk 1:1—2:4," 442.

59. See Berlin's emphasis on meter and rhythm in her definition of Hebrew poetry, "Introduction to Hebrew Poetry," 308–9, also Alonso Schökel, *A Manual of Hebrew Poetics*, 33, and Kuntz, who comments that recognition of the poet's use of sound is a "needful corrective to the approach taken by those scholars who, perhaps unknowingly, assume that biblical texts should be seen and not heard," "Biblical Hebrew Poetry," 36.

60. Alter, *The Art of Biblical Poetry*, 146.

situation a transcendence that also allows it to speak to later audiences, an observation that is reminiscent of the performance theme of re-enactment.

Translation Principles

Overall, translation of the MT has been left as literal as possible in order to highlight the changes in speaker and addressee, number and person of verbal forms, the many conjunctives, and the frequent personification. As will be seen below, Hab 1:2–4 is written with first person singular forms from the perspective of prophet, Hab 1:5–11 uses second person plural address forms while in Hab 1:6 the first person singular perspective probably identifies Yahweh as the speaker who refers in third person to the Chaldeans, although third person singular verbs are mostly used in that scene. Habakkuk 1:12–17 also uses second person singular forms, but here Yahweh is identified as addressee, the first person forms in Hab 1:12a identify the prophet as the speaker referring in third person to another group, probably the Chaldeans. Habakkuk 2:1–20 again uses first person singular forms to identify Habakkuk as the speaker, who describes in third person a report of Yahweh's response to the complaints. Despite the fact that Habakkuk is reporting Yahweh's words, the perspective of the woes is sometimes that of the vanquished nations and sometimes that of the prophet, with interruptions in the third person in reference to Yahweh's glory and holiness (Hab 2:14, 20).

In relation to translation of New Testament texts, Thomas and Thomas assert that lexical consistency was purposely used by New Testament composers to make cognitive connections with the audience as well as provide mnemonic aids to the performer of the text. Translators, therefore, should aim to maintain such consistency.[61] Rhoads also devotes a section of his essay on performance criticism to "The Art of Translation," noting that translating for performance "leads one to notice aspects of the text often overlooked—repetition, word associations, rhyme and rhythm, historical presents, word order, verbal threads, alliteration, and so on."[62] My translation has aimed for high iconicity including lexical consistency to enhance performance features

---

61. Thomas and Thomas, *Structure and Orality in 1 Peter*, quoted in Maxey, "Performance Criticism—Part 2," 171.

62. Rhoads, "Performance Criticism—Part 2," 171.

in the text, including cognitive connections in the manner of 'ready-mades' as well as mnemonic devices.

Translations and commentaries often alter the original forms in order to harmonize the changes in forms or make the Hebrew more understandable. For example, almost all translations and commentaries use the parallel terms 'the wicked' and 'the righteous' in Hab 1:4 while the MT has a definite article only on the second. G, NIV and a variety of commentators[63] add an 'I' into Hab 1:5 on the assumption that the speaker is Yahweh although the pronoun does not occur until Hab 1:6 in the MT. The NRSV and NIV use third person plural forms throughout Hab 1:6–11 when in fact most are third person singular. In modern English it is not possible to distinguish between singular and plural 'you' and so the translation of Hab 1:5 has indicated plural verb forms by beginning the verse with 'All of you.' Many translations omit the recurring *waw* at the beginning of clauses, but maintaining it in translation gives a greater sense of the movement of the script. When modifications of the sort that have been described are made in translation, important features of the text may be obscured in the process. In several instances, a high level of iconicity has been employed whereby there is close correspondence between the translation and the original Hebrew word-sign—seen clearly, for example, in examples of onomatopoeia.

A performative analysis that wishes to pay attention to features such as script, actors, audience, scene, and improvisation will need to take cognizance of the particularities of these features in the original text.

---

63. For example, Ward, *A Critical and Exegetical Commentary*, 8; Robertson, *The Books of Nahum, Habakkuk, and Zephaniah*, 142; Andersen, *Habakkuk*, 135.

Translation

Prelude (1:1)—Announcement of the Performance

¹ The revelation that Habakkuk the prophet saw.

ACT ONE—CRISIS

Scene One (1:2-4)

² How long, Yahweh, shall I call and you not hear?
I cry out to you 'violence!' and you do not save?
³ Why do you make me look at sorrow
and to trouble you pay attention?
And devastation and violence are before me
and there is strife, and contention carries on.
⁴ Therefore [the] Torah is paralyzed
and justice never goes forth.
For wickedness surrounds the righteous one.
Therefore crooked justice goes forth.

Scene Two (1:5-11)

⁵ All of you, look at the nations and pay attention!
And be profoundly astounded!
For a work is being worked in your days
— you would not believe it if it was recounted!
⁶ For behold, I am raising the Chaldeans,
that nation hurtful and hasty,
the man who marches across expanses of earth
to possess dwelling places not his own.
⁷ Terrible and fearful is he,
from himself his justice and his dignity go forth.
⁸ And swifter than leopards are his horses,
and keener than wolves of the evening.

And they gallop his gallopers and his gallopers.
From far they come, they fly,
like a vulture he hastens to eat.
⁹ Every one comes for violence.
The eagerness of their faces goes forward.
And he gathered captives like sand.
¹⁰ And as for him, at the kings he scoffs
and rulers are an object of derision to him.
As for him, at every fortress he laughs.
And he heaped up dust and he captured her.
¹¹ Then he swept through [as] wind,
and he passed by and was guilty.
This is his strength for his god.

Scene Three (1:12–17)

¹² Are you not from old, Yahweh?
My God of holiness, you will not die!
Yahweh, for justice you set him;
and Rock, for rebuke you established him.
¹³ Your eyes are too pure to look at evil.
And you are not able to pay attention to trouble.
Why do you pay attention to those who act treacherously?
[Why do] you keep silence when wickedness swallows [the] righteous one?
¹⁴ And you made humankind like the fish of the sea,
like a lowly sea-creature with no-one ruling over it.
¹⁵ Every one he brought up with a fishing hook,
he drags him away with his net,
and gathers him with his fish-trap.
Therefore he is glad and rejoices.
¹⁶ Therefore he sacrifices to his net,

> and offers smoke to his fish-trap.
> For with them his portion grew rich,
> and his food was fat.
> ⁷ Shall he therefore empty his net and continue
> to slay nations without mercy?

Introduction to Scene Four (2:1)

> ¹ On my guard let me stand,
> and let me set myself on siege works,
> and let me keep watch to see what he says to me,
> and what I will bring back concerning my rebuke.

Scene Four (2:2–5)

> ² And Yahweh answered me and said:
> Write [the] vision and make plain on the tablets
> so that [the] reader will run with it.
> ³ For [the] vision is yet for the appointed time,
> and it breathes to the end and does not lie.
> If it tarries, wait for it, for it surely comes, it will not delay.
> ⁴ Behold, it is swollen: his soul is not upright in him,
> but [the] righteous one in his faithfulness will live.
> ⁵ And moreover the wine is treacherous!
> A mighty man is haughty and does not abide,
> who widens his soul like Sheol,
> and he is like death and is not sated.
> And he gathered to himself all the nations,
> and collected to himself all the peoples.

Scene Five—Part One (2:6–13)

⁶ Are not all these lifting up a taunt against him?
And satirical riddles about him? And he says:
Woe to him who piles up what is not his
—How long?
And the one making heavy debts upon himself.
⁷ Will not the ones biting you suddenly arise?
And will not the ones violently shaking you wake?
And you will be their spoil.
⁸ Because you plundered many nations
let the remaining peoples plunder you —
On account of blood of man and violence of earth,
a town and all who live in it.
⁹ Woe to him who violently gains unjust gain!
Evil belongs to his house
who has set his nest in the heights
to be delivered from the grasp of evil.
¹⁰ You counseled shame for your house,
to cut off many people, and your soul is sinning.
¹¹ For a stone from a wall will cry out,
and a rafter from the woodwork will answer it.
¹² Woe to him who builds a city with bloodshed
and establishes a town with iniquity!
¹³ Behold! Is it not from Yahweh of Hosts?
And peoples labor for fire and nations grow faint for nothing.

Interjection (2:14)

¹⁴ But the earth will be filled
with the knowledge of the glory of Yahweh
as the waters cover the sea!

Scene Five—Part Two (2:15-19)

> [15] Woe to him making his neighbor drink;
> Who clings to your rage and even drunkenness
> in order to gaze upon their nakedness!
> [16] You are sated with shame rather than glory.
> Drink, you also, and be counted as uncircumcised!
> A cup in the right hand of Yahweh will turn around upon you,
> and shameful shame will be upon your glory.
> [17] For the violence of Lebanon covers you,
> and the devastation of beasts causes them to be terrified —
> On account of blood of man and violence of earth,
> a town and all who live in it.
> [18] Of what benefit is an idol when he who hewed it made it?
> — an image and a teacher of deception?
> For the maker who makes it trusted on it,
> To make dumb worthless idols.
> [19] Woe to him who says to a tree 'wake up!'
> 'awake!' to the mute stone. 'It is teaching!'
> Behold it, overlaid with gold and silver
> and full of wind? There is nothing in it!

Interlude (2:20)

> [20] And Yahweh is in his temple of holiness.
> Hush before him all the earth.

ACT TWO—FAITH

Prelude (3:1)

> [1] A prayer of Habakkuk the prophet according to Shigionoth.

Scene One (3:2)

² Yahweh, I have heard of your reputation,
I am in awe, Yahweh, of your work.
In the midst of years you will make it live.
In the midst of years you will make yourself known.
In turmoil, you will remember compassion.

Scene Two (3:3–15)

³ God comes from Teman
and [the] Holy One from Mount Paran. *Selah*.
His splendor has clothed the heavens
and his praise has filled the earth.
⁴ And bright as the light it is,
rays from his hand has he.
And there is a hiding place for his strength.
⁵ Before him Pestilence marches
and Fire-bolt goes forth before his feet.
⁶ He has taken his stand and he measures earth.
He has looked, and he makes nations free.
And has shattered the mountains of old,
bent down are the ancient hills.
The ways of old are his.
⁷ Below I saw trouble at the tents of Cushan.
Let curtains be in turmoil in the earth of Midian.
⁸ Has Yahweh burned against the Rivers?
Is your face against the Rivers?
Is your fury against the Sea?
For you ride on your horses,
on your chariots of salvation.
⁹ Indeed laid bare is your bow.

Sworn are the spears of your word. *Selah.*

With streams you cleave the earth.

¹⁰ Having looked at you, mountains shake.

A downpour of waters has passed by.

Deep has given its voice,

Sun has lifted its hands on high.

¹¹ Moon has stood in its lofty abode.

As light your arrows dart,

as brightness, your glittering spear.

¹² In indignation you stride through the earth.

In anger you tread down nations.

¹³ You go forth to save your people,

to save your anointed one.

You have smitten the head of the house of wickedness,

to lay bare foundation to neck. *Selah.*

¹⁴ You have pierced with his spears the head of his warriors

They storm out to scatter me.

Their exultation was like he who devours the poor in secret.

¹⁵ You have walked through the Sea (with) your horses,

a heap of great waters.

Scene Three (3:16–19a)

¹⁶ I heard and my belly is in turmoil,

at a voice my lips tingled.

Decay comes into my bones,

and in my place I am in turmoil,

where I wait for a day of distress

to come up to a people who will invade us.

¹⁷ If the fig tree does not sprout,

and no produce is on the vines,

if the yield of the olive tree has failed
and fields have not produced food,
the flock has been cut off from the fold
and no cattle are in the stalls,
¹⁸ yet I will exult in Yahweh,
I will rejoice in the God of my salvation.
¹⁹ᵃ Yahweh my Lord is my strength.
He places my feet like the hinds'
and on my high places he makes me walk.

Postlude (3:19b)—Final Performance Instructions

¹⁹ᵇ To the Director, according to my Niginoth.

FIVE

A Performance Reading of Habakkuk 1

IN THIS AND THE following two chapters the 'script' of Habakkuk will be read in the light of the performance themes and features that were identified in Chapter 2. For ease of reference and in order to keep the chapters of a similar length my performance analysis will be applied to the three chapters of the book of Habakkuk sequentially, despite my presentation of the script as comprising two acts.

Habakkuk 1 forms the beginning of Act One and is introduced by a prelude (1:1). The three scenes that follow are divided on the basis of a change in speaker from the prophet (Scene One, 1:2–4) to Yahweh (Scene Two, 1:5–11) and returning to the prophet in Scene Three (1:12–19).

PERFORMANCE FEATURES IN HABAKKUK 1

Prelude (1:1)

¹ The revelation that Habakkuk the prophet saw.

Author and Script

Applying performance theory to the book of Habakkuk suggests that the entire book may be read as a 'script.' There is evidence that a redactor, probably in the Persian era, drew together disparate materials, linked them thematically and attributed them to the prophetic *persona* 'Habakkuk' (compare 1:1 and 3:1). The term משׂא (*revelation*), must therefore be understood as relating to the entire book. The use of the definite article gives weight to this assertion. "The revelation" includes visions, taunts, prayers of complaint, and songs of praise.

Use of the verb חזה (*he saw*), places an emphasis on the visual at the expense of the literary. This is not a revelation to be only read, but one to be visualized; a scene to be drawn for an attentive audience. Admittedly the script makes use of auditory features such as onomatopoeia (e.g., הס [*hush* v. 20]) and word play (e.g., ופשו פרשיו ופרשיו [*they gallop his gallopers and his gallopers* v. 8], המר והנמהר [*hurtful and hasty* v. 6]), but even these poetic devices suggest a composition to be performed orally, and not just read silently.[1]

Actors

No clear expectations are given in the prelude as to what sort of prophetic *persona* Habakkuk will be. Will he be an announcer of judgment or mercy? Will he be a prophet whose work will be proven by the fulfillment of his word, as the Deuteronomistic History describes prophets? Or will he be a teacher of the Torah as was the dominant role of the prophet in the Persian period? It is not even clear at this point whether Habakkuk is a cultic prophet as no temple setting is given in the prologue. Habakkuk's name may give a hint of the thrust of the book if its meaning as "the one embraced" is accepted, although the first words of the character—a prayer of complaint—belie such a self-understanding as Habakkuk clearly does not feel embraced, but rather abandoned (see discussion of Scene One below). Despite the early ambiguity, this book's main character reveals more about himself than many of the other prophets of the Hebrew Bible, as will be shown in the unfolding performance.

Interestingly, Yahweh has not yet appeared as an actor. The source of the revelation is not revealed. Many translations evidence discomfort with this fact (see CEV, GNT, NIrV, RSV, *The Message*); indeed Clark and Hatton recommend that translators add "of the LORD" to the word "oracle" because "The Hebrew word implies that the message is a religious one."[2] Comparison with the use of the term elsewhere in the prophetic literature shows that it is frequently coupled with a reference

---

1. In his book *The Performance of Reading*, Kivy makes a case for a performative element in literature, including novels. Silent reading, he argues, is analogous to reading musical scores where a work is performed in the head as a token of the original work. Although the vast majority of current readers of the Bible do so silently, many have argued that Biblical literature was presented and received orally by the majority of its adherents historically and so was not intended primarily for silent reading.

2. Clark and Hatton, *A Handbook on the Books of Nahum, Habakkuk, and Zephaniah*, 68.

to Yahweh (Jer 23:33; Ezek 12:10; Zech 9:1; 12:1; Mal 1:1). Thus the lack of reference to Yahweh in Habakkuk 1:1 leaves the term ambiguous, a significant observation from the perspective of performance analysis.

Audience

The prelude does not indicate who the audience is, but an audience is implicit in the announcement of "the revelation." This is clearly a message that requires an audience as the author has taken trouble to present it in this form. At this stage the audience remains distant, but is ready to be drawn in as the script unfolds.

Setting

Despite the lack of physical setting, the term מַשָּׂא (*revelation*), puts this author's material in a frame—it sets it apart as unusual, to be noticed, drawing attention to itself. The prelude is presented in the third person, but is immediately followed by first-person speech. The prelude therefore, simply through its lexical choices, introduces the audience to the context (a prophetic word) and content (a revelation that was seen) of what is to follow.

Given that the material and socio-historical context of the audience should be considered as part of the setting, the assumption that this composition was finally put together in the Persian period would mean that the events of Neo-Babylonian attack, exile under Neo-Babylonian rule and return under Persian colonial rule would be included in the experiences, memories and stories that formed the identity of the audience. They would be aware of competing claims for authority amongst the fifth century Yehud community that was "not unified but experienced substantial social conflict."[3] The acceptance or otherwise of this "revelation" by the listening audience may depend on whether it is presented as being delivered from within the temple by an institutionally sanctioned official or outside of it by a self-appointed spokesman, thereby running the risk of being considered a false prophet.[4] Clues later in the performance may help to determine its setting.

---

3. Berquist, *Approaching Yehud*, 3.
4. As characterized by Meyers and Meyers, *Zechariah 9–14*, 371.

Improvisation

As noted earlier, the term משא (*revelation*), is a word commonly used in the prophetic literature. The use of it here, however, is unusual in that it is not immediately followed by a message *from* Yahweh, but instead by a complaint *to* Yahweh regarding the situation the prophet observes. It appears the author has taken a common prophetic term and broadened its application to cover the entire book with its wide variety of form and content.

Act One—Scene One (1:2–4)

> ² How long, Yahweh, shall I call and you not hear?
> I cry out to you 'violence!' and you do not save?
> ³ Why do you make me look at sorrow
> and to trouble you pay attention?
> And devastation and violence are before me
> and there is strife, and contention carries on.
> ⁴ Therefore [the] Torah is paralyzed
> and justice never goes forth.
> For wickedness surrounds the righteous one.
> Therefore crooked justice goes forth.

Author and Script

Those listening have been told to expect a revelation and the implications of the use of משא (*revelation)*, would give the impression that this is the prophet's report of the words of Yahweh. Immediately, however, there is an irregularity in the script that might be called 'a twist in the plot' since the next words are those of a prayer of the prophet addressed *to* Yahweh. Furthermore, it is a prayer of complaint! Can this be seen as part of the "revelation"?

Actors

The change from third person report to first and second person address brings the actors into sharp focus, with "I" presumably being the prophet Habakkuk whose presence was reported in the Prelude and "Yahweh" being the addressee of the prayer. As the first introduction of Yahweh this is somewhat shocking: rather than naming the virtues of Yahweh, accusations are hurled against him: "you do not hear," "you do not save," "you make me look at sorrow." The audience is receiving a very negative image of Yahweh as an uncaring, impotent, capricious deity.

It is possible that "Torah" is introduced as a personified character here—an idea that became more common in later Jewish literature.[5] Unlike many other references to the term in the prophetic literature, it is not affixed to Yahweh in this script but stands as an entity on its own. There would have been an understanding of Torah as a written form of the will of Yahweh for the community and by the Persian period it would not be uncommon to refer to "the Torah" as an entity containing Yahweh's teaching. The speaker implies that the uncaring attitude of Yahweh has a direct impact upon "Torah," rendering it "paralyzed." Torah sits immobile on the stage as an accusing presence in the face of Yahweh's callousness.

Into this general atmosphere of violence, sorrow, trouble, and strife, a new character is placed. הצדיק (*the righteous one*), is identified by the definite article in contrast to the nebulous wickedness that surrounds him. Is "the righteous one" to be associated with the speaker, the prophet Habakkuk? If so, there is a blurring of distinction between the actors. Could there even be a blurring between Yahweh and "the righteous one"? Is the perceived willful impotency of Yahweh to be better understood as an inability to act due to imprisonment by "wickedness"? As "the righteous one" is given no speech the identity of the character remains ambiguous.

Audience

At this stage the audience is still distant, eavesdropping on one side of a complaint. The verbs of the address are singular so the effect is that there is an audience of one, but this is still subsumed under the genre "the revelation" and so an audience is expected.

---

5. This is shown in Deuterocanonical works (Sir 24; Bar 3:9—4:4). This concept has been picked up in scholarship seeking antecedents for the "Logos" as divine intermediary in the Gospel of John. For example, Schoneveld translates "Logos" as "Torah" in the prologue of John's gospel, arguing that the prologue refers to Jesus as "Torah in the flesh" with its allusions to Gen 1:1 and Prov 8:22 as well as Deuterocanonical and rabbinic literature ("Torah in the Flesh," 81–85).

The immediate twist in the plot ensures that the audience's attention is engaged. Surprise is a necessity in performance, according to De Marinis, ensuring a spectator's attention.[6] He asserts that the ability of a performance to hold attention is dependent upon its ability to create expectations in the audience and then disrupt them through "sudden leaps, rapid changes of direction, tone, atmosphere, rhythm, etc."[7] Thus the use of surprise is a key element of performance and can be seen to be integral to this performance of Habakkuk where an unexpected genre is utilized following the announcement of a "revelation."

The term ריב (v. 3) has been used here in a general sense of "strife" as a pair with "contention," but for a fifth century audience there may well be echoes of a legal court in which matters are brought before a judge or council of elders for judgment. Thus the audience may be encouraged to join the prophetic *persona* in questioning the wisdom and faithfulness of Yahweh at this point in their history.

Setting

The characters have been set in a tumultuous world: one of turmoil and strife where the only forward movement is negative. All elements that would be expected to be good—Yahweh, Torah, the righteous one—are inactive, paralyzed, and hemmed in. Does this surrounding (framing) have the effect of highlighting the righteous one or, alternatively, of rendering any righteousness void? The scene ends with movement, but it is "crooked" justice that is going forth, not justice as normally understood as the God-given norm for a well-ordered society.

Improvisation

As well as challenging the expectations of the audience by commencing "the revelation" with a prayer of complaint, the author has subtly altered the usual use of this form. As previously stated, a complaint may be defined as a direct challenge or protest to Yahweh about the way he has acted or threatened to act (compare Pss 44:9; 88:8)—in this case Yahweh, it is claimed, has *not* acted but has stood by idly watching. The complaint is thus about inaction rather than action. Complaints, often used elsewhere in the Hebrew Bible, are usually accompanied by an

---

6. De Marinis, "Dramaturgy of the Spectator," 109.
7. Ibid., 111.

expression of trust or a vow of praise. Psalm 13:1–2 has the most obvious echoes of the complaint here, but the psalm is completed by a statement of trust and praise. The lack of any such element here is notable. Mandolfo's work on psalms of lament, that are closely related to prayers of complaint, suggests that such forms may be read dialogically, where two voices collide: the supplicant offering the voice of experience, often in first person address, while the 'didactic voice' presents the voice of tradition, usually in 'objective' third person speech. Her argument is that by recognizing the voices as divergent one might listen more attentively, especially to the more vulnerable—the supplicant—whose view is often subsumed by the more authoritative voice.[8] The author of Habakkuk's complaint refuses to allow the chance of it being subsumed by leaving out the voice of tradition in this scene.

A number of terms in this scene are common terms used in Biblical literature and thus could be viewed as ready-mades—terms such as ישׁע (save), תורה (Torah), רשׁע (wickedness), צדיק (righteous), משׁפט (justice).[9] Their use here, however, has the effect of overturning prior expectations: Yahweh does not seem inclined to perform mighty acts to save his people: Torah is paralyzed, the wicked have the upper hand, the righteous one is surrounded and justice has become crooked. The audience would be uncertain of the outcome of the situation.

Act One—Scene Two (1:5–11)

> [5] All of you, look at the nations and pay attention!
>
> And be profoundly astounded!
>
> For a work is being worked in your days
>
> — you would not believe it if it was recounted!
>
> [6] For behold, I am raising the Chaldeans,
>
> that nation hurtful and hasty,
>
> the man who marches across expanses of earth
>
> to possess dwelling places not his own.

---

8. See Mandolfo, *God in the Dock*; Mandolfo, *Daughter Zion Talks Back to the Prophets*; Mandolfo, "Talking Back."

9. The word משׁפט (*justice*) occurs four times in the first chapter of Habakkuk (1:4 [x2], 7, 12).

⁷ Terrible and fearful is he,
from himself his justice and his dignity go forth.
⁸ And swifter than leopards are his horses,
and keener than wolves of the evening.
And they gallop his gallopers and his gallopers.
From far they come, they fly,
like a vulture he hastens to eat.
⁹ Every one comes for violence.
The eagerness of their faces goes forward.
And he gathered captives like sand.
¹⁰ And as for him, at the kings he scoffs
and rulers are an object of derision to him.
As for him, at every fortress he laughs.
And he heaped up dust and he captured her.
¹¹ Then he swept through [as] wind,
and he passed by and was guilty.
This is his strength for his god.

Author and Script

Either this description is an example of the "crooked justice" mentioned in Hab 1:4 or there is another twist in the plot here. Given the tendency of this author to keep the audience guessing, the latter option is the more likely. The decisive but devastating poem with its emphatic verbs and graphic imagery builds a picture of an unrelenting destructive force, perhaps even with an underlying association with the locust plagues that are mentioned elsewhere in the Book of the Twelve (Joel 2:4–10; Nah 3:15–17; Mal 3:10–11). Whether real or metaphorical, the destruction of a locust plague gave an image of enemy invasion that was distressingly familiar to the Yehud community.

Yet by personifying this force into an individual enemy the author is able to bring the image to some sort of closure at the end of the poem with the declared judgment "he was guilty" (v. 11). This judgment is reinforced by the use of wordplay in that the verb יעבר (*he swept through*) can also be translated *he transgressed*. The uncertainty with which the previous scene finished has now been resolved in that the enemy described has been judged and found wanting.

Actors

A new and authoritative actor suddenly enters the stage, addressing a wider audience as indicated by the use of plural verbs in v. 5. The complaint of the prophet in Scene One (1:2–4) is ignored. Instead, the subject of the verse is making a public announcement about his action, seen in the plural imperative verbs ראו (*Look!*), התמהו תמהו (*be profoundly astounded*), לא תאמינו (*you would not believe it*), and the use of הנה—best translated by the old-fashioned word *behold*—a dramatic word used to draw attention to what follows. Astonishment would not be an unexpected response in the light of the earlier perceived helplessness of the deity. Can this speaker possibly be the same "Yahweh" addressed in v. 2 who had been accused of disinterest at best, impotence at worst? Such a question is further enhanced by the lack of connection between the scenes. There is no acknowledgement of the prophet or his complaint other than to view him as part of the general audience being addressed. If this is indeed the same Yahweh, it is as if the actor has suddenly woken up and remembered his lines, firmly taking center stage. Habakkuk is marginalized in this scene.

There is an argument for understanding this whole scene as having happened in the past, an earlier prophecy to the nation being presented here as a 'flashback.'[10] Such a reading would resolve the problem of the 'non-answer' to the prophet's complaint and it could plausibly be presented in dramatic fashion. The staging would necessitate the prophet taking center stage, presenting an earlier word of Yahweh as reminiscence. Film technology rather than dramatic presentation would more easily allow such a reading. The 'I' would be the prophet speaking *in lieu* of Yahweh, allowing Yahweh the actor to remain passively sidelined as in the previous scene. While this is an attractive theory that resolves some grammatical and theological issues, there is arguably far more dramatic interest in the sudden appearance of Yahweh as part of the *dramatis personae*. Whereas the 'flashback' theory protects Yahweh's reputation, my reading of it as 'a twist in the plot' introduces the character of

---

10. Ward, *A Critical and Exegetical Commentary*, 5–6; Cleaver-Bartholomew, "An Alternative Approach," 216.

Yahweh as an authoritative and yet perplexing *persona*. This allows for interesting character development and the potential for conflict between the main actors that makes for compelling drama.

The Chaldeans are introduced as new actors in this scene. Although some commentators have suggested the source of trouble, strife, and wickedness in Scene One (1:2–4) is the Chaldeans, the majority view the 'wicked' of Scene One as wrongdoers in Judean society. The Chaldeans, therefore, are a surprise act flamboyantly introduced by Yahweh who takes on somewhat of a directorial role. They are personified in a single entity with masculine verbs implying the king is their representative.[11] This individual is introduced as a force to be reckoned with: hurtful, hasty, terrible, and fearful. Despite another mention of the invaders in the plural (v. 9), the use of כלה (*every one*) maintains the sense of a representative individual. The animal metaphors of v. 8 compound the frightening nature of this character who is likened to leopards, wolves, vultures, and stampeding horses. The feminine suffix at the end of v. 10 further highlights the destructive power of the invading (male) king of the Chaldeans although the identity of the object captured is unclear—perhaps a (feminine) fortified city[12] or perhaps the nation of Judah herself. A cast of extras is also mentioned—"the nations" in v. 5 and "kings and rulers" whose power amounts to nothing as the Chaldean torrent sweeps by (v. 10).

Finally, v. 11 introduces a shadowy figure—"his god"—who might or might not re-appear at the end of the next scene. There is a suggestion that the violent action of the personified enemy is an offering to this god (v. 11), although the fact that strength (v. 11), justice and dignity (v. 7) come "from himself" and not "his god" keeps this character a marginal actor in the scene.

11. In fact the personification of the enemy continues to be typical of the rhetoric of war, as evidenced in excerpts from a news conference given by General Schwarzkopf during the Gulf War in 1991: "As you know, very early on, we took out the Iraqi Air Force. We knew that he had very very limited reconnaissance means. And therefore, when we took out his air force, for all intents and purposes, we took out his ability to see what we were doing down here in Saudi Arabia. Once we had taken out his eyes . . . we knew he couldn't see us any more, we did a massive movement of troops all the way out to the west, to the extreme west, because at that time we knew he was still fixed in this area with the vast majority of his forces, and once the air campaign started, he would be incapable of moving out to counter this move, even if he knew we made it" (*New York Times Online*).

12. As proposed by Roberts, *Nahum, Habakkuk, and Zephaniah*, 93.

Audience

As noted, the plural imperative verbs at the beginning of this scene explicitly draw in the audience at this point. The first imperative of v. 5, ראו (*Look!*) and the הנה (*behold*) of v. 6 re-emphasize the visual nature of the revelation, and in the following scene a frightening picture is graphically portrayed for the audience. The response of the audience would depend upon their view of Yahweh, as it is he who has claimed responsibility for this terrible eventuality. Can they trust Yahweh to act for their benefit despite this pronouncement? The final word of judgment of v. 11 suggests Yahweh can be depended upon to resolve the situation in favor of his people, but the prophet's subsequent speech suggests that he, for one, cannot come to the same conclusion just yet. There is an impression given, therefore, of a divided audience, including the prophet. The declaration of decisive action heard by the communal majority is undermined by the individual aside that admits the possibility of disbelief, and the confident assertion "he was guilty" is placed in doubt by a further set of questions addressed to Yahweh in the next scene.

Setting

The plural verb forms of v. 5 mark this off as a new scene following the prophet's individual complaint.[13] The focus shifts away from Yehud-specific "Torah" (v. 4) to "the nations" (v. 5), in particular the Chaldean nation (v. 6). The verses that follow are a description of the nation linked with similar ideas and metaphors and bound together with conjunctions, closing with three past tense verbs, providing a conclusion to the section.

As noted above, Yahweh claims responsibility for the surprising introduction of the Chaldeans in this scene. Any Persian-era audience, however, would be familiar with the warfare setting of the description and would not be surprised at the imagery. Imperial armies were known to invade neighboring territories and seize the land (v. 6), to use horses for power and speed (v. 8), to take citizens into captivity (v. 9) and commonly to lay siege to walled cities by constructing earthen ramps to assault the walls (v. 10).[14] The Neo-Babylonian army, in particular,

13. I disagree with Peckham who argues it is a continuation of the complaint; see "The Vision of Habakkuk," 624.

14. See Yadin, *The Art of Warfare in Biblical Lands*, for a discussion of ancient Near Eastern warfare techniques that would have been familiar to the Israelites.

was known to have engaged in many military campaigns, with at least twenty-one campaigns recorded in the space of seventeen years.[15]

Improvisation

The description of the invading Chaldean king/nation fits that of a powerful enemy with the exception of v. 7b: "From himself his justice and his dignity go forth." Here terms are used that are familiar to the audience of Yahweh worshippers and Torah adherents as descriptors of Yahweh. משפט (*justice*) is an attribute ascribed to Yahweh himself (Deut 32:4; Ps 97:2). Indeed, it has already been introduced in this performance (Hab 1:4), but there the reference to "crooked justice" unsettles the expected meaning. Here "justice" is being attributed to the enemy who is sweeping through the nation dispensing his own form of justice. שאת (*dignity*) is far less common but is used elsewhere in reference to the majesty of God (Job 13:11; 31:23) or a person whose position is one of prominence (Gen 49:3; Ps 62:5). Such elevation is a result of the enemy's own self-perception and thus the usual understanding of these terms by the audience is mocked by the invader. Secondary meanings of שאת as *swelling* due to disease (Lev 13:2, 10, 19, 28; 14:56) or *uprising* as the action of Leviathan the sea-monster (Job 41:17) might also have influenced the use of this term, through the author's subtle reference to the invader either as an unwelcome disease or as a frightening monstrous presence. Many English translations translate the term as *pride*, pre-empting the judgment of the nation that is suggested in Hab 2:6, 9, 12, 15, 19 but removing the mocking tone of its use in this scene. A further nuance is Yahweh's reference to "a work being worked in your days" (v. 5), raising connotations of the great deeds of the Exodus tradition—perhaps this is the answer to the accusing cry "you do not save" (v. 2). But the astounding event which Yahweh goes on to reveal is the raising of the Chaldeans, not a miraculous intervention on behalf of his people. Is Yahweh allowing this Chaldean king to take his place in their society as acknowledged leader and dispenser of justice? It seems that "crooked" justice continues to move forward in this scene, further highlighted by the repetition of the verb יצא (*to go forth*, v. 7, compare with v. 4).

The re-introduction of חמס (*violence*) is further evidence of "crooked" justice and a Yahweh who acts completely out of character. In

---

15. Wiseman, *Chronicles of Chaldean Kings*, 95–96.

Scene One the prophet's complaint mentioned violence twice (vv. 2, 3), pointing it out to a seemingly blind Yahweh. In this scene Yahweh goes further it seems: directing a new set of actors who come specifically *for* violence (v. 9).

Another potential ready-made in this scene is רוח (*spirit, wind*). Although used later in Habakkuk to suggest the presence or absence of life (Hab 2:19), here the word might be used for its onomatopoeic impact further emphasizing the speed and excitement of the scene. The destructive force is sweeping through "as wind" but this description hints at an equally fleeting impact—the force may leave as quickly as it came.

Act One—Scene Three (1:12–17)

> [12] Are you not from old, Yahweh?
> My God of holiness, you will not die!
> Yahweh, for justice you set him;
> and Rock, for rebuke you established him.
> [13] Your eyes are too pure to look at evil.
> And you are not able to pay attention to trouble.
> Why do you pay attention to those who act treacherously?
> [Why do] you keep silence when wickedness swallows [the] righteous one?
> [14] And you made humankind like the fish of the sea,
> like a lowly sea-creature with no-one ruling over it.
> [15] Every one he brought up with a fishing hook,
> he drags him away with his net,
> and gathers him with his fish-trap.
> Therefore he is glad and rejoices.
> [16] Therefore he sacrifices to his net,
> and offers smoke to his fish-trap.
> For with them his portion grew rich,
> and his food was fat.
> [17] Shall he therefore empty his net and continue
> to slay nations without mercy?

Author and Script

Another surprising twist in the plot is shown in an abrupt change of scene. The confident performative voice of Yahweh in Scene Two (Hab 1:5–11) with its closing words of judgment of the enemy is immediately challenged by the prophet with sarcasm and a damning accusation of silence in the face of trouble. This accusation indicates that for the prophet the scene just witnessed does not serve as an answer to his first complaint. Furthermore, the prophet's speech draws on a wealth of traditions regarding Yahweh's character and history with his people through the use of titles, salvation and creation themes, judgment, and even an allusion to cultic worship. This rich background casts the character of Yahweh into sharp relief, begging for a resolution to the problematic *persona* that is building up around the character of Yahweh. The way Yahweh moves from uninterested, impotent spectator to decisive, energetic actor and then back to silent observer who refuses to live up to his reputation sets up an interesting plot line, leaving one with the sense that this character (and this drama) could develop in any direction.

Actors

The prophet again steps onto the stage with another prayer of complaint addressed directly to Yahweh. The prophet acknowledges the ability of Yahweh to rise above human troubles and manipulate events from a distance, so the phrase "you will not die" can be seen as a sarcastic comeback to the confident announcement of Yahweh in the previous scene. It is worth noting that this is a shocking phrase to describe Yahweh, as evidenced by the *tiqqun* in the MT where ancient scribes have 'corrected' the phrase to read in the first person plural form, stating "we will not die," even though that makes little sense in the context of a destructive Chaldean invasion. The multiple addresses to Yahweh (*Yahweh, my God of Holiness, Yahweh, Rock*) possibly continue the sarcasm as the prophet 'reminds' Yahweh of the characteristics he expects from his God (compare with Deut 32:4; 1 Sam 2:2; 2 Sam 22:32; Ps 18:2). The designation "from old" is perhaps included to remind Yahweh of his role as creator and master of the world (compare with Pss 74:12; 77:12; Prov 8:22–23).[16]

Yahweh's announcement has suggested he will act out of character and bring disaster upon his own people through the menacing 'he'

---

16. Sweeney, "Structure, Genre, and Intent," 230.

in the scene who presumably is the same figure as the representative Chaldean king from the previous scene. The absence of a proper name for this character increases trepidation—he cannot be pinned down but represents personified and relentless evil. It also allows him to be an archetype, a character that can reappear at subsequent readings of this experience and represent the 'face' of evil threatening the current audience.[17]

צדיך (*[the] righteous one*) makes another appearance in this scene (v. 13). Unlike the earlier reference (v. 4), there is no question here that one could understand the designation to refer to Yahweh. The term comes in the context of a direct question to Yahweh unlike the third person report speech of Hab 1:4. There remains the possibility, however, that צדיך could be identified with the prophet.

A new cast of extras are employed in this scene also: the amorphous mass of humankind who are being treated no better than animals by the all-powerful enemy. That their plight is seemingly ignored by Yahweh is emphasized by the vocabulary of this scene. After all, it is Yahweh who made them (possibly another sarcastic use of a traditional concept), but it is Yahweh who allows "him" to drag them away. The vocabulary used in vv. 12–13 emphasize this irony: reference to Yahweh as צור (*Rock*) ironically highlights the changeableness of his character, more like shifting sand than rock. The reference to Yahweh's origins as being "from old" (מקדם) echoes the previous scene where the destructive force is described as "coming forward" (קדימה, v. 9). This choice of words gives the tantalizing suggestion that Yahweh and the enemy have a similar origin. Yahweh is expected to be the eternal and dependable creative force but instead turns a blind eye to the evil and trouble of his own people, while at the same time "pay[ing] attention" to "those who act treacherously" (v. 13).

The mention of "sacrifice" and "smoke offerings" evoke a scene of worship, but whether "he" is acknowledging his god—the shadowy figure from Scene Two (v. 11)—or treating his nets (figurative language for

---

17. It is also possible to interpret the third person report as continued reference to Yahweh, as if the prophet has turned back to the audience and described the actions of the character who has taken on the enemy's *persona*. Without definite character identification one could read in the phrases a reference to Yahweh as the one "bringing up with a fishing hook, dragging away in his net, gathering them in a fish-trap" (v. 15). The following verse, however, makes this unlikely, since a sacrifice would not be performed by a deity.

weapons of war) as deities who have brought him success is ambiguous. Either way, there seems to be an acknowledgement that his life of luxury (riches and fatness) is attributable to something outside of himself.

The attention returns to the prophet at the end of the scene as he poses his plaintive question, *Shall he therefore empty his net and continue to slay nations without mercy?* The third person format provides some ambiguity—is this question addressed to Yahweh or to the audience who are invited to judge Yahweh along with the prophet? It is a question that even raises the suggestion that it is Yahweh who is ultimately responsible for the success of the enemy.

Audience

The second person address of the first two questions and the use of the second person singular pronoun אתה (*you*) means that the audience is again predominantly eavesdropping rather than being directly involved at the beginning of this scene. The final question, however, has a more ambiguous address and is intended to engage the audience's participation. The emotive language employed by the prophet ensures that even if the audience is removed grammatically, it cannot fail to be moved emotionally by the complaint. The audience is reminded of Yahweh's character by using traditional concepts for Yahweh, thus setting up an expectation that he will continue to act in these ways. The prophet's complaint interrupts those expectations and would have the effect of unsettling the audience by showing them how inconsistent these expectations are with Yahweh's present actions.

Setting

The abrupt move from a reference to "his god" to a prayer addressed in second person to Yahweh not only marks this as a new scene but also highlights Yahweh as the predominant character in the composition who completely overshadows any other potential 'deities' in the performance.

The change in verb forms divides the scene into two sections, so that vv. 12–14 are a prayer addressed to Yahweh and vv. 15–17 are a report of the hostile actions of the other character already introduced in the previous scene. The two sections are held together with the common metaphor of fish. Yahweh made humankind "like the fish of the sea" and the enemy is also treating them like fish, using traps, hooks, and nets to subdue and slay the nations. Once again the imagery would not be unfamiliar to a Persian audience—in the Hebrew Bible 'hooks' and 'net' were common metaphors describing actions of an oppressor (Ezek 12:13; 17:20; Amos 4:2) and pictorial depictions of captives being taken away following battle include images of nets, hooks, and ropes through lips and noses.[18]

Improvisation

In similar fashion to the first scene, the use of the traditional form of a prayer of complaint by Habakkuk has nonetheless been innovatively modified. Here there is a confusing mixture of action and inaction on the part of Yahweh—he who supposedly cannot see evil nevertheless pays attention to the troublemakers while at the same time keeping silent in the face of injustice (v. 12). The reference to רשׁע (*wicked*) and צדיק (*righteous*), links this to the earlier complaint—there the wicked surrounded the righteous but now wickedness has *swallowed* the righteous (v. 13). Once again, there is no expression of trust or vow of praise in the prayer. In actual fact 'prayer' may not be the right word at all for Habakkuk's complaints. His use of sarcasm implies provocation and challenge, by which he speaks with Yahweh on equal terms. He is not exactly "talking back,"[19] as Yahweh has not directly addressed him, but he is certainly allowing his complaint to be front and center in the scene.

The use of creation imagery in this scene is striking, particularly as it uses the language of Genesis 1 while subverting the accepted meaning of Genesis 1. Humankind is described in two parallel terms: "like the fish of the sea" and "like a lowly sea-creature." The latter term—רמשׂ—is the same term found in Gen 1:24. Given that the Genesis verse refers to "cattle and wild animals of every kind" alongside "creeping things" it is likely that the latter term should be understood as the 'low life' of the animal world, such as the insects or rodents. Hill notes that while רמשׂ ordinarily refers to small creeping rodents and reptiles, in Ps 104:25 and Hab 1:14 the reference is to sea creatures.[20] Both of these verses have the sea as the context and elsewhere the verb רמשׂ is used to describe movement of water creatures (Gen 1:21; Ps 69:35). Even if רמשׂ is to

---

18. Ahlström, *The History of Ancient Palestine*, 746.
19. Compare with Mandolfo, "Talking Back."
20. Hill, "רמשׂ," 1128.

be understood as sea creatures here, it stands in contrast to Genesis 1 where humankind is created to have dominion over the animal world including "the fish of the sea" and "every creeping thing" (Gen 1:26). Here humankind *are* these creatures, without anyone ruling over them and therefore are completely vulnerable and susceptible to domination by the enemy. The merging of the creation motif with a fishing metaphor also raises allusions of Yahweh subduing Leviathan as part of his acts of creation (Isa 27:1; Ps 74:13–14; Job 40:24—41:1). The same imagery is being used here, however, to emphasize that Yahweh is allowing the monstrous enemy free reign over his people.

PERFORMANCE THEMES IN HABAKKUK 1

Pelias speaks of the evocative power of language in the performance of aesthetic texts: "Expressive language avoids the ordinary, the cliché, the everyday. Striking in effect, it surprises, delights, enriches, moves, and compels listeners. In short, it commands attention and it is keenly felt. Its power arises from reliance upon the sensuous, figurative, rhythmic, and reflexive."[21]

This description fits a performative reading of chapter one of Habakkuk and picks up two of the common performance themes that have been isolated. Engaging the senses through figurative and rhythmic language such as the use of colorful metaphors, wordplay, and emotive language is an aspect of embodiment. Pelias claims that the reflexive nature of aesthetic texts allows them not only to examine themselves, but to be used vicariously by an audience who can be drawn in to share the experiences and emotions of the actors.[22] A careful examination of Habakkuk 1 will show that these aspects of self-reflexivity and embodiment are present, along with process, re-enactment, and universality.

Autobiography is understood as an especially self-reflective form of performance, comparable to self-portraits in the visual arts.[23] The prophetic literature is usually presented in autobiographical form, where the *persona* of the prophet sets out his experience of receiving and transmitting the Word of God. Nissinen claims that the prophetic experience requires four components: the deity, the message, the transmitter of the

---

21. Pelias, *Performance Studies*, 109.
22. Ibid.
23. Levy, "The Performance of Creation," 194.

message and an audience.[24] The role of the prophet as intermediary, then, is the primary identification. The theme of self-reflexivity is therefore a fundamental theme in prophetic communication.

The traditional role of the prophet as intermediary is self-consciously altered when the prophet questions the character and motives of Yahweh in Scenes One (1:2–4) and Three (1:12–17). Scene Three especially throws the spotlight on perceived shortcomings in Yahweh's role, with the prophet sarcastically referring to traditional expectations that are being ignored and demanding answers to his anguished questions. In Scene Two (1:5–11) Yahweh had claimed to act decisively in raising up the Chaldeans. But the scenes that are focused on the prophet's complaints—Scene One (1:2–4) and Scene Three (1:12–17)—draw attention to the inaction of Yahweh who remains silent in the face of injustice.

The prophet also reflects on the nature of humankind as he pursues his role of intermediary. The reference to humankind as "fish of the sea" and "creeping things" shows an alertness to the creatureliness of the human actor, but the particular choice of metaphors emphasizes the sense of helplessness in the face of the onslaught of the enemy and the prophet's perception of himself and his community as victims in the scenario.

Conquergood speaks of "two different domains of knowledge: one official, objective and abstract . . . ; the other one practical, embodied and popular."[25] The "participatory knowing" of the latter highlights the theme of embodiment, a theme well developed in Habakkuk 1. The immersion of the speaker in a violent and destructive world suggests that he is not an impartial observer but an embodied participant. The prophet's speech is anguished and his pain escalates in intensity as shown through the use of the verbs שׁוע (*call*) and זעק (*cry out*) in 1:4. If "the righteous one" (v. 4) is to be understood as the prophet, then righteousness has been embodied in him, further emphasizing his helplessness in the face of the enemy onslaught.

The text suggests that Yahweh is physically present in the drama. Despite the use of the title "Rock" for Yahweh (v. 12), human attributes are ascribed to him whose "eyes" cannot see evil and who "keeps silence" when one might expect him to speak out (v. 13). The enemy is also embodied, both in the reference to the oppressor as a representative

---

24. Nissinen, "What is Prophecy?" 20.
25. Conquergood, "Performance Studies," 311–12.

individual in Scene Two (1:6–11) and via the multitude of verbs ascribed to "him" in Scene Three (1:12–17). He brings up, drags away, gathers, rejoices, sacrifices, grows rich and fat (1:15–16). The lack of name ensures that this enemy remains a universal oppressor, but the concrete actions described enable him to be visualized and 'experienced.'

The theme of embodiment can also apply to the implied audience. The scenes lose impact when merely read as a text. Verbs of seeing and hearing suggest these scenes need to be visualized and experienced as well as heard. The audience would be impacted by the fast pace and apprehensive emotion evoked by the colorful imagery of Scene Two (1:5–11), where the impression of whirlwind destruction is emphasized by the use of swift carnivorous animal metaphors (leopards, wolves, vultures) and verbs of speed (swift and keen, they gallop, they fly, he hastens, goes forward, sweeps through). Alliteration adds to the sense of movement and menace, such as פעל פעל (*a work is being worked*, v. 5); המר והנמהר (*hurtful and hasty*, v. 6); פשו פרשיו (*they gallop his gallopers*, v. 8). There is excitement but also trepidation. Who would not fail to be moved to anxiety by such a description?

The theme of process is enhanced by the grammatical elements of the text. Examples include the repeated use of the conjunction "and" in Scene One (1:2–4), creating the impression of bad things piling up; the use of present-tense verbs and a swift concluding change to past-tense in Scene Two (1:5–11); and the sustained use of present-tense verbs in Scene Three (1:12–17), ending with the question "shall he continue?" These grammatical elements contribute to an emphasis on the activity of the enemy with an open-ended future. The audience does not have the sense of this oppressor being only a past memory, but an ever present reality. In addition there is a sense of open-endedness prior to the events of the text shown by the first complaint beginning with the words "how long?" There is an implication that this is not a new thought, but one which has already troubled the speaker for a long time. The intensifying of verbs within the complaint from "I call" to "I cry out" (v. 2) and the repetition and build up of words around the idea "you pay attention to trouble" (v. 3, v. 13) suggests an escalating process.

Analysis of the first three scenes in Act One reveals a new and unprecedented way of using traditional forms and terminology. The 're-enactment' of these elements enable the surprise that is essential in maintaining interest and involvement by the audience. The improvisation of known forms shows that while these scenes are located in a particular time, they are applicable to any time of crisis. Thus the theme of universality is also present in this text. The prophet's complaints, while individual in expression, are set in general terms. The sources of strife and violence are not provided and "the righteous one" is not named so that other hearers and readers can identify both with the experience of the prophet and the sense of helplessness of being a "righteous one" who is trapped in such a setting.

Members of a Persian audience would have been only too familiar with the description of violent invasion, their territory having been the location of similar invasions several times in their history. The despair and helplessness evoked in these scenes are likely to be re-lived in other times of crisis. The description of this oppressor may be consistent with the warfare practices of a Neo-Babylonian army, but generic terms such as "those who act treacherously" (v. 13) and "he drags them away with his net" (v. 15) accentuate the universal nature of any oppression that leaves its victims feeling helpless and trapped. Each re-enactment of such an experience would have familiarity despite new circumstances, exemplified by the Qumran community some centuries after the Persian Yehud group relating the prophecy to their own fear of Roman invasion.

SIX

A Performance Reading of Habakkuk 2

THIS CHAPTER CONTINUES TO analyze the book of Habakkuk with the aid of performance criticism, focusing on Habakkuk 2. Act One continues in Habakkuk 2 and divides into two scenes, Scene Four (vv. 2–5) and Scene Five (vv. 6–19), identified by different settings and grammatical links. There is an introduction to Scene Four (v. 1), and an interlude (v. 20) that divides Acts One and Two. Scene Five of Act One is interrupted by an interjection (v. 14).

PERFORMANCE FEATURES IN HABAKKUK 2

Act One—Introduction to Scene Four (2:1)

¹ On my guard let me stand,
and let me set myself on siege works,
and let me keep watch to see what he says to me,
and what I will bring back concerning my rebuke.

Author and Script

The emphasis on watching and listening again underscores the value of a performance reading of Habakkuk as a new scene begins. Although it is a single voice speaking in the first person, it is clear from the location that this is a public announcement in a public place. Thus far in this performance abrupt shifts between genre and presentation of characters leave a very open plot line that could develop in different directions. The introduction to Scene Four (Hab 2:1) continues to keep the plot open with its future verbs and its portrayal of a watchful and alert guard.

Actors

In this short introduction the only actor is the prophet. Although Habakkuk is not specifically identified (unlike the preludes to Acts One and Two), the reference to Yahweh's answer in the next verse (Hab 2:2) clearly shows that it is the prophet speaking. Although absent in this introduction, Yahweh's role is defined through the prophet's expectant statement. For the prophet, Yahweh has a role to perform even if that role is still unknown.

It is possible to discern character development in the prophet between the end of Scene Three and this statement. The self description of the prophet in military terms ("on my guard," "siege works") suggests that he has self-consciously moved from being a helpless victim of circumstances to an active player in the drama. Furthermore, the use of first person verbs and pronouns, "what *I* will bring back concerning *my* argument," suggests that the prophet himself has a contribution to make to the discussion.[1] Earlier Habakkuk was described as 'sarcastic' and 'judging' of Yahweh, but here the prophet presents himself as one who is prepared to wait patiently for an answer to his own arguments. This, of course, indicates that the earlier 'answer' given by Yahweh was a 'non-answer' for the prophet, but there is a new sense of self-confidence in his right to expect further communication. Examination of the ancient versions shows a discomfort with the idea that a prophet could either argue with Yahweh or demand an answer from Yahweh, and modern commentaries often comment on the prophet's 'audacious' claim.[2] Such discomfort notwithstanding, the hitherto capricious nature of Yahweh's *persona* justifies the prophet's assumption that he has not yet heard the full story from Yahweh.

---

1. Boyle, *The Rhetoric of Taunt Language*, 178-90, translates Hab 2:1 in a similar fashion: "I will watch closely to see what he will say to me/and what I will say back for my rebuke." He understands this to be Habakkuk's invitation to Yahweh for an ongoing disputation in the manner of the first chapter. He views Yahweh's command to "write the vision" (Hab 2:2), however, as reducing the anticipated dispute to a monologue: "[the prophet] is decisively brought down from his posture of indignant challenger to that of obedient secretary."

2. For example, Robertson, *The Books of Nahum, Habakkuk, and Zephaniah*, 165–66; Roberts, *Nahum, Habakkuk, and Zephaniah*, 105; Anderson, *Habakkuk*, 194; Hiebert, "The Book of Habakkuk," 639.

Audience

An audience is not explicitly mentioned, but the presence of an audience can be assumed given the public setting. Those who are part of the prophet's community have already been drawn into the debate, specifically through the general final question of the previous scene. Can it be assumed that they side with the prophet's dissatisfaction of Yahweh's first answer and an expectation that more will be said? This introduction implies the presence of another audience, however, in that the public setting in the midst of warfare suggests the Chaldean army will also hear what Yahweh says.

Setting

The siege works provide a new setting, justifying a new scene division, but retaining the overall warfare imagery established in Scene Two (Hab 1:5–11). If the performance was being filmed, one could imagine a panning view of marching armies sweeping through a vast landscape intent on destruction with a gradual focusing-in on a lone figure standing on guard, alert to anything that would signify the arrival of friend or enemy. The word מצור (*siege* or *siege works*) also occurs in the context of narrative descriptions of the Babylonian attack on Jerusalem (2 Kgs 24:10; 25:2) and is an appropriate translation here given the context of the invasion of the Chaldean king with his army. The warfare theme is further enhanced by the verb "keep watch," used elsewhere in the context of watching for signs of warfare (1 Sam 14:16; Isa 21:6; Ezek 33:1–4; Nah 2:2) or spying on an enemy (Ps 37:32). The setting suggests that Jerusalem still stands despite the announcement in Scene Two of her capture by the Chaldean king.

The staging of this introduction is significant. The prophet is raised on a structure at the edge of the city and his elevated position outside of the normal constraints again emphasizes his shocking claim to being an (almost?) equal conversation partner with Yahweh.

Improvisation

The traditional role of the prophet is again challenged and modified in the way the prophet is presented here. Remembering that the primary quality of prophecy is that of intermediation between the divine word and the human audience, it is significant that in this case the prophet continues to take on a more proactive role in challenging Yahweh's answers and demanding more from him. In addition, the prophet assumes his own contribution is valid and on par with that of Yahweh's. As was seen in Scene Three (Hab 1:12–17), the impudence inherent in complaint and sarcasm is typical of this prophet, despite its rarity in the prophetic literature.

Act One—Scene Four (2:2–5)

> ² And Yahweh answered me and said:
> Write [the] vision and make plain on the tablets
> so that [the] reader will run with it.
> ³ For [the] vision is yet for the appointed time,
> and it breathes to the end and does not lie.
> If it tarries, wait for it, for it surely comes, it will not delay.
> ⁴ Behold, it is swollen: his soul is not upright in him,
> but [the] righteous one in his faithfulness will live.
> ⁵ And moreover the wine is treacherous!
> A mighty man is haughty and does not abide,
> who widens his soul like Sheol,
> and he is like death and is not sated.
> And he gathered to himself all the nations,
> and collected to himself all the peoples.

Author and Script

Scene Four begins with an 'answer.' Despite the requirement of patience implied in the introduction, there is an immediate response from Yahweh. A חזון (*vision*) is mentioned, which is ironic given the accusation against Yahweh in Scene Three that he is not able to see (Hab 1:13). The use of הנה (*behold*) suggests the vision begins at v. 4. What is not clear is whether the חזון is the content of v. 4 only, vv. 4–5 (these verses belong together by virtue of the particles ואף כי, *and moreover*), or inclusive of the scenes that follow. The choice of a different word suggests that the חזון is only one part of the entire משא announced at the beginning of the performance. This vision is to be public, easily seen and inspiring action in those who read it (v. 2). Its significance is underscored by the reference to הלחות (*the tablets*), the same word used for the stones that carried the Decalogue (Exod 24:12). The verb באר (*to make plain*) also evokes Moses' reception of the law in that it is only used in two other places in the Hebrew Bible, both of which are related to the Horeb/Sinai experience (Deut 1:5; 27:8).

Actors

As anticipated, Yahweh re-enters the drama in the scene. Unlike his earlier appearances, however, Yahweh is now acting as expected. In the introduction to this scene the prophet had announced he would wait for an answer (Hab 2:1). Scene Four begins with "he answered me," a phrase reiterated with the typical narrative form ויאמר (*and he said*). Furthermore, Yahweh relates to the prophet in the expected manner, commanding him (with imperatives) to clearly communicate the vision as would be expected of a deity's instructions to an intermediary.

That Yahweh expects an audience to this vision is shown in the statement "so that [the] reader may run with it" (v. 2). קורא (*reader*) is introduced as an actor in this scene. This active participle implies a proclamation, not silent reading. It is not necessary to be reminded of the intimate interplay between oral and written cultures in the ancient world because attentiveness to the roles presented in the drama suggest action that is seen and heard. The lack of a clear identification of קורא, however, means that those listening in the audience are able to identify themselves in that role.

The third person singular verbs that follow draw attention once again to the Chaldean king. The use of the unusual verb עפל (*to be swollen*) in a feminine form, in relation to the king (or perhaps his [feminine] soul), suggests a character to be made fun of: a 'bighead' who has already been described in arrogant terms (Hab 1:7, 10) and who continues to be described as "haughty" (v. 5) and overly greedy, with an appetite for conquering and destroying as large as that of Sheol who swallows the dead without discrimination (v. 5; compare with Isa 5:14). Even in the English translation a double meaning is obvious with the description of the king as גבר (*a mighty man*) who will be put in his place. In this vision the king of the Chaldeans need no longer be feared, because he will "not abide" (v. 5).

While first person pronouns imply the continuing presence of Habakkuk in this scene, the reappearance of צדיק ([*the*] *righteous one*) can also be understood as referring to the prophet, although the title is somewhat provocative given the presumptuousness the prophet has shown.[3] Nonetheless, the prophet has shown both assertiveness *and* patience (notice the exhortation to "wait" in Hab 2:1 and 2:3) and has been vindicated by the lack of reprimand by Yahweh despite repeated questions and complaints. With the designation צדיק the prophet draws attention to himself as a principal character in the scene. The phrase in v. 4: "But the righteous one in his faithfulness will live" is out of place in the discourse about the haughty one and may be understood as an interjection, arguably by the prophet himself. When הצדיק first appeared in Scene One (Hab 1:4) he was surrounded by wickedness but now patient waiting has resulted in vindication for the righteous one who will live and judgment for the haughty man who will not abide!

Audience

If the audience have been awaiting Yahweh's response along with the prophet then they will be alert to the announcement of a vision and would remain expectant and attentive even if it is not immediately forthcoming (v. 3). An explicit taunt is mentioned at the beginning of Scene Five (Hab 2:6) but already the language includes a mocking tone that would be apparent to the audience and would begin to raise the emotional level of a crowd. The reference to כל־הגוים, (*all the nations*) and כל־העמים (*all the peoples*), emphasized by the rhyming word play, raises the possibility that those in the audience are implicated in the events that are being brought to a head. In addition, כל־הגוים is a reminder of the presence of the Chaldeans and an acknowledgement that they, too, are part of the audience. The vision of Yahweh is to be unveiled before the enemy who has so arrogantly acted against Yahweh's people.

---

3. See Pinker, "Was Habakkuk Presumptuous?" 27. Pinker considers Hab 1:3 "to be an expression of insolence" and that the prophet's words in Hab 1:6 and 2:1–2 "exemplify taking liberties in making his case and being presumptuous." Pinker's views support midrashic sources that take exception to the identification between Habakkuk and Moses as well as to the thought that a prophet might question Yahweh's judgment.

Setting

For the first time in Habakkuk explicit stage directions are given: the prophet is to write the vision and the reader is to run with it. The references to writing and running suggest that the action has moved down from the siege works to the marketplace where such events are commonplace and public proclamation makes sense. The puzzling reference to wine (v. 5)[4] can also be understood as belonging in a public area. One can imagine carousing Chaldeans who are celebrating their victory becoming the objects of public ridicule when over-consumption leads to uncontrolled behavior.

Mention of Sheol adds a further dimension to the setting and suggests that this drama is not relevant only for this time and this world but has implications for the future. The righteous one will live, but the one who is haughty and crooked enters a living death where satisfaction is never possible.

Improvisation

The term חזון (*vision*) is one closely associated with prophetic activity[5] and is used in the introductions to Isaiah, Obadiah, and Nahum. The instruction to write the vision on tablets is a variation on the usual use of the word, although Isa 30:8 is an instruction to write prophetic words on a tablet for future reference. The emphasis in Habakkuk on writing "so that [the] reader will run with it" (v. 2) suggests the activity of writing is not only for future posterity or vindication but also for the benefit of the present audience.

As noted above, the reference to הלחות (*the tablets*) uses the ready-made association of Moses and the Law. Midrashic sources appear to note this with some unease. *Bavli Makkot* 3.15–16 II begins: "Therefore he gave them abundant Torah and numerous commandments . . . Six hundred and thirteen commandments were given to Moses." The long discussion that follows concludes: "Habakkuk further came and based

---

4. Many translations have followed Q and read "wealth deceives." Both suggestions are valid renderings as both serve the intention of the author in ridiculing arrogant power that does not recognize the greater might of Yahweh. The later reference to drunkenness (Hab 2:15), however, suggests that this forms an intentional link between Scenes Four and Five ensuring that the "mighty man" of Hab 2:5 is associated with the one misusing drink in Hab 2:15–16.

5. Naudé, "חזון," 56.

them on one, as it is said, 'But the righteous shall live by his faith' (Habakkuk 2:4)."[6] Despite the skepticism of the Midrash, such an acute understanding on the part of the author of Habakkuk, which might even be called a 'vision,' has been enthusiastically received by the ongoing tradition as evidenced by the quotation of this text in Rom 1:17; Gal 3:11; and Heb 10:38.

Act One—Scene Five, Part One (2:6-13)

> [6] Are not all these lifting up a taunt against him?
> And satirical riddles about him? And he says:
> Woe to him who piles up what is not his
> — How long?
> And the one making heavy debts upon himself.
> [7] Will not the ones biting you suddenly arise?
> And will not the ones violently shaking you wake?
> And you will be their spoil.
> [8] Because you plundered many nations
> let the remaining peoples plunder you —
> On account of blood of man and violence of earth,
> a town and all who live in it.
> [9] Woe to him who violently gains unjust gain!
> Evil belongs to his house
> who has set his nest in the heights
> to be delivered from the grasp of evil.
> [10] You counseled shame for your house,
> to cut off many people, and your soul is sinning.
> [11] For a stone from a wall will cry out,
> and a rafter from the woodwork will answer it.
> [12] Woe to him who builds a city with bloodshed
> and establishes a town with iniquity!

---

6. Neusner, *Habakkuk, Jonah, Nahum and Obadiah in Talmud and Midrash*, 49-52; see also Pinker, "Was Habakkuk Presumptuous?" 33.

¹³ Behold! Is it not from Yahweh of Hosts?

And peoples labor for fire and nations grow faint for nothing.

Interjection (2:14)

¹⁴ But the earth will be filled

with the knowledge of the glory of Yahweh

as the waters cover the sea!

Act One—Scene Five, Part Two (2:15-19)

¹⁵ Woe to him making his neighbor drink;

Who clings to your rage and even drunkenness

in order to gaze upon their nakedness!

¹⁶ You are sated with shame rather than glory.

Drink, you also, and be counted as uncircumcised!

A cup in the right hand of Yahweh will turn around upon you,

and shameful shame will be upon your glory.

¹⁷ For the violence of Lebanon covers you,

and the devastation of beasts causes them to be terrified —

On account of blood of man and violence of earth,

a town and all who live in it.

¹⁸ Of what benefit is an idol when he who hewed it made it?

— an image and a teacher of deception?

For the maker who makes it trusted on it,

To make dumb worthless idols.

¹⁹ Woe to him who says to a tree 'wake up!'

'awake!' to the mute stone. 'It is teaching!'

Behold it, overlaid with gold and silver

and full of wind? There is nothing in it!

Author and Script

Scene Five is divided into two parts by an interjection and is followed by an interlude. Undoubtedly it was originally designed as a coherent scene with its series of five taunts introduced by the particle הוי (*woe*). These woe oracles predominantly follow a pattern including a rhythmic shift between third-person and second-person address. Despite being "rather awkward in English"[7] this pattern functions to add vividness to the scene and explicitly draw the audience into the action.[8]

The scene is introduced by an explicit stage instruction: everyone is invited to join in a series of taunts. The object of the taunts is surely the Chaldean king—that arrogant and puffed up tormentor who is now to be put in his place. The use of singular verbs underscores this interpretation. But as the verbs change from third person to second person some ambiguity is introduced into the script. Is the author turning on individuals in the Israelite audience and including them in his condemnation? Or are "all these," as representatives of the righteous one, turning their attention directly to the king, now in the judgment seat to hear their accusation directly? Both interpretations are possible and the decision lies with the director of this scene.

The script is especially full of word play devices in this scene, suggesting an underlying wisdom background in which sayings are constructed to be remembered.[9] Thus in the Hebrew script several instances of alliteration and assonance can be found including לא־לו (*not his own*, v. 6), בצע בצע (*who violently gains unjust gain*, v. 9), אלילים אלמים (*dumb worthless idols*, v. 18); repetitive use of צ (the sound *ts*) that would sound like hissing in the second woe oracle (vv. 9–11); three rhyming phrases in vv. 7–9 and two examples of compound words constructed by repeating the first syllable to intensify the concept: מזעזעיך (*the ones violently shaking you*, v. 7) and קיקלון (*shameful shame*, v. 16).

---

7. Clark and Hatton, *A Handbook on the Books of Nahum, Habakkuk, and Zephaniah*, 100.

8. Renewal of the audience's attention is one of the reasons for person shifts in prophetic texts according to de Regt, "Person Shifts in Prophetic Texts," 231, who states: "Against the background of non-face threatening third person forms, second person forms renew the audience's involvement, addressing Israel anew."

9. Robertson, *The Books of Nahum, Habakkuk, and Zephaniah*, 186–88.

Actors

The scene begins with a reference to אלה כלם (*all these*), an inclusive term that draws in all who have suffered at the hand of the invader. The attention has shifted away from the prophet as the concerned representative to the community as a whole. But the singular verb that follows the invitation ויאמר (*and he says*) concentrates the taunts in an individual speaker—Yahweh. In addition, although the stage has been envisaged full of Chaldean enemies along with the Israelite audience so that all are participants in the action, the singular verbs in the five woes ensure that the individual enemy—the Chaldean king—is the main focus of attention. This distinction is not as obvious in English translation where the pronoun 'you' can be either singular or plural. But from the perspective of performance it is significant. Two principal actors remain in the spotlight throughout the scene. That this enemy is the same king introduced in Scene Two (Hab 1:5–11) is indicated by the repeated phrase לא־לו (*not his own*, 1:6; 2:6). This is the one who "possesses" and "piles up" what is not his own and he will be called to account.

A host of other characters are introduced in this scene, but all make only brief appearances after which attention is drawn back again to the speaker and recipient of the woes.

The first woe mentions "the ones biting you" and "the ones violently shaking you" (v. 7)—parallel participles that can be understood as characters. They arise "suddenly," but evidently as a result of poetic justice, to claim back from the Chaldean king what he has arrogantly and wrongfully plundered. Likewise "Lebanon" (v. 17) functions as a character, with the construct form of חמס (*violence*), allowing it to be read as a characteristic of Lebanon rather than an action taken against Lebanon as is often read (e.g., the NRSV translation: "violence done to Lebanon"). The speaker of the woes announces that the dreaded enemy will be pursued and overtaken by his own enemies. The reference to "a town and all who live in it" (v. 8), repeated in v. 17, further suggests the relentless pursuit of justice.

Retribution and shame will come upon not only the enemy but also his "house" (v. 9). The second woe plays with the term "house" by referring to aspects of a building; stones in the wall and woodwork from the rafters (v. 10). These inanimate objects are given a voice and so become characters in their own right, adding their cry to those outraged by the actions of the enemy.

The two stars of this scene come to the fore again in the third woe. "He who builds a city with bloodshed and establishes a town with iniquity" (v. 12) is the Chaldean king, held up for scrutiny and contrasted with a magnified Yahweh, יהוה צבאות (*Yahweh of Hosts*, v. 13). This is a new attribute for Yahweh in this performance, although one that will resonate with the Israelite audience (compare with Isa 47:4; Jer 7:3; Mic 4:4; Nah 2:14; Zeph 2:10). It could be viewed as another taunt at the Chaldean members of the audience with its military overtones, poking fun at their now depleted power. Indeed, the "peoples" and "nations" (v. 13) are references to those aligned with the Chaldean king. Their efforts amount to nothing in contrast to Yahweh of Hosts.

The third woe ends abruptly, without a shift to second person singular verbs as is the usual pattern. It is interrupted by another pious statement—surely the interjection comes again from the prophet. Could it be that the author sees the prophet as the true star of the show, ensuring that he makes an appearance in every scene? The self-designation by Yahweh of his status as commander of hosts (note the הנה, [*behold!*] in v. 13, that draws attention to the statement) prompts the prophet to endorse enthusiastically the perceived power of Yahweh. Habakkuk is now on the side of the winners, vindicated by his patience despite his earlier anguish.

The fourth and fifth woes present additional minor characters. A degree of titillation is introduced via the naked and drunken neighbors of the Chaldean king (v. 15), undoubtedly another taunt against non-Israelite nations as evidenced in the reference to the "uncircumcised" (v. 16). The maker of idols is mentioned (v. 18) but does not come on stage. In contrast to the stone and woodwork of v. 10 that were able to speak, the hand-crafted stone and wooden idols are dumb and mute (v. 19) and the mocking reference to them functions as another means of poking fun at the Chaldean king.

Notable in this scene is the lack of speech on the part of the accused. With the possible exception of Hab 2:19, which quotes speech offered to idols, the subject of the woe oracles is silent. A non-speaking actor can achieve a powerful dramatic effect.[10] In this scene, however, such silence functions not to elicit sympathy for the character but rather

---

10. Levy, *The Bible as Theatre*, 24, uses the examples of Hannah in 1 Samuel 1, the concubine at Gibeah in Judges 19, and Dinah in Genesis 34 to point out the power of silence in drama that itself can be described as "non-verbal (theatrical) language."

to highlight the guilty nature of the accused. His silence in the face of accusation can only be the result of his inexcusable behavior.

Audience

The introduction to the scene with the question "Are not all these lifting up a taunt?" and the rhythmic shift from third-person to second-person forms in the verbs deliberately involves the audience in this scene. Despite the ongoing presence of the main characters, this performance has become more like performance art than a conventional production, as the audience inadvertently discovers it has been brought on-stage. The audience is not given an active role, however, as the taunts are spoken by one person. One can imagine members of the audience taking the role of 'seconds' to the leader of the group, jeering and affirming the taunts that are voiced by an individual and enthusiastically cheering at the public judgment and condemnation made of the Chaldean king on their behalf.

Anstey refers to the role of the audience as that of 'chorus'[11] but, as has been noted, the audience on stage includes the Chaldeans and cannot therefore be seen as a unified entity supporting the action on-stage. Nor does their role function as that of a classic Greek chorus, commenting on themes and showing an ideal response to the drama. They are drawn in via אלה כלם (*all these*), but predominantly remain observers of the unfolding dialogue. It is the prophet, possibly "the righteous one," who voices an 'ideal response' to the drama via his interjections (Hab 2:4b, 14, 20).

Setting

The woe oracles belong together and have been grouped in a series similar to that seen in other prophetic contexts (especially Isa 5:8, 11, 18, 20, 22, where five comparable woes are listed). They are framed by an introductory exhortation (Hab 2:6a) and an affirmation about Yahweh (Hab 2:20). The latter verse functions as an interlude between the second and third chapters of Habakkuk and thus merits individual analysis.

The introduction to this series speaks of משל (*a taunt*), מליצה (*a satire*) and חידות (*riddles*). This combination of terms is uncommon and will be discussed below. The verbal taunts in the text are obvious, but

---

11. Anstey, "Habakkuk the Faithful Dissident," 53.

the verb נשׂא (*to lift up*), suggests insulting physical gestures may have accompanied the taunt songs and therefore been an integral part of this scene.

This scene calls for a number of props. The stone and rafter (v. 11) are given voices and thus could be considered actors. The tree and stone idols (v. 19), however, are clearly mere objects. Their presence on the stage would effectively emphasize their uselessness as sources of glory or power, especially in contrast to the living Yahweh active on stage throughout the scene. Drawing attention to their appearance as "overlaid with gold and silver" emphasizes the irony that these attractive coverings nonetheless smother them, rendering them breathless and lifeless. A significant prop is the "cup in the right hand of Yahweh" (v. 16), a metaphor with both positive and negative connotations but in this scene accompanied by words that present it as a menacing threat against the Chaldean king.

The script suggests that the scenery is continually changing as the taunts play out. As is common in poetry, the words paint pictures in the imagination, but from a performance perspective one can envisage a more tangible setting being offered. As the background shifts from nations to land to towns to individual houses to Lebanon and finally to the natural world of trees and stones one can imagine, in a modern retelling, an interactive media presentation[12] of changing images flicking past on a backdrop, bewildering in its variety but building up the idea that all the world is joined in condemnation of the Chaldean king. The concluding statement "Hush before him all the earth" (v. 20) is a fitting end to such a scenario, where all experience is relativized in the presence of Yahweh.

Improvisation

The term משׁל, often translated *proverb*, has its roots in the verb משׁל (*to be like*).[13] It is thus a word used for comparison, as proverbs often are, both positively and negatively. The prophetic literature predominantly uses the term for negative comparison as shown here in Habakkuk. The woes are a list of actions a condemned person might have done: plundering, gaining by illicit means, violently shedding blood, showing no respect for neighbors and putting faith in idols.

12. See the description of InterVarsity's multi-media presentation of the book of Habakkuk in Chapter 8.

13. Beyse, "משׁל," 47.

The combination of משל (*a taunt*), מליצה (*a satire*), and חידות (*riddles*), occurs elsewhere only in Prov 1:6 but there is used positively in reference to חכמים (*the wise*). The author of Habakkuk chooses to be influenced by the wisdom tradition to highlight the misdemeanors of the Chaldeans rather than the more common metaphor in the prophetic literature of a legal dispute (for example, Isa 5:1–7; Jer 2:5–9; Hos 4:1–3; Mic 6:1–8). The Chaldean king is not only being held up for contempt owing to his actions, but also for his lack of common wisdom (common sense?) that would have shown him that taking a stand against Yahweh of Hosts is futile.[14]

The use of הוי (*woe*), in each oracle further emphasizes the comparative thrust of the sayings. The author of Habakkuk has taken a word used often in funeral laments (1 Kgs 13:30; Jer 22:18; 34:5) in order to cast the shadow of death over the reported behavior of the king, thus condemning him in the very words spoken to him. Gowan's suggestion that the author parodies a funeral song in order to taunt the Chaldean king may well be correct.[15]

The revelation that the prophet Habakkuk saw began with the evocative words עד־אנה (*how long?*, Hab 1:2). A similar phrase that can be translated the same way is found in the middle of the first woe of Scene Five, עד־מתי (*how long?*, v. 6). This repetition spoken by Yahweh functions as a ready-made—an ironic reference back to the complaint of the prophet—reminding him that the time of inaction perceived by the prophet is relativized by the control now shown over the condemned man. "How long" will you go on piling up what is not yours? Only until judged by Yahweh. He who seemed impotent and inactive in Scene One is now firmly in control.

Another ready-made used by the author is the prophetic formula of v. 12, *who builds a city with bloodshed and establishes a town with iniquity*. In a parallel verse in Micah the condemnation is of the rulers and chiefs of the houses of Jacob and Israel who have "built Zion with bloodshed and Jerusalem with iniquity" (Mic 3:10). By taking out

---

14. Affinities between Habakkuk and the wisdom writings can be seen through the use of wisdom terminology, the exploration of questions of theodicy and the structure of the book beginning with complaint expressed through dialogue between a human and God and ending with theophany. Studies that highlight this link between Habakkuk and the wisdom tradition include Gowan, "Habakkuk and Wisdom"; Thompson, "Prayer, Oracle and Theophany"; and Hiebert, "The Book of Habakkuk."

15. Gowan, *The Triumph of Faith*, 54.

specific references to the city of Jerusalem the author has reworked an earlier judgment of Yahweh's own people to apply to the outsider and broadened the misdemeanor to cover injustices against many nations. This improvisation further strengthens the sovereignty of Yahweh whose judgments are able to extend beyond his own people and apply to others.

The interjection (Hab 2:14) had the sound of a slogan due to its appearance in a number of different contexts in the Hebrew Bible. As such it can also be viewed as a ready-made: a familiar phrase reminding the audience of the sovereignty of Yahweh who will ultimately triumph over the present crisis. The addition of "glory" to the phrase as it is found in Isa 11:9 (which reads "the earth will be filled with the knowledge of Yahweh as the waters cover the sea") evidences the interjector's intention of contrasting the futile aggrandizement of the recipient of the woe oracles with the natural glory of "Yahweh of hosts" (Hab 2:13).

Interlude (2:20)

> [20] And Yahweh is in his temple of holiness.
> Hush before him all the earth.

Author and Script

Habakkuk 2:20 has been characterized in this script as an 'Interlude' in recognition of the fact that the performance continues with further scenes. Arguably, it would have been a fitting conclusion to the drama, serving as a climax to the preceding scenes. The prophet's questions have been answered: Yahweh has heard and saved (Hab 1:2), paid attention to the violence troubling the prophet (Hab 1:3) and broken his silence to bring accusations against the wicked (Hab 1:13), thus interrupting the continual slaughter of the Chaldean king (the rhetorical question of Hab 1:17). This statement is also an answer to the question of Hab 1:12, "Are you not from old, Yahweh?" The main character in the drama, Yahweh, can now be found in his right place, his "temple of holiness," set over against all the earth. Does anything more need to be said?

The preceding scene has combined forms in an entertaining manner. The scene was introduced by encouraging the crowd to join in "taunts, satires and riddles" and indeed several speeches poked fun at the Chaldean king and his army, by contrasting the king with Yahweh of

Hosts, who now has the upper hand, and ridiculing the dumb and silent idols they serve. But the choice of the funereal הוי resulted in each taunt holding within it an expectation of judgment. The word הס (*hush*), adds to this expectation of judgment given its use in other prophetic contexts (Amos 6:10, 8:3; Zeph 1:7; Zech 2:13). Despite the verdict of "guilty" in Scene Two (Hab 1:11) and several dire warnings in Scene Four ("you will be their spoil" in v. 7; "shameful shame will be upon your glory" in v. 16; "the violence of Lebanon covers you" in v. 17), no direct words of judgment have been stated.

Habakkuk 2:20 thus functions as a 'peak' in this script, the point at which a problem has been considered and a solution is expected to be formulated.[16] In anticipation of the solution, then, Hab 2:20 needs not be seen as the climax to the drama, but instead is well placed as the climax to Act One.

Actors

Attention is concentrated on a single character—Yahweh—although he is not active but merely present. The statement *Yahweh is in his temple of holiness* and the command *Hush before him all the earth* is not a stage direction but is an announcement, probably spoken by the 'righteous one.' The announcement is made to 'all the earth.' In similar fashion to the beginning of Scene Five, a large audience is envisaged. But unlike the earlier scene there is only one spotlight and only one actor in focus. Somewhat surprisingly one becomes aware that at this point in the performance the Chaldean king is no longer in view. Is he shrouded in darkness awaiting a dramatic final judgment or has he exited the stage completely?

---

16. In Discourse Analysis 'peak' can be recognised by a number of identifiable features: "*concentration of participants, rhetorical underlining, locus underlining and grammatical underlining*" (Cotterell, "Linguistics, Meaning, Semantics, and Discourse Analysis," 156, author's italics). This verse conforms to these insofar as there is a concentration of characters so that the verse is spoken by "the righteous one" who gives his name to the book but is focused on "Yahweh" the principle character in the drama; the move from a series of woes to a command to be silent has a profound rhetorical effect; a change of locus noted by the sudden introduction of the temple; and the lack of verbs grammatically underline the phrase by giving it an immediate presence.

Audience

The announcement to כל־הארץ (*all the earth*), suggests that the audience is intended to be broader than the on-stage audience, even though the on-stage audience includes the Jerusalem community and the Chaldean invaders. This verse, while acting as a 'peak' in the drama, also reaches beyond the drama to address itself to future audiences.

The immediate audience, however, would be drawn in by this announcement to expect a word of judgment from Yahweh. The scene has built up the expectation of imminent judgment by the use of the woe oracles, the public denouncement of the Chaldean king and the incorporation of the image of the cup, a metaphor of judgment common in the prophetic tradition (Isa 51:17; Jer 25:15; Ezek 23:32). Until this point the accused has been notably silent, while the audience had been encouraged to 'lift up' taunts. Now all are instructed to be silent—is there an implication that all are under judgment? The removal of Yahweh from the midst of the action to an inaccessible place היכל קדשו (*his temple of holiness*), separates him from the audience and increases the sense of the audience as passive spectators waiting for further events to unfold.

Setting

Nothing has prepared the audience of this performance for the setting of the temple that is shown here. The performance introduced its first actor as a 'prophet' whose opening words were addressed to Yahweh, so a member of the audience familiar with the cultic life of the Yehud community might have been led to expect a liturgical setting, but the succeeding dialogue with its elements of complaint, questioning, and sarcasm was not conventional liturgical prayer. Furthermore, the earlier settings of battleground, fishing ground, watchtower, and public square mean that Yahweh's presence in the temple marks an abrupt change of scene.

The re-location of a major actor, Yahweh, in היכל קדשו (*his temple of holiness*), functions to highlight this part of the script and magnify the character of Yahweh. It was noted at the beginning of this performance that no physical location was specified for the revelation that came to the prophet. Here, however, the setting is crucial to the drama and the change of setting contributes to the characterization of this interlude as the 'peak' of the performance.

Improvisation

This sentence evokes Ps 11:4a—יהוה בהיכל קדשו (*Yahweh is in his temple of holiness*)—but in fact the whole psalm is evoked by the author. Key words in this performance, such as: הנה (*behold*, Ps 11:2); הרשעים (*the wicked*, Ps 11:2, 5); צדיק (*[the] righteous*, Ps 11:3, 5, 7); חמס (*violence*, Ps 11:5); נפש (*soul*, Ps 11:5); רוח (*wind*, Ps 11:6); כוס (*cup*, Ps 11:6); ישר (*upright*, Ps 11:7); and the idea of Yahweh looking on and judging evil is common to both compositions.

The trust and confidence of the psalmist contrast with the earlier uncertainty of the prophet, seen especially in Scenes One (1:2–4) and Three (1:12–17). The author has capitalized on the newly discovered assurance in the prophet, evidenced by his interjections and by co-opting the liturgical tradition of an individual psalm of trust. By doing this he effectively removes the ambiguity of Yahweh's character and replaces it with the familiar image of a powerful and awe-inspiring deity. By the time the curtain falls at the end of Act One of this drama the audience is fully expectant of a decisive divine resolution to the complaints of the prophet.

PERFORMANCE THEMES IN HABAKKUK 2

Self-reflexivity is an obvious theme in the introduction to Scene Four (Hab 2:1). The prophet is self-consciously commenting on his actions and his intentions, explaining what he will do and what he expects. He evidently intends to contribute to the drama himself, with the parallel statements "let me keep watch to see what he says to me / and what I will bring back concerning my argument" (v. 1) indicating a perception on the part of the prophet that he has an equal contribution to make. Some have argued that this statement should be interpreted as what the prophet will repeat as Yahweh's answer[17] but this would also be an act of self-reflexivity in which the prophet would take on the role of spokesperson for another character and thus consciously step outside of his own role. In fact this development is seen in the character's self-understanding as Scenes Four and Five unfold: if it is the prophet who is 'the righteous one,' he has moved away from his earlier role of questioning, complaining and rebuking Yahweh and taken on the role of prophet who transmits the message of Yahweh and represents an orthodox theologi-

---

17. For example, Andersen, *Habakkuk*, 194.

cal position that assigns glory and sovereignty to the deity. Through his interjections the prophet recognizes that his earlier frustration is now removed and his vision expands as he asserts: 'the righteous one' will live by faithfulness (v. 4), knowledge of the glory of Yahweh pervades the earth (v. 14) and ultimately 'all the earth' will be brought to silence before him (v. 20).

Self-awareness also occurs for the anti-hero in this drama. The use of third person references to 'him' (the Chaldean king) forces that character to step outside of his role and see how his actions have affected others. He is made to see both his deeds and the ramifications that will result from them: retaliatory violence (vv. 7–8) and shame (vv. 10, 16).

Members of the audience are invited to self-examination in Scene Four (2:2–5) when the 'swollen' (v. 4) 'mighty man' (v. 5) is described as 'haughty' (v. 5) and spoken of in terms of death while the 'righteous one in his faithfulness will live' (v. 4). With which of these comparative figures will the listeners identify? Will they stay on the side of life as the prophet has done or will they choose the path that 'does not abide' (v. 5)? The lack of precise identification of 'the righteous one' and 'the mighty man' allows them to be paradigmatic figures. The character of Yahweh is precisely identified, despite some shifting in his *persona* through the performance, so that members of the audience are not expected to recognize in him their own thoughts and feelings. The other major characters, however, are positioned in relation to Yahweh and exemplify possible responses to him. The characters thus become universally accessible so that an observer or reader of any era might find themselves responding with either 'faithfulness' or 'haughtiness'—a choice leading ultimately to life or death.[18] That the choice is made universally available is underscored by the visions proclaimed by both Yahweh and the prophet: Yahweh's vision is 'made plain' (v. 2) and the subsequent visions of the prophet are for 'all the earth' (vv. 14, 20). Similarly, the misdemeanors that are the subject of the woe oracles are of a sufficiently generalized nature that they serve as universally applicable descriptors of behavior inconsistent with Yahweh's justice. Just as the Chaldean king is to be condemned for these behaviors, so later oppressors would similarly be

---

18. The only other use of יהיר (*haughty*) in the Hebrew Bible occurs in Prov 21:24. Here "haughty" is included with "proud, scoffers, scorners, and fools" and contrasts these with the "wise" who practice righteousness, justice, and equity. It contributes to the overall message that wisdom leads to life whereas folly leads to death.

judged. The vagueness in referents, then, serves the theme of universality typical in performance analysis. Because of the lack of detail it is possible to restage the production in other settings and thereby retain the relevance of its themes and characterizations.

Embodiment is a strong theme in Habakkuk 2. In the introduction to Scene Four the prophet repeatedly announces that he has placed himself on siege works: 'Let me stand... let me set myself... let me keep watch,' (v. 1). His raised expectation and his audacious claim to equality with Yahweh as a conversation partner are thus emphasized physically as well as verbally. The answer that comes from Yahweh is an embodied vision. Though the words are to be written on tablets, the intention is that they will be proclaimed, shown in the use of a participle, '[the] reader will run with it' (v. 2).

English translations of the Hebrew miss the subtle examples of embodiment in the words. The verb root underlying יפחו (*and it breathes*, v. 3) can also mean 'to puff or pant.'[19] Because this verb describes the vision of Yahweh there is identification between it and the reader who is running with it.[20] Likewise, the term נפש (*soul*, vv. 4, 5) has multiple possible translations including 'throat'—an image that is evoked in v. 5, where the mighty man cannot be sated even though swallowing multitudes of nations and peoples.

The likelihood of gestures accompanying the verb נשא (*to lift up*) was suggested earlier. The verb can also be translated *to bear, to carry*. The close relationship between this verb and the noun משא (*revelation*) was noted earlier and has led some to translate the revelation given to the prophet as a 'burden.' Such embodied language is a reminder that the conversation between the prophet, Yahweh and the other actors is weighty and should not be easily dismissed.

By choosing to use the participles נשכיך (*the ones biting you*), and מזעזעיך (*the ones violently shaking you*, v. 7), the author has put flesh onto the verbs, embodying the action in real people. He also personifies building materials (stone and rafter, v. 11) by having them זעק (*cry out*) and ענה (*answer*). By contrast he imposes his judgment on the stone and wood idols by rendering them אלמים (*dumb*) and דומם (*mute*, vv. 18–19).

19. Clark and Hatton, *A Handbook on the Books of Nahum, Habakkuk, and Zephaniah*, 91.

20. Hence the translation in the NEB: "it will come in breathless haste."

References to nakedness (v. 15) and circumcision (v. 16) draw attention to the body and probably function to elicit sympathetic reactions from the audience. From the beginning of Scene Five, moreover, the device of the second person address has resulted in the audience 'feeling' the accusations of the woe oracles.

Scene Four (2:2-5) is a dynamic scene with several changes of tempo. There is anticipation at the beginning and a sense of waiting set up in the introduction to the scene, then the immediate answer (v. 2) and the instruction to 'run with it' quickens the pace. In the very next verse, however, the possibility of delay is raised, but an assurance is given that 'it surely comes' (v. 3). The audience is left wondering exactly what the vision is and whether or not it has arrived.

Scene Five (2:6-19) maintains a steady pace through its series of woes despite the interruption in v. 14. The changes in verb tenses in the woe oracles, however, give a sense of an intertwined present and future. The large number of participles translated as progressive present together with a number of past tense verbs gives the impression that the ongoing future will be a result both of actions in the past and in the present. There is an escalation of the severity of offences in the five woes so that the scene builds up in intensity: the first woe oracle is concerned with greed, the second with extravagant private building, the third with extravagant public building that relies on the use of violence, the fourth showing the impact on the community of drunkenness and the last relating to idol worship, a question of ultimate allegiance. All this movement comes to an end at v. 19 and the impression that all action ceases as Yahweh takes his place in his temple of holiness is accentuated by the lack of a verbal form in v. 20.

This dynamism in timing and tempo exhibits the typical performance theme of process. Another example of process in Habakkuk 2 is the change in the prophet's stance. In the earlier scenes he was impatient with the lack of answers to his questions, whereas at the introduction to Scene Four (2:1) he is ready to wait patiently for answers. His demeanor changes too from what has been described as 'presumptuous' in offering his views and aligning himself with Moses (2:1-2) to presenting himself as the representative of an orthodox stance of worship and eschatological expectation (2:4, 14, 20). Act One, then, ends with a sense of anticipation and hushed expectation. This openness to the future is also characteristic of the theme of process.

Habakkuk 2 has several examples of allusions to other Biblical traditions but includes two specific re-adaptations of prophetic formulae. The phrase 'who builds a city with bloodshed and establishes a town with iniquity' (v. 12) quotes Mic 3:10 but removes the references to Zion and Jerusalem in order to be applicable to other nations and at the same time to stress the sovereignty of Yahweh who has the right to judge non-Israelite communities. The interjection in v. 14, "But the earth will be filled with the knowledge of the glory of Yahweh as the waters cover the sea!" is an adaptation of Isa 11:9b, which reads "For the earth is filled with knowledge of Yahweh as the waters cover the sea." The phrase in Isaiah occurs in the context of an eschatological vision of a new ruler who will arise and instigate an era of peace and harmony. Isaiah's use of the particle 'for' implies that this situation is made possible through the knowledge of Yahweh. In Habakkuk the phrase interrupts a woe spoken against the Chaldean oppressor, before a consequence can be expressed. It comes as an enthusiastic assertion of an established eschatological vision offered as a contrast to the behavior being described, hence the choice of translation of כי as 'but' in this context. In comparison with the Isaiah statement, the words have been rearranged slightly but the major innovation on the part of the interjector is the introduction of כבוד (*glory*). This word comes up in the next woe oracle, used twice in v. 16 in reference to the accused whose glory will be removed and replaced with shame. 'Knowledge of the glory of Yahweh' thus precedes any pretensions to glory on the part of the accused.

The re-use and adaptation of existing formulae are examples of the re-enactment theme in performance criticism. Re-enactment is not merely repetition, but often integrates small changes or innovations that achieve a new purpose. In the light of this, the exact repetition of the phrase מדמי אדם וחמס־ארץ קריה וכל־יישבי בה, (*on account of blood of man and violence of earth, a town and all who live in it*, vv. 8b, 17b) warrants comment. This is a generalized statement of accusation in that all other grievances against the enemy can be summed up this way. At the beginning of the performance the prophet complained about Yahweh's refusal to save in the face of blatant חמס (*violence*, 1:2). Descriptions of the enemy's devastation included violence against humans (1:9, 15, 17; 2:5, 6, 9, 12, 15)[21] and against the earth (1:6, 10; 2:17). Such acts are

---

21. Roberts, *Nahum, Habakkuk, and Zephaniah*, 114, notes that the expression דמי אדם refers to human blood shed in violent acts.

summarized in this phrase and one can imagine the audience joining in and repeating it as a refrain.

Turner speaks of social drama in which communal 'rules' are broken by an individual or sub-group, resulting in crisis.[22] The community enters into a 'liminal phase' where normal structures are broken down. The response taken by the community is some form of redressive action, either through legal or religious institutions, often making use of rituals, symbolic action, humor, and so forth. Following this the community either restores peace and normality or recognizes an irreversible change that the crisis has brought upon the community. Scene Five follows the first two elements of this pattern with the Chaldean king being publicly accused of violence against the community by Yahweh in the context of a people's court. The series of woe oracles act as a dramatic presentation of the crimes that have been committed, underscored by the repeated summary statement noting the bloodshed of many and devastation of earth (vv. 8, 17). As has been seen, these oracles introduce sapiential elements by the theme of reversal. The enemy will be brought low by having the same crimes committed against him as he has committed against others. The one who is 'swollen' (big-headed!) and 'haughty' (vv. 4–5) will be 'shamed' (v. 16). The one whose 'justice and dignity' went forth 'from himself' (1:7) is now brought to justice and in the process loses all dignity and in addition loses the power of speech.

Despite the forward movement in the plot, however, the crisis is not fully resolved in this chapter. A clear statement of judgment has not been made and although the audience in this performance are expectant of resolution Act One ends with a command to 'hush!' The use of silence can have a powerful dramatic effect as has been seen in this performance where the accused individual is speechless, highlighting his guilt. The command for silence to 'all the earth,' however, implies that to some degree all share a measure of guilt and must await resolution. The chapter ends at a 'peak' and thus sets up keen anticipation for the ongoing drama.

---

22. Turner, "Universals of Performance," 11.

SEVEN

A Performance Reading of Habakkuk 3

THIS CHAPTER FOCUSES ON Habakkuk 3, which forms Act Two of the performance. Act Two commences with a Prelude (v. 1) and finishes with a Postlude (v. 19b). In between are three scenes: Scene One (v. 2), Scene Two (vv. 3–15) and Scene Three (vv. 16–19a) identified by changes in perspective and grammar. Scene Two arguably could be divided into two parts on the basis of a change in verb forms midway through the poem from third person report (vv. 2–6) to second person address (vv. 8–15). Its thematic unity in theophanic language, however, justifies viewing it as one scene.

PERFORMANCE FEATURES IN HABAKKUK 3

Act Two—Prelude (3:1)

[1] A prayer of Habakkuk the prophet according to Shigionoth.

Author and Script

This sentence is a prelude to Act Two of this performance, mirroring the prelude to Act One (Hab 1:1). Both statements announce "Habakkuk the prophet" in the third person and both could have been included as a final addition to the otherwise completed script in a similar fashion to adding an 'introduction' and 'conclusion' to an essay. For this reason text critics have tended to view the superscriptions as anachronistic and evidence that two disparate works were combined at a later date rather than the book of Habakkuk being understood as a unified composition.[1]

---

1. For example, Hiebert, *God of My Victory*, 130-31; Roberts, *Nahum, Habakkuk, and Zephaniah*, 148-49.

From a performance critical point of view it can be argued that the author deliberately chose to introduce the two acts of the performance in this way, partly to link them together through the common character of the prophet and partly to highlight the surprise content for the audience. As already noted, in 1:1 a משׂא (*revelation*) was announced but rather than following the announcement with a divine message, the first scene was of the prophet complaining to Yahweh. A similar twist in the plot takes place at this juncture also. The audience has been set up to expect an announcement of judgment (through the use of the language of a psalm of trust and the command to keep silence at the end of Act One) but what immediately follows is a particular form of prayer ("according to Shigionoth"). Perhaps, then, the script provides a call to worship rather than an announcement of judgment. This is a fascinating author who does not write 'according to script' but who nonetheless conveys a sense of unity through the actions, speeches, and psychological development of the main character.

Actors

The actor in focus in this scene is again Habakkuk the prophet. This is the beginning of Act Two and much about this character is now known. Unlike his first introduction (1:1), a picture has been provided as to what type of prophet he is. From the models available, Habakkuk fits best into the role of a cult prophet, since he has not announced judgment or mercy, nor proven to have had his word fulfilled, nor been a teacher of the Torah. On the other hand, he has acted as an intermediary: setting the case of injustice before Yahweh and demanding a response (1:2–4, 13); setting himself in a place appropriate for waiting and watching for the word of Yahweh (2:1); and living an exemplary life of faith as expected of הצדיק (*the righteous one*, 2:4). The most recent setting mentioned in this performance—"the temple of his holiness" (2:20)—and the literary form תפלה (*prayer*) further emphasize his role as a cult prophet.

Audience

Given that an announcement has been made, an audience is again implicit in the performance. After a short second-person address directed to Yahweh, the words of the prophet that follow include a poem referring to Yahweh in the third person and therefore are intended to be heard by an audience.

Setting

Although no setting is asserted at the beginning of Act Two, the reference to prayer implies a cultic setting. The designation "Shigionoth," however, adds some uncertainty as to what liturgical performance is expected. This word in plural form occurs only here in the Hebrew Bible and the word in singular form only once in the superscription to Psalm 7, a lament psalm. The content of Psalm 7 has led some scholars to determine the meaning to be a technical term for a lament,[2] while others look to the possible verbal roots and find a meaning based on the root שנה (*to stagger*) or שׁגע (*to be mad*), suggesting a wild, passionate song.[3] The similarity to the word "Niginoth" in the Postlude (Hab 3:19b) also suggests it is a musical term. Whichever idea is adopted in the rendering of "Shigionoth," a liturgical setting is presupposed rather than the battleground or public square of Act One.

Improvisation

As has already been noted, the previous scene set up an expectation of a judgment. Instead of a judgment speech, however, this prelude introduces a prayer. The audience had been commanded to "hush" before Yahweh but, rather than an ensuing silence, more words are spoken, or rather, sung. Moreover, the use of the mysterious "Shigionoth" means that whatever the audience might expect by way of prayer also could be overturned. A wild, passionate song would be surprising after the command to keep silence. But equally unexpected would be a lament given that the previous scene had condemned the Chaldean oppressors and given an expectation that justice would be brought about. The confident statements of faith expressed in the prophet's interjections would be undermined by further expressions of lament. And while the last scene of this performance has some of the characteristics of the lament form, the scenes that immediately follow the prelude are better characterized as a theophany and a prayer of praise.

---

2. See Sweeney, *The Twelve Prophets*, 430.
3. See *HALOT*, 1414.

Act Two—Scene One (3:2)

> ² Yahweh, I have heard of your reputation,
> I am in awe, Yahweh, of your work.
> In the midst of years you will make it live.
> In the midst of years you will make yourself known.
> In turmoil, you will remember compassion.

Author and Script

First person speech addressed to Yahweh identifies this scene as the prophet in prayer. Although such a grammatical structure was also seen in Scene One of Act One (1:2–4), the tone is markedly different here. In the earlier scene accusatory words were flung against Yahweh and the anguished verbs increased in intensity. Here the verbs are in positive form rather than negative. Earlier Yahweh was accused by "you do not hear" and "you do not save"—here the prophet says "I have heard" and "I am in awe." Repetition of the name of Yahweh and of the phrase בקרב שנים (*in the midst of years*) adds a rhythmic character to the prayer. Mention of the פעל (*work*) of Yahweh provides a further lexical connection to the earlier scenes. Most importantly, the concept רחם (*compassion*) is introduced to the script for the first time.

Actors

The prelude that introduces this scene and the grammatical and lexical elements found in it suggest continuity between the two actors of this scene, the prophet and Yahweh, with earlier scenes. Both characters, however, disclose new aspects of their *personae*. Both have, in the space of a relatively short script, evolved significantly.

The prophet began in Act One as an angry, accusing, and sarcastic challenger to Yahweh, questioning Yahweh's lack of action in the face of injustice in the light of his character and history with his people (1:2–4, 12–17). The prophet himself felt surrounded and trapped by injustice (1:4, 15) and perplexed at the way Yahweh seemed to be ignoring his plight. A change is shown as Scene Four (2:2–5) is introduced, with the prophet's speech showing a self-confidence (even presumption) in which he viewed himself as an equal dialogue partner with Yahweh

(2:1). Alongside this assertiveness are patience and an expectation that his questions would be answered. The prophet's possible self-identification as "the righteous one" further developed his character as a model of faithfulness and piety. In this first scene of Act Two he has recognized his human limitations in contrast to Yahweh and he expresses a sense of awe in the work of Yahweh and an acknowledgement that life and understanding are to be set in the context of a temporal dimension ("in the midst of years"). The faith of earlier scenes is still expressed but the prophet no longer demands immediate answers.

Yahweh has shown himself to be a perplexing character in this drama. Alternating between passivity and decisive action in Act One, he seems at times to ignore events and at other times to mastermind them. When on stage his presence is commanding, his speeches and actions accentuated by particles such as הנה (*behold*, 1:6; 2:13) and הוי (*Woe to him*, 2:6, 9, 12, 15, 19). Although Yahweh takes a central and decisive role in Scene Five of Act One (2:6–19), taunting and condemning the actions of the Chaldean king, there is a sudden scene change at the end of Act One that removes him from the action (2:20). This impression of inaccessibility is maintained in the present scene through the prophet's reference to Yahweh's awe-inspiring "work" and his use of the word רגז (*turmoil*). This unusual word is found elsewhere to describe the confusion of the exiled Israelites (Isa 14:3) or the trouble that comes to Job (Job 3:26) but also in reference to God's thunder-like voice (Job 37:2) and the demeanor of a warhorse (Job 39:24). Such a description inspires fear and disquiet. The reputation of Yahweh is at stake (Hab 3:2). Repetition of the verb שמע (*to hear*) emphasizes the process by which a reputation lives or dies. Will Yahweh live up to what has been previously heard about him, either positively or negatively? The prophet's next words indicate that he has a positive view of Yahweh's character as one who reveals himself in the midst of turmoil and offers רחם (*compassion*). This concept adds a softer dimension to the *persona* of Yahweh than hitherto seen. The verb shares its root with the noun רחם (*womb*) and often portrays the love of God as that of a parent for a child. With this characteristic Yahweh is further differentiated from the Chaldean king, another major actor in Act One of this performance, who had shown no compassion on his enemy.

Audience

No clues are given about audience involvement in this scene, but it can again be assumed an audience is present and hearing the words of the prophet. Reference to Yahweh's "work" already mentioned in Act One and the important concept of רחם (*compassion*), would engage its attention and interest because these are attributes of Yahweh well known to the Israelite audience. Repetition of the phrase בקרב שנים (*in the midst of years*), draws attention to the words and so has a rhetorical impact even in a monologue.

Setting

The prophet at prayer assumes a continuation of the liturgical setting. The words of the prayer, however, belie a static location. The combination of past and non-past verbs and concepts ensure that this is a prayer that could be spoken in many settings.

Improvisation

The words פעל (*work*) and רחם (*compassion*) act as ready-mades in this scene. In Act One Yahweh had announced a work that would be done and that would be astounding, even unbelievable (1:5). The fact that this announcement was made in response to the prophet's complaint did render it almost incomprehensible. Raising a fearful foreign army to invade an already suffering nation was not the expected action of Yahweh. Allusion to this fearful "work" would raise anxiety again in the audience listening to this prayer, except for the fact that the prophet re-interprets it in the context of Yahweh's long history of relating to his people ("in the midst of years"). The work may have been extraordinary in the circumstances of the Chaldean invasion, but with the benefit of hindsight it has a purpose that leads to life for his people.

The use of רחם (*compassion*) reinforces this interpretation. Throughout the Hebrew Bible it is used to refer to the covenant relationship between Yahweh and his people. Notably, it is always used when a relationship has already been established,[4] making the reference here to Yahweh "remembering" compassion significant. When רחם (*compassion*) is used in the psalms it is very often associated with a plea for

---

4. Sakenfeld, "Love (OT)," 378.

deliverance from enemies so its use by the prophet would remind the audience that they will be delivered from the threat of the Chaldeans.

Act Two—Scene Two (3:3–15)

> ³ God comes from Teman
> and [the] Holy One from Mount Paran. *Selah*.
> His splendor has clothed the heavens
> and his praise has filled the earth.
> ⁴ And bright as the light it is,
> rays from his hand has he.
> And there is a hiding place for his strength.
> ⁵ Before him Pestilence marches
> and Fire-bolt goes forth before his feet.
> ⁶ He has taken his stand and he measures earth.
> He has looked, and he makes nations free.
> And has shattered the mountains of old,
> bent down are the ancient hills.
> The ways of old are his.
> ⁷ Below I saw trouble at the tents of Cushan.
> Let curtains be in turmoil in the earth of Midian.
> ⁸ Has Yahweh burned against the Rivers?
> Is your face against the Rivers?
> Is your fury against the Sea?
> For you ride on your horses,
> on your chariots of salvation.
> ⁹ Indeed laid bare is your bow.
> Sworn are the spears of your word. *Selah*.
> With streams you cleave the earth.
> ¹⁰ Having looked at you, mountains shake.
> A downpour of waters has passed by.
> Deep has given its voice,
> Sun has lifted its hands on high.

¹¹ Moon has stood in its lofty abode.

As light your arrows dart,

as brightness, your glittering spear.

¹² In indignation you stride through the earth.

In anger you tread down nations.

¹³ You go forth to save your people,

to save your anointed one.

You have smitten the head of the house of wickedness,

to lay bare foundation to neck. *Selah.*

¹⁴ You have pierced with his spears the head of his warriors

They storm out to scatter me.

Their exultation was like he who devours the poor in secret.

¹⁵ You have walked through the Sea (with) your horses,

a heap of great waters.

Author and Script

The script breaks into a theophanic poem/hymn at this point. Like other theophanies in the Hebrew Bible (e.g., Judg 5:4–5; Pss 18:7–16; 29; 68:8–9; Mic 1:3–4), there is a description of the effect of the presence of the deity on the natural world. Up until this point greater attention has been given to relationships: between the prophet and Yahweh; Yahweh and the Chaldean king; the prophet, his community, and their enemies. Here the attention is broadened to include the natural world of mountains, seas, and celestial bodies. As will be seen below, these natural phenomena are given proper names and thus also become entities to be related to rather than just acted upon.

It is not entirely clear whether this theophany is to be understood as part of the "prayer" announced at the beginning of Act Two. The reference to אלוה (*God*), in v. 3 could suggest the insertion of a separate poem (vv. 3–6) for it is Yahweh who is addressed in v. 2 and again in v. 8. In support of this idea the verb forms change midway through the poem from third person report (vv. 2–6) to second person address (vv. 8–15). The geographical references also divide the poem into two, in that the first part forms an *inclusio* beginning with references to Teman and Paran (v. 2) and ending with Cushan and Midian (v. 7). On the other hand, v. 7 includes a first person reference suggesting the speaker of the theophany is the same person as the one offering the prayer that continues from v. 8. This speaker, the prophet, has addressed Yahweh as אלהי קדשי (*my God of holiness*) earlier in the performance (1:12) so it is not an entirely new element. The composition therefore is of the praying prophet caught up in a theophanic vision that is reported as it unfolds, and so is treated as one scene. This scenario is heightened by the scene that follows (3:16–19), in which the prophet is visibly shaken by his experience.

As will be shown below, the poem has many intertextual links with other parts of the Hebrew Bible and has some grammatical features that suggest the author has drawn on ancient sources. The lack of regularity shows that it is not 'classic' Hebrew poetry, perhaps due to the influence of the supposedly staggering "Shigionoth" rhythm.[5] The many variations in translation and the uncertainty of the text render it open to a variety of interpretations. Like any good performance, the script can be interpreted in a number of ways, each of which can remain 'authentic' to the text and its range of meanings.[6]

Actors

This poem presents yet more characteristics of Yahweh, assuming that the term אלוה (*God*), is referring to Yahweh as addressed by the prophet in Scene Three of Act One (Hab 1:12). The parallel term קדוש (*[the] Holy One*), reiterates the title אלהי קדשי (*my God of holiness*), although there is no trace of the earlier sarcasm indicated here. Yahweh's presence is larger than life. He thunders onto the stage with such force that mountains are "shattered" and earth is "cleaved." The frequent references to light (rays in v. 4, fire-bolts in v. 5 and arrows of light and spear of brightness

---

5. This poem departs from the classical patterns due to its irregular colonic structure and uncertainty of parallelism in some verses. For example, vv. 4, 6, 9, and 14 each have an additional line following parallel bicola. Széles, *Wrath and Mercy*, 44-45, suggests the irregularity may be explained by the "Shigionoth" verse-form "in which not only the rhythm rambles but so also does the versifier."

6. For instance, some scholars interpret the theophany as consistent with the Exodus story (Patterson, "The Psalm of Habakkuk") while others understand Canaanite mythology to lie behind the poem (Day, "New Light on the Mythological Background"). I refer again to Friedman, "In Defense of Authenticity," 38, who defines authentic performances as "*enactment[s] that express one version of the significance of a text that demonstrably falls within that text's range of meaning*" (author's italics).

in v. 12) show that his presence cannot be ignored. He dominates the scene. The overriding *persona* of Yahweh in this scene is that of a warrior: marching into battle; riding on horses and chariots; brandishing bow, arrows and spear; vanquishing enemies. The fearful enemy of Act One has been overshadowed by an even fiercer warrior. The attribute of רחם (*compassion*) has disappeared and in its place indignation and anger are seen as Yahweh's motivation for saving his people (v. 12). The stage is overwhelmed by his forceful presence.

Yahweh, however, is not alone on the stage. A valid portrayal of this scene could include a number of other deities—personified natural forces—such as Deber (דבר, *Pestilence*) and Resheph (רשף, *Firebolt*) in v. 5, Neharim (נהרים, *Rivers*) and Yam (ים, *Sea*) in v. 8; and Tehom (תהום, *Deep*), Shemesh (שמש, *Sun*) and Yareh (ירח, *Moon*) in vv. 10-11. Each of these is subordinated to Yahweh in some way. Deber and Resheph are portrayed as part of the retinue accompanying him in his theophanic march.[7] Neharim and Yam have been subdued by his power. Tahom, Shemesh and Yareh all pay tribute to his commanding presence as he marches by.

Another actor in this scene is ראש מבית רשע (*the head of the house of wickedness*) in v. 13. This phrase draws together the nebulous "wickedness" found in Scenes One and Three of Act One (1:4, 13) with the house of the enemy mentioned in Scene Five (2:9). In the light of these earlier scenes, the character mentioned here is best understood as the Chaldean king. The next verse refers to "his warriors" who would then be identified as the Chaldean army, a force that has been present throughout this performance although not always active. Here they are envisaged "storming out" against the speaker of the poem but despite their threatening stance they are vulnerable to the superior might of Yahweh.

With all these characters, the stage is potentially rather crowded in this scene. But the prophet can still make his presence felt. The first person pronouns "I" (v. 7) and "me" (v. 14) place him in the midst of the action. In this scene he does not express his emotions but merely reports the events. Only in the subsequent scene is his reaction seen.

---

7. Hiebert, *God of My Victory*, 19.

Audience

First person pronouns are used in v. 7 and v. 14, indicating the poem is offered by a single speaker or singer. The threefold use of *Selah* from the tradition of the Psalms, however, suggests it is a community hymn to be used in public worship. Although there is no clear consensus on the meaning of *Selah*, it is usually thought of as musical annotation or an affirmative particle similar to 'Amen.' Either explanation implies a performance incorporating an audience. The rhetorical questions of v. 8 are another device for drawing the audience into the experience. The collective noun in v. 13—עמך (*your people*)—would further embrace the listening audience and allow it to identify with the words expressing faith in Yahweh who has proven stronger than the feared enemy of Act One. This view concurs with that of Watts who examines the impact of an 'inset hymn' in the book of Habakkuk. He writes: "Since ancient readers customarily read aloud, usually to an audience, the inclusion of an old and clearly marked hymn in a text might evoke audience participation. So Habakkuk 3's literary effect might well move towards liturgical actualization, not just suggesting the identification of prophetic vision with corporate worship, but realizing it through the experience of reading the book publicly."[8]

Setting

One might assume that Act Two (3:1–19) opens in a liturgical setting, due to the mention of "his temple of holiness" at the end of Act One (2:20) and the announcement of the prayer of the prophet. The beginning of Scene Two, however, offers an entirely different location with the specific geographical referents of Teman and Paran (v. 3). The listening audience would be familiar with the tradition of Yahweh leaving his temple to answer a cry of help, as shown in Mic 1:2–3 and Ps 18:7, both of which are followed by a theophany. The claim that God "comes" from Teman and Mount Paran would therefore be surprising. These historical referents are probably used to evoke memories of the Exodus tradition of the salvation march from Egypt in the south through the wilderness to Judah, the description of Yahweh's saving action *par excellence* for an Israelite audience. Reference to Cushan and Midian in v. 7 further establishes this connection due to their association with the wife of Moses.

---

8. Watts, "Psalmody in Prophecy," 222.

Yahweh as a warrior makes use of horses, chariots, and weapons. The descriptions of these in the poem overlap with descriptions of natural phenomena: his garments display the colours of the rising sun in the sky (v. 3); thunder and earthquakes shake the mountains (vv. 6, 7, 10); the chariot is the storm cloud, bringing torrents of rain and churning up the waters to form whitecaps in the waves (vv. 8, 10, 15); and his arrows and spear are lightning bolts that shoot to earth (vv. 4, 9, 11). These descriptions suggest this scene is an impressive sound and light show! Yahweh's presence is not to be merely read about but is to be seen, heard, and experienced.

The whole scene, of course, could be understood as a vision of the prophet. Again, in a contemporary performance, this vision could be portrayed with the use of a series of visual images flashed above the solitary prophet. The poem is of a warrior on the move, with geographical locations and verbs of motion giving the impression that the scene is unfolding before the eyes of the prophet. It has a temporal dimension also, with mention of sun and moon suggesting a change from day to night. Despite this impression of movement there are no specific stage directions given by the script. The use of the *Selah* instruction, as has been noted, functions to draw in the audience, but does not divide the poem into logical sections.

Improvisation

Multiple examples of intertextuality can be found in this scene and show that the author has adapted older material. Similarity to other theophanic poems where the coming of God has a cataclysmic effect on the natural world has already been noted (Judg 5:4–5; 2 Sam 22:8–17// Pss 18:7–16; 29; 68:8–9; Mic 1:3–4). In addition, the poem evokes the Exodus motif in its geographical references but also in the description of walking through the sea to save the Israelites (compare with Exodus 15). To this may be added intertextual links with Joshua, Job, and Psalms. Joshua 10:12–13 records a tradition of the sun and moon standing still at the command of Yahweh. Connections with Yahweh's primordial battle with the Sea (*Yam*) can be found in Job 7:12; 9:8; and Ps 74:13, among others. The image of Yahweh "going forth" to save his people (v. 13) is one used frequently in descriptions of Yahweh's advance into battle (Judg 5:4; 2 Sam 5:24; Ps 108:12; Isa 42:13; Zech 14:3) but also draws on the earlier scenes of this performance where this verb was used ironically to suggest Yahweh's justice was not forthcoming (Hab 1:4 and 1:7). As such it functions as a ready-made, emphasizing the decisive action of Yahweh in the light of his earlier perceived impotency.

Another ready-made that has been modified in this scene is the use of the term משיחך (*your anointed one*, v. 13). Although the singular form of this term is common in the Hebrew Bible, it usually refers to the Davidic king (1 Sam 2:35; 24:6; Pss 89:20; 132:17). Psalm 105:15 (repeated in 1 Chr 16:22) uses the term in the plural and associates it with "my prophets." With no mention of a Davidic king in this performance but several references to הצדיק (*the righteous one*), it is possible that the prophet is also claiming this title for himself.

Psalm 77 forms a parallel to Habakkuk in structure and in some textual details. The psalmist begins with a "cry" to God (Ps 77:2//Hab 1:2) and wonders if God's רחם (*compassion*), will be available (Ps 77:10//Hab 3:2). The psalmist then recalls the פעל (*work*) of Yahweh (Ps 77:13//Hab 1:5 and 3:2), recounting the effect of Yahweh's presence on the waters, the deep, the clouds and the sea, in thunder and arrows of lightning. The author of Habakkuk seems to have drawn on other material to present an image of Yahweh that is consistent with Israel's traditions but is integrated into this new performance.

In addition to connections to other Biblical material, several ancient near-eastern mythical motifs are found in this poem. Canaanite poetry commemorating Baal's conflict with the sea uses similar language and probably forms the background to the passage. Influence from solar cults can also be seen with the emphasis on light and the mention of "rays from his hand" (v. 4). The storm-god was a common motif in the ancient Near East and traces of this imagery is seen in this poem. The combination of solar and storm imagery, as attributes of a deity, was also common to other cultures. There is slippage between natural phenomena and names for deities in this poem, but the description of Yahweh's superiority has been noted. Thus the author has drawn from other traditions but has reshaped them to present a consistent picture of Yahweh as a victorious conqueror, able to vanquish his foes and vindicate his people.

Act Two—Scene Three (3:16–19a)

> ¹⁶ I heard and my belly is in turmoil,
> at a voice my lips tingled.
> Decay comes into my bones,
> and in my place I am in turmoil,
> where I wait for a day of distress
> to come up to a people who will invade us.
> ¹⁷ If the fig tree does not sprout,
> and no produce is on the vines,
> if the yield of the olive tree has failed
> and fields have not produced food,
> the flock has been cut off from the fold
> and no cattle are in the stalls,
> ¹⁸ yet I will exult in Yahweh,
> I will rejoice in the God of my salvation.
> ¹⁹ᵃ Yahweh my Lord is my strength.
> He places my feet like the hinds'
> and on my high places he makes me walk.

Author and Script

This speech leaves the realm of theophany and returns to the experiential perspective of the prophet. The use of שמע (*to hear*), the same verb as at the beginning of Hab 3:2, forms a striking frame to the theophany. At the beginning of the prayer the prophet says "I have heard of your reputation." In the theophany he both hears and sees the manifest works and nature of Yahweh and so here the 'hearing' has a new significance. He had formerly admitted to a sense of awe, but had positively and confidently placed that awe in the context of a temporal relationship ("through the years") that would culminate in רחם (*compassion*). Now the 'hearing' causes a physical reaction with symptoms of fear graphically described in terms of רגז (*turmoil* [of the belly]) and צלל (*tingling* [of the lips]). Strikingly, the hope of justice is here expressed as a future phenomenon, as is the expectation of invasion (v. 16). This puts the theophany that has just been related into perspective as a vision of the future and places the prophet back in the same place as at the beginning of the performance—amongst his community awaiting an inevitable attack from their enemy. Mention of a יום צרה (*day of distress*, v. 16) draws on a common prophetic motif related to the action of Yahweh in the world, but a day that is not usually good news for Yahweh's people. The subsequent verse does nothing to dispel this apprehension as it paints a picture of hardship and famine, although the move away from military disaster to environmental/economic disaster places the experience of the prophet in a much broader sphere.

Continuing to revel in twists in the plot, the author finishes his script on a surprising note. In view of the description of a fearful future, the response of עלז (*exultation*) and גיל (*joy*) on the part of the prophet (3:18) is almost completely unexpected. The closing sentiment is one of faith and trust, in striking contrast to the opening scene of the performance where the prophet's response to a troubled situation was bitter complaint.

Actors

The only actor on stage in this scene is the prophet. Yahweh has thundered on his way and left a visibly shaken prophet in his wake. The prophet's soliloquy gives the effect of private thoughts to which the audience eavesdrops, although any speech in performance is intended to be heard. The prophet is self-directed in this scene, waiting for future events to unfold. Despite his admission of inner agitation, the personal pronoun ואני (*yet I*, 3:18) is an emphatic statement of trust. Moreover, there is a strong identification with Yahweh on the part of the prophet. A triple designation of Yahweh as אלהי ישעי (*the God of my salvation*), אדני (*my Lord*), and חילי (*my strength*, 3:18–19a) shows that the prophet's identity is tied up in his relationship with Yahweh. Thus the *persona* of Yahweh remains present in the performance until the very conclusion of Act Two.

Audience

The majority of pronouns in this scene are first person singular, leaving the audience predominantly in a passive role as eavesdroppers on the prophet's private contemplation. The reference to "a people who will invade *us*" however, draws the audience in as part of the prophet's community who, along with him, will await the future calamity of an enemy invasion. This phrase strikingly shifts the temporal perception of the audience. The woe oracles spoken against the enemy in Scene Five of Act One and Yahweh's victory march in Scene Two of Act Two suggest a post-victory setting, yet here the audience is taken back to the time prior to the enemy's invasion. The performance thus offers those in the audience the opportunity to identify with the faith of the prophet despite the likelihood of a bleak future.

Setting

First-person verbs mark this as a new scene but together with Scene One (3:2) it forms a frame for the theophany. In an imaginative way the prophet conjures up familiar scenarios for the attentive audience. Mention of the future invasion envisages the city awaiting attack from a hostile army poised at the gates. The reference to barren trees, fields, and denuded flocks is a reminder of the natural disasters of drought or plague all too familiar to the agriculturally based Yehud communities. Finally, reference to במות (*high places*), using a phrase familiar from the psalm tradition (2 Sam 22:34//Ps 18:34), would evoke ideas of worship and/or idolatry. Bringing all of these together in one short scene concentrates major themes of this performance effectively. In the midst of disaster the prophet questions the ways of Yahweh, contemplates scenarios in which disaster threatens to overwhelm, expresses faith in the saving ability of Yahweh and concludes on a note of worship. Yet mention of the "heights" forms an echo to the introduction to Scene Four (Hab 2:1), suggesting that the prophet's status continues to be that of an active player in this performance and a star of comparable billing to Yahweh. Although this is the closing scene, the plot remains open, shown by the concluding verb דרך (*to walk*).

Improvisation

The frequency of the occurrences of the term יום צרה (*day of distress*) in the Hebrew Bible indicates it is a ready-made for the listening audience.[9] As pointed out by Andersen, however, the phrase "never describes the trouble experienced by the wicked when justice is done to them in retri-

---

9. For example: Judg 10:14; Pss 20:2; 50:15; Jer 15:11; 16:19; Obad 12, 14; Nah 1:7.

bution. It always describes the distress of the LORD's people, caused by an oppressor, a distress from which he should deliver them."[10] The author of this performance has thus taken a common phrase and refashioned it to refer to the Chaldean invaders. The day of distress will "come up to a people who will invade us" (v. 16). Despite the continued expectation of attack, the prophet has taken to heart the judgment of Scene Five in Act One and the theophany of the scene immediately preceding this one and has confidence that the attack will be turned upon the attacker.

This confidence is underlined by the multiple use of the root ישע (*salvation*), in Act Two (3:8, 13 [x2], 18). Act One began with the prophet's cry of complaint against Yahweh and an accusation that he refuses to save (1:2). By the end of the performance, however, the prophet is confidently giving Yahweh the name אלהי ישעי (*the God of my salvation*, 3:18). The fact that deliverance is still in the future indicates the way the term has been subtly altered from the beginning of the performance to the end, with the reality of salvation being removed from the present to the future.

There is also a subtle shift in the use of the agricultural terms in this scene in comparison to other Hebrew Bible uses. Elsewhere a connection is found between the action of Yahweh in the natural world, where he can either stop fertility as punishment (e.g., Amos 4:9) or re-establish fertility as symbolic of a promise of restoration (e.g., Joel 2:22). Habakkuk 3:17–18 does not attribute infertility to Yahweh, but asserts that even if such disasters should occur, the worship of Yahweh would continue unabated. The return to a situation of crisis as the location for an exploration of faith ensures that the earlier scenes are not dismissed as irrelevant, but show they have made a contribution to this exploration. In the light of the expected disaster, the prophet has become a conversation partner with Yahweh and has been privileged to glimpse an eschatological vision that puts crisis into perspective. Out of the entire experience he is able to assert confidence in the character of Yahweh. As such it stands as a powerful and inspiring statement of trust and faith.[11] In this regard, Hiebert is correct in emphasizing the intro-

---

10. Andersen, *Habakkuk*, 345.

11. This conclusion is not shared by Snyman, "Non-violent Prophet and Violent God," 433, who argues that the book of Habakkuk describes a 'non-violent' prophet who has had to submit to a 'violent' God. Rather than viewing the prophet as a conversation partner with Yahweh whose complaints are taken seriously, Snyman concludes: "Habakkuk made his point although he eventually had to submit to the overwhelming power of Yahweh."

duction of apocalyptic thought in Habakkuk 3, since it has the function of "[raising] the prophet's hope for justice to another dimension, a new dimension of reality that entered biblical thought with the dawn of the apocalyptic consciousness in the post-exilic era."[12]

Postlude (3:19b)

19b To the Director, according to my Niginoth.

Author and Script

The postlude to the book emphatically justifies a performance reading. This is a script that is intended to be thoughtfully directed and enacted. The probable connection of the terms "Niginoth" (v. 19b) and "Shigionoth" (v. 1) suggest a musical aspect to this performance, although it is not clear from related words elsewhere in the Hebrew Bible whether the term is indicative of a mocking song (Ps 69:13; Job 30:9; Lam 3:14) or the use of stringed instruments (Isa 38:20; Lam 5:14). The suggestion of a mocking song undermines the conclusions reached by the prophet and may be evidence of irony on the part of the author. In a script that has continually surprised its audience, this truly would be a twist in the tail. In such an interpretation, the confident faith of the prophet in the last scene would be viewed as delusional and the entire performance would fade away to nothing in similar fashion to an absurdist play. The lack of conclusive evidence of the meaning of "Niginoth," however, means this must remain only a tantalizing possibility.

Actors

Given that this colophon is understood to be a postlude, the "Director" is probably not being presented as a new character but instead as part of the 'support crew.' If such a performance is to take place it will require direction and interpretation. The term מנצח (*Director*), whether with connotations of music (2 Chr 34:13) or supervision of labor (2 Chr 2:1, 17), implies a position of some authority and control, but the first person suffix attached to "Niginoth" retains an overarching authority with the author as well as the prophet who is performing the script. The Director should be guided by the script and the prophet. This is further under-

---

12. Hiebert, "The Book of Habakkuk," 654.

scored by the positioning of the phrase at the very end of the script. In the Psalter מנצח (*Director*) is found fifty-five times, always at the beginning of the psalm. Its position at the end of the book of Habakkuk, therefore, significantly turns the concept upside-down. One would only know how to sing the script after hearing it!

Audience

As well as implying the necessity for performance, the reference to a Director also implies the necessity of an audience. The theophany in Scene Two (Hab 3:3–15) has been designated a 'community hymn' to be used in public worship, evidenced by the use of *Selah* from the tradition of the Psalter. There is also a sense of an audience being drawn into the performance through rhetorical questions and occasional plural pronouns. As was noted in chapter 2, when audiences are drawn into the world of a drama so that it becomes merged with an audience's own stories, the performance does not finish at the conclusion of the script but continues to have an influence in the lives of those who have witnessed it. Attentive audience members who have remained part of a worshipping community despite periods of national crisis—either political or natural—will continue to interpret, reflect on, and engage in such a performance as this.

Setting

The setting for this Postlude will be determined by the interpretation of "Niginoth." As a musical term it is connected to the temple, the place of community worship. If considered a mocking song, however, the context may return to the public square. Whichever setting is determined, there is an expectation that this script will be re-performed. Because performance is affected by the experiences of actors and audience, each new performance will have a new setting. This postlude keeps the possibilities for re-enactment open.

Improvisation

Greek and Aramaic versions of Habakkuk use the terminology of victory and conquering in translating the final phrase. This may be due to the similarity of the root נצח to the Aramaic root *nsh, to conquer*. The association may be intentional, since much of the script has been focused on warfare imagery.

The positioning of this colophon is unusual in comparison to its usual placement prior to a psalm. It could be seen as a dedication rather than an instruction, although the first person pronoun suffix on "Niginoth" ("according to *my* Niginoth") speaks against this interpretation. More likely is that the placement of this instruction as a postlude ensures that it is intended to be re-enacted, like a song with no end.

PERFORMANCE THEMES IN HABAKKUK 3

The liturgical instructions included in Habakkuk 3 indicate awareness that this text has not appeared by accident or arisen out of habitual use, but instead is a script that must be interpreted and thoughtfully re-enacted. Although the precise meaning of the liturgical terms is not clear, self-reflexivity on the part of the author and the performers is clearly a necessary process. The prayer/poem/song is to be performed according to "Shigionoth" and "Niginoth," terms that frame Act Two. Performers must determine how this impacts the presentation and act accordingly. The lack of clarity provides a degree of freedom in interpretation that means this performance will be altered over time, a characteristic of performances that has been identified as 'process.' Audience participation is intended as shown by the *Selah* instruction that interrupts the poem (vv. 3, 9, 13) and therefore interpretation and re-enactment of this script will always be a community event.

The theophanic poem as a unit (Hab 3:3–15) displays several of the performance themes identified. Given that theophany is a familiar genre in the Hebrew Bible the whole poem can be viewed as a re-enactment of a traditional motif of Biblical faith, that of the victory march of the warrior following the liberating Exodus from Egypt. Thus Yahweh comes from the south, walks through the seas, destroys his enemies and provides salvation for his people. This is a creative re-enactment, however, that also draws on other motifs. Elements of creation hymns can be detected, so that Yahweh is not only a warrior who conquers human enemies but also has power over natural forces. Attributes of sun gods, storm gods, and sea gods can all be discerned in the descriptions of Yahweh in this poem. At the same time, Yahweh stands over against the forces of nature, acting upon them (vv. 6, 9, 10) and eliciting respect from them (vv. 10–11).

These forces of nature are embodied in this poem to such an extent that attributing proper names to them is a reasonable translation option.

Recognition of the theme of process in performance emphasizes the actual activity as opposed to a finished static product. Meaning grows and changes through time and has the potential for culture to be altered as a result of the performance. There is a sense of movement and change in the theophanic poem with its description of a march from one geographical location to another, the frequent use of ו (*and*), that transmits the idea of a vision unfolding, and the effects of nature's upheaval akin to a 'sound and light show' as suggested above. The more important recognition of the effect of process comes in noticing the framework of the poem with the prophet's anticipation and reaction to it. During the theophany, the first person pronoun of v. 7 suggests that the prophet is present, caught up in the action. As the theophany concludes, the prophet describes his mental and physical reaction to Yahweh's "work" (v. 2) and presence (vv. 3–15), including re-using the word רגז (*turmoil*) from v. 7. Hiebert notes that the basic meaning of the root רגז is "to be in an agitated, disturbed, or unsettled state . . . the general disruption caused by the theophany."[13] The fact that רגז also occurs in v. 2, describing Yahweh's demeanor, forms a link between Yahweh's action and the prophet's reaction. The prophet's self-descriptions form a frame for the poem and are evidence of his own conscious response to events. The final soliloquy (vv. 17–19) provides an example of an actor standing back from the action, conscious of his own separateness, reflecting on his experience. This characterizes self-reflexivity. Actions and reactions are not just reflected *in* performance, but are shaped *by* the performance. The prophet's claim to maintain faith, shown so clearly in the use of the particle with the personal pronoun ואני (*yet I*, v. 18), not only reflects a "completely orthodox and traditional response to the painful questions raised in earlier chapters"[14] but also provides the potential to shape the response of an attentive audience or later reader who have the opportunity to measure their own response against his.

The prophet's response of faith in the midst of crisis or disaster is one that can be reapplied to any crisis and indeed has been applied throughout the history of Jewish and Christian communities who

---

13. Hiebert, *God of My Victory*, 14.
14. Watts, "Psalmody in Prophecy," 216.

draw on the Hebrew Bible as a source for shaping and preserving faith. Habakkuk 3 thus has a universal appeal and application.

Habakkuk's faith in the midst of crisis is all the more remarkable for his graphic description of physical terror. Verse 16 is one of the clearest examples of embodiment in this performance where fear is manifested as a physiological response. The author has carefully chosen unusual words to describe the experience. רגז (*turmoil*) is usually descriptive of convulsions of nature, such as earthquakes. Here it is "the only place where the verb is given a psychological connection with organs of the body."[15] Similarly, the verb צלל (*tingle*) is associated with lips only in this passage (elsewhere it is used to describe the ears that hear words of judgment; see 1 Sam 3:11; 2 Kgs 21:12; Jer 19:3). In Hebrew, expressions describing the state of bones metaphorically signify well-being (Prov 15:30) or disease and decay (Prov 14.30). The prophet thus describes himself as paralyzed and speechless. Embodiment as 'participatory knowledge' is manifested clearly in Habakkuk 3.

In relation to the prophet's visceral response, Andersen points out that similar language is used in the *Enuma Elish* of Tiamat.[16] In addition to the descriptions of Yahweh's presence in the theophany, the author has drawn on motifs from other ancient near-eastern traditions to describe the prophet's reaction to it. These are examples of the universal nature of performance whereby one can find common motifs across cultural and ethnic divisions. Even modern readers can share the experiences of the prophet, by sensing the transcendent in natural forces[17] and by being physically affected by shock and fear. Descriptions of such liminal encounters have a universal familiarity.

Returning to the theme of process, the grammar and vocabulary of the first and third scenes of Act Two (3:2 and 3:16–19), scenes that enclose the theophany, indicate how important Habakkuk 3 is for reframing reality and potentially altering the cultural framework of the prophet and his audience. The combination of past and non-past verbs in vv. 2 and 16 give the sense of the past and future impacting upon the present. In Scene Three (3:16–19) the prophet returns to the theme of crisis that was present at the beginning of the performance, but his reaction to it

---

15. Andersen, *Habakkuk*, 344.
16. Ibid.
17. For instance, a universally common expression for sunbeams shining through clouds is "the fingers of God" as used by Courtenay in *April Fool's Day*, 344.

is markedly different. Rather than complaint and sarcasm he expresses a quiet and confident faith in the ability of Yahweh to save. Thus the vision of Scene Two (3:3–15) has altered the prophet's world view and reinterpreted his experience. The choice of a verb of movement (הלך, *to walk*) as a final word from the prophet ensures that the script remains open. The prophet is enabled to "walk" where before he was paralyzed, quaking, and speechless. Moreover, he walks on the high places, returning to the theme of the introduction to Scene Four in Act One (Hab 2:1) where the prophet's elevated stance emphasized his speaking as an equal with Yahweh. In the Hebrew Bible "walking" with Yahweh is metaphorical for living within the ways of God, evidenced by the term *Halakha* in reference to the body of Jewish law still followed by contemporary communities. If this script has ended on a note of worship, it is active worship that is intended to impact the worshipper and the prevailing culture of those attending to the performance.

EIGHT

Reading Habakkuk through a Performance Lens

This study has taken a unique approach to the book of Habakkuk. It recognizes that Habakkuk belongs to the genre of prophetic literature, and that current issues pertaining to the prophetic literature are important in an analysis of the book. These include the role of the prophet as intermediary, the growth of the prophetic books through oral and literary stages with a final form emerging in the Persian period, and an examination of its place in the Book of the Twelve. Performance criticism introduces a new way of reading the book. This is a relatively recent approach in Biblical studies and the breadth of interpretive and disciplinary uses of the terms 'performance' and 'performance criticism' has resulted in a variety of interpretive approaches to Biblical material. The approach I have taken has been to identify several recognizably performative features and themes and analyze the text according to these criteria. Reading the text from a performance perspective allows for a new appreciation of the inherently 'dramatic' nature of prophecy in general and the book of Habakkuk in particular. In this final chapter I intend to review the performance themes in Habakkuk before reflecting more deeply on performance features and then to examine the insights that can be gained by reading the book through the lens of performance criticism.

HABAKKUK AS A 'PERFORMANCE'

Performance Themes in Habakkuk

It is clear that the performance themes identified in chapter 2 can be found when reading an ancient text like Habakkuk. The theme of self-reflexivity is exemplified in the prophet's self-understanding as an intermediary between Yahweh and an audience. The prophet stands outside himself and reflects on his experience as a human creature, while simultaneously carrying the "revelation" of Yahweh (1:1) to his audience. The audience is also encouraged to engage in self-reflexivity by being offered paradigmatic characters whose attitudes and actions can be models for the audience, both positively and negatively.

Embodiment has also been shown to be a strong theme in this prophetic book, with the prophet present in the midst of crisis and experiencing Yahweh's revelation visually, audibly and even viscerally (3:16). A feature of prophetic literature in general is recognition of the embodiment of the word of Yahweh in the person of the prophet who acts as an intermediary.[1] In the same way that embodiment distinguishes the performance arts from other visual arts such as painting, sculpture, and literature, God's message through the prophets distinguishes this form of Biblical literature from law codes, narratives, and historiography. Without the prophet the message would not be conveyed. Amongst the prophets Jeremiah stands out as the supreme example of the prophet becoming the message, whose life is identified with his mission. Although less celebrated in discussions of the prophets, the words attributed to the prophet in the book of Habakkuk suggest that he too embodies his message. The anguish of the crisis faced by the prophet is integrated into his being, as are his questions and doubts over the role of Yahweh and ultimately his calm trust amidst crisis. My suggestion that the term הצדיק (*the righteous one*) could be identified with the prophet indicates a further degree of embodiment in that the attitude and conduct of the prophet becomes exemplary for the audience. Furthermore, by reading the book of Habakkuk as a performance, one becomes aware of embodiment via the physical presence of both Yahweh and the enemy, conveyed through the human attributes and active verbs ascribed to them.

It was noted in Chapter 2 that the field of performance studies has a holistic world-view that results in recognizing universality as a key

---

1. House, "The Character of God," 129.

characteristic. Commentaries on the book of Habakkuk note the lack of specific historical detail, which frequently raises questions about the historical setting for the book, but at the same time lifts the message to a more universal application. Gowan, for example, says in relation to the woe oracles: "It is my conclusion that no effort has been made in this song to refer to any specific situation in history; rather that it has purposely been expressed in general terms that could apply again and again to tyranny in many forms."[2] Childs comments that precise historical details of the original oracles have been "sacrificed" for a particular theological perspective,[3] and O'Brien states that the "generic style is one of the features that allows Habakkuk to communicate powerfully at different times and places."[4] My own observations have shown that characters and situations are deliberately vague in order that later audiences may be able to identify with the challenges and hopes conveyed in the text.

Process is another characteristic in performance wherein the actual activity of the artist or actor is in focus, not just the finished product. Several thematic and grammatical features of the book of Habakkuk show that this characteristic is integral to the book, particularly the open-ended nature of the text. Questions are left unanswered, expected judgment does not come, the situation of the prophet at the end of Act Two (3:16–19) combines a testimony of triumphant faith with fearful anticipation of imminent invasion, the text ends on the active verb דרך (*to walk*), and the postlude encourages renewed performance (3:19b). Changes in verb tenses at various points throughout the text give a sense of timelessness, with past, present, and future merging into each other. Indeed, O'Brien comments specifically on Habakkuk 3: "Perhaps it is no accident that . . . the past and the present seem indistinguishable."[5] The lack of complete resolution in the book and its openness to being re-applied to new situations highlights the theme of process, as does the associated theme of re-enactment.

A strong tenet in performance criticism is the claim that all performance leans toward re-performance.[6] The author of Habakkuk has

---

2. Gowan, *The Triumph of Faith*, 57.

3. Childs, *Introduction*, 453.

4. O'Brien, *Nahum, Habakkuk, Zephaniah, Haggai, Zechariah, Malachi*, 62.

5. Ibid., 82.

6. For example, MacAloon, *Rite, Drama, Festival, Spectacle*, 9; Carlson, *Performance*, 5; Schechner, *Performance Studies*, 34.

been innovative in his re-use of conventional forms and themes, such as adaptations of existing prophetic formulae, creative use of the complaint form and the theophanic poem, and surprising conjunction of terms and forms (e.g., in 1:2–4 a complaint follows the announcement of a revelation; and in 3:1–2 a prayer follows an expectation of judgment). The liturgical elements in Act Two demand ongoing use by the community, a conclusion shared by many commentators. Robertson describes Habakkuk 3 as "in a form appropriate for a continual corporate celebration in the worshiping community of Israel"[7] and Sweeney states, "Like the Psalms, Habakkuk 3 was apparently intended to be performed as part of the Temple liturgy."[8] I have argued that the colophon (3:19b) specifically invites re-enactment, giving it a significance that may otherwise be overlooked. In a survey of studies of superscriptions and incipits Watts notes that colophons differ from superscriptions in that they are generally written by copyists in relation to the copying process, so that: "The reader is not involved or interested."[9] My interpretation would suggest otherwise.

As has been demonstrated, the themes of self-reflexivity, embodiment, universality, process, and re-enactment, commonly found in performance studies, are as relevant to a prophetic book in the Hebrew Bible as they are to any contemporary performance in culture, society or the arts.

Performance Features in Habakkuk

My approach to Habakkuk is similar to Levy who, in his book *The Bible as Theatre*, seeks "the intrinsic theatrical qualities in the biblical texts themselves."[10] Levy analyzes several Biblical passages as 'theatrical,' distinguishing his approach from that of narrative criticism which focuses on drama as a genre. Rather than concentrating on plot structures, narration and dialogue, characters, and significant use of time and place,[11] Levy "shifts the focus from a literary genre-oriented discussion

---

7. Robertson, *The Books of Nahum, Habakkuk, and Zephaniah*, 214.
8. Sweeney, *The Twelve Prophets*, 488.
9. Watts, "Superscriptions and Incipits," 110.
10. Levy, *The Bible as Theatre*, 2.
11. See Alter, *The Art of Biblical Narrative*; Berlin, *Poetics and Interpretation of Biblical Narrative*; and Amit, *Reading Biblical Narratives*, for typical approaches to narrative criticism.

to a medium-oriented one."¹² He looks for the theatrical components ("biblical stage-directions") that are built into the texts such as time, space, movement, costumes, props, and lighting. In a similar exploration of the "intrinsic theatrical qualities" in the book of Habakkuk, this commentary has taken as its starting point the performance features of script, actor, audience, setting, and improvisation established in a review of literature from the diverse field of performance studies (see Chapter 2). The poetic form of many of the prophetic books resists narrative analysis, but remains open to performative analysis. Regarding the text as a script to be performed enables the questions: Who are the actors? What role does the audience play? Are there identifiable scenes? Is the performance open to interpretation and re-enactment?

Chapters 5–7 show that it is possible to divide the book of Habakkuk into scenes marked by changes in speaker, location, and focus. With the exception of the introductory preludes to each act, no consistent narrator's voice is identifiable. Frequent changes between first, second, and third person address imply that the identity of the actors changes frequently and is at times ambiguous. In addition, the audience plays a critical role, not only because the public nature of prophecy requires an audience but also because the script's use of rhetorical devices such as questions and plural verb forms invites the audience to participate in the performance. In translating the text from the original Hebrew it is notable that textual difficulties give rise to a variety of translations, both ancient and modern, suggesting that this is a performance open to a diversity of faithful interpretations and re-enactments.

The identification of the five performance features in the book of Habakkuk indicates that it is appropriate to read the book as a 'performance.' Before drawing together some of the insights that have been discerned in this particular method of reading Habakkuk, it is necessary to establish what the author wanted to communicate through this performance and to show how the performance features that have been identified contribute to this.

THE 'DRAMA' OF HABAKKUK

An emphasis on performance engages readers of Scripture more fully than interaction with 'text' alone. In order to convey this I have chosen

12. Levy, *The Bible as Theatre*, 5.

to substitute the term 'drama' for the idea of the 'message' of Habakkuk. My sub-title distils the drama of the book of Habakkuk: "Faithful Re-enactment in the Midst of Crisis." The context of crisis is unquestionable. Almost all recent commentaries agree that the mention of הכשׂדים (*the Chaldeans*) in Hab 1:6 is a reference to the Neo-Babylonian threat that came upon Judah in the late-seventh century BCE. The prophet's bitter complaints in Scenes One (1:2–4) and Three (1:12–17) of Act One presuppose a situation of oppression, and the woes of Scene Five (2:6–19) describe the actions of an oppressor against weaker victims, leading to the conclusion that such actions are describing the fate of Judah and other nations at the hands of the Neo-Babylonian army. Despite the context of communal worship in Act Two, the prophet returns to the pressing situation of "a people who will invade us" (3:16); thus the entire book must be seen in the context of a military crisis. This military invasion, however, is not the only form of crisis envisaged. Habakkuk 3:17 describes a natural disaster of drought, plague or famine, which results in a dearth of food and livelihood. It is a reminder that even when military crises pass, a community is still susceptible to other forms of trauma.

In such a context the ways of Yahweh are openly questioned by the prophet. His complaints in Scenes One (1:2–4) and Three (1:12–17) have been described by others as "exceedingly bold"[13] and "risky."[14] In my own assessment the prophet uses sarcasm in these complaints. From the time of the earliest textual witnesses discomfort has been shown at the prophet's boldness, but the script gives no evidence of reproof by Yahweh. This suggests that the language is acceptable, even appropriate given the situation in which the prophet finds himself and his community. Furthermore, the prophet is given a voice equal to Yahweh. The 'stage directions' that suggest his physical elevation at the introduction to Scene Four correspond to an expectation that he has a contribution to make to the situation of injustice, seen in the parallelism of "let me keep watch to see what he says to me / and what I will bring back concerning my rebuke" (2:1). There is a development in the character of the prophet through the performance that suggests a decrease in frustration and an increase in trust, but his initial complaints are in no way minimized or

---

13. Robertson, *The Books of Nahum, Habakkuk, and Zephaniah*, 156.
14. Andersen, *Habakkuk*, 175.

dismissed by this change. The 'faithfulness' of the prophet is therefore not undermined by his freedom to speak his mind.[15]

The fact that faithfulness continues in the midst of crisis is shown by the open-endedness of the conversation. An examination of the exchange between the prophet and Yahweh in Act One shows that Yahweh does not directly answer the prophet's charges that he is unable to see injustice. Nevertheless, Yahweh's "answer" in Scene Four (Hab 2:2–5) and the woe oracles of Scene Five (2:6–19) show that Yahweh is aware of injustice and the inevitability of retribution. Already in Scene Two a verdict of "guilty" has been passed (1:11) but the ongoing description of heedless devastation by the enemy keeps the question of judgment alive. The contrast between life and death established in Scene Four (2:2–5) and the use of woe oracles in the manner of funeral rites in Scene Five (2:6–19) suggest that the way of oppression leads to death. There is also an assurance that the way of faithfulness leads to life. Interruptions to the woe oracles by interjections (2:14, 20) exemplify the faithful attitude of the prophet, and at the end of Act One the drama is poised for decisive divine resolution. But the expected judgment against the enemy does not come in Act Two, only a reminder of Yahweh's saving ability (3:8, 13, 18). This is enough, however, for the prophet. His response is that of prayer and finally joyful worship, worship that is to be continually re-enacted by the prophet and his community as indicated by the liturgical rubrics and the final instruction for performance (3:19b).

In this prophetic book there is an openness to the future that invites re-enactment. As has been stated, the questions of justice/judgment are not fully resolved. Yahweh's 'control' of the situation is expressed by recalling past deeds of salvation (particularly in allusions to the Exodus event), thus merging past, present, and future events into ever-present realities. Faithfulness becomes trust in Yahweh's salvation despite an uncertain future. The prophet resolves to continue to "walk" (3:19) in

---

15. This conclusion that the prophet has an independent contribution to make is in remarkable contrast to Achtemeier's statement, "Prophets have no independent wisdom of their own—they are dependent on the word of God" (*Nahum—Malachi*, 42). In this context Achtemeier approvingly refers to Calvin whose commentary on Habakkuk asserts that human judgment is the work of Satan: "As long as we judge according to our own perceptions, we walk on the earth; and while we do so, many clouds arise, and Satan scatters ashes in our eyes, and wholly darkens our judgment" (Calvin, *Commentaries on the Twelve Volume IV*, 59). Such a suggestion is not supported in this reading of Habakkuk in which the prophet's independent thought is promoted.

the knowledge of Yahweh's presence in his life, specified in the multiplication of possessive pronouns (the God of my salvation, my Lord, my strength, my high places—3:18–19). This resolution marked by an active verb epitomizes faithful re-enactment and thus continues to emphasize the drama of the book as "faithful re-enactment in the midst of crisis."

HOW PERFORMANCE FEATURES ENHANCE THE DRAMA OF HABAKKUK

Reading the book of Habakkuk through the lens of performance criticism elucidates the drama of the book with greater clarity than traditional historical-critical methods. Lexical and grammatical choices made by the author of the script enhance the sense of crisis as a present reality, demanding active response. The presentation of the prophet as the main actor provides an example of faithfulness. An audience is assumed and is drawn into the action. Despite several scholars and commentators of the book of Habakkuk noting dramatic and liturgical elements in the structure of the book,[16] little attention has been given to its dramatic features, or, indeed, to drama in the prophetic literature as a whole. As Stacey notes, "a page or two is usually sufficient to dispose of the prophet's actions."[17] There is undoubtedly a widely-held assumption that the actions of the prophets 'merely' illustrate their words but, as I have argued, the neglect of performance features may also be due to the traditional Judeo-Christian disparagement of theatre on the one hand[18] and the scholarly turn to the text on the other.[19] The recent interest in performance criticism across many disciplines, including Biblical studies, has focused attention on such dramatic features, demonstrating how they help to open up the prophetic book of Habakkuk.

Vanhoozer recognizes a dramatic character to Israelite prophecy when he states, "The prophets were neither philosophers nor moralists but speech agents and symbolic actors concerned with what God was doing in history and with how the people ought to respond. At times

---

16. For example, Ewald, *Commentary on the Prophets*, 31; Eaton, "Origin and Meaning of Habakkuk 3," 160-63; Watts, *Books of Joel, Obadiah, Jonah, Nahum, Habakkuk, and Zephaniah*, 5-7; Watts, "Psalmody in Prophecy," 210; Floyd, *Minor Prophets, Part 2*, 89.

17. Stacey, *Prophetic Drama*, 4.

18. Bruch, "The Prejudice against Theatre," 4.

19. Walker, "Why Performance?" 150.

they proclaimed; at other times they enacted minidramas of God's relationship to Israel."[20] This description, however, still fails to fully integrate word and deed in the prophets as embodied mediators.

Script in the Drama of Habakkuk

Commentaries often make mention of the disparate materials collected in the book of Habakkuk that suggest several layers of editing. Although many argue that the material has been deliberately shaped to link the different materials thematically, one observation to be drawn from viewing a text such as Habakkuk as a 'script' is that the emphasis remains on the composition as a complete unit. When read in its entirety, repeated words and themes are noticed more readily. Wordplay in the text and the use of ready-mades that evoke memories, emotion or expectations from those in the audience also come to the fore. The shape of the performance is seen through those changes in actors, setting, and voice that divide the script into scenes.

Proponents of Biblical performance criticism emphasize the importance of reading the Biblical texts aloud in order to appreciate fully the subtleties of the composition. Thus Bennet points out in relation to the book of Ecclesiastes: "The text itself, in the way it is structured with repetition, suggests that it is to be heard, and not just read or spoken."[21] Ararat argues for a dramatic perspective in the Hebrew Bible but states that the texts are "principally meant to be read aloud rather than be performed."[22] Scholars in the field of rhetorical studies have stressed the unique contribution an oral performance makes by its use of such features as assonance, pauses, pitch, and volume; features easily missed when texts are read silently.[23] Tone of voice can convey attitudes such as sarcasm or taunting that might otherwise be unheeded.

Physical features other than hearing the words spoken aloud can also contribute significant meaning to the text. Physical gestures, facial expressions, movement, posture, and body language are all aspects that

---

20. Vanhoozer, *The Drama of Doctrine*, 51.

21. Bennet, "On Reading the Whole of Ecclesiastes," 310.

22. Ararat, *Drama in the Bible*, 2, quoted by Levy, *The Bible as Theatre*, 6. Levy suggests that the sensitivities of Ararat's Jewish faith lie behind such reticence to 'perform' Biblical texts.

23. Maxey, "Performance Criticism—Part 1," 41; Rhoads, "Performance Criticism—Part 2," 174.

affect performance. For example, in Scene Five of Act One (2:6–19) the verb נשׂא (*to lift up*), when combined with taunts and satirical riddles, implies physical gestures that add to the mockery conveyed in the words. Moreover, "all" are encouraged to participate in this action. As noted earlier, Levy encourages us to pay particular attention to 'stage-instructions' implicit in the text.[24] Such implicit stage instructions can be seen in Habakkuk at the beginning of Scene Four in Act One (2:1) where mention of the elevation of the prophet physically as well as figuratively gives him a particular importance in the drama and re-imagines his relationship to Yahweh. In a similar way, the posture of the prophet in the final scene of Habakkuk (3:16–19a) significantly enhances his words, moving from physical symptoms of utter fear manifested in trembling, tingling lips and melting bones to confident assertions of joy and strength and an ability to walk forward in the presence of Yahweh on "high places" (3:19a).

The script of Habakkuk invites readers to see as well as to hear its message. Indeed, verbs pertaining to sight occur throughout the script: the announcement that the prophet "saw" a revelation (1:1); Yahweh's injunction to "look" (1:5); the prophet's resolve to "keep watch" (2:1); reference to a "vision" to be written and made "plain" (2:2); the report that Yahweh stood and "looked" over creation (3:6) and the prophet "saw" trouble (3:7). Hence vision is integral to the presentation. Furthermore, the poetic imagery of the invading army and the theophanic description of Yahweh that has been characterized as a 'sound and light show' are evocative, lively, and easily visualized.[25] This emphasis in the script on visual performance as well as auditory characteristics invites response from the audience.

The choice of verbs used in this script leans towards performance and re-enactment. Active verbs are frequently used, even in relation to negative observations, such as "crooked justice goes forth" (1:4), "everyone comes for violence" (1:9), "you pay attention to those who act wickedly" (1:13). The significance of the final verb ידרכני (*he makes me walk*, 3:19a) is not often noticed. Roberts speaks of the prophet's determination "to stay on the path";[26] Smith suggests the verse means that the

---

24. Levy, *The Bible as Theatre*, 5.

25. Széles, *Wrath and Mercy*, 6, notes this emphasis on seeing, connecting it to the role of Habakkuk as a cult prophet who sees visions while he prays.

26. Roberts, *Nahum, Habakkuk, and Zephaniah*, 158.

prophet can be "faithful to God in his living"[27]; and Széles places priority on the action of Yahweh's earlier march rather than the prophet at this point.[28] Comparing this verse with a very similar formulation found in 2 Sam 22:34 shows a deliberate emphasis in the Habakkuk script. The poet in Second Samuel attests על במותי יעמדני (*on my high places he sets me secure*), suggesting passive faithfulness, while the script of Habakkuk states על במותי ידרכני (*on my high places he makes me walk*), stressing active faithfulness, particularly notable as this is the last word of the performance prior to the postlude.

Throughout the script there is a mixing of past and non-past verbs, giving the impression that the past and future impact upon the present. This is a device of the script that keeps the drama current and allows for continual re-enactment. The audience is also impacted by grammatical elements in the script. In Act One, the introduction of second person plural verbs in Scene Two (1:5) and the use of third person plural references at the beginning and end of Scene Five (2:6 and 20) draw the listening audience in to the action. It is the community who should look and be astounded, it is all those affected by the deeds of the Chaldean oppressor who will lift up taunts, it is all the earth who will keep silence in the presence of Yahweh. Similarly, the demonstrative particle הנה (*behold!*) is used to draw attention to the oppressor—first to the surprising introduction of the Chaldean army personified by its king (1:6), then to his crooked soul that will lead to his demise and become the subject of taunt woes (2:4) and finally to his practice of idolatry with its impotent, silent idols (2:19).

Moreover, the language keeps the audience on their toes as the woes are announced. The rhythmic movement from third person singular to second person singular could have the effect of leaving the audience wondering: am I the one who is being addressed? Or the king could be present amongst the crowd, so that "all these" turn and focus on him as the address becomes more pointed. Such ambiguity in the script invites interpretation.

Further ambiguity is introduced through the absence of a narrative voice. As new actors appear and speak, their identity is not entirely clear. The prophet and Yahweh are the only clearly identified characters, but even the speeches commonly attributed to them can be questioned. For

27. Smith, *Micah—Malachi*, 117.
28. Széles, *Wrath and Mercy*, 57.

example, with no "usual formula of quotation . . . to mark the change of speaker"[29] the identity of the speaker at the beginning of Scene Two of Act One is unclear. The "I" of Hab 1:6 is certainly not the "I" already identified as the prophet who offers the preceding prayer. Although commentators almost universally attribute the speech of 1:5–11 to Yahweh, Robertson admits "the reader is left to his own devices to determine who happens to be the speaker at any given point in the dialogue. Not until 2:2 is a speaker specifically identified."[30] Another unidentified voice is that of the speaker in 2:14, that may be characterized as an 'interjection.'[31] The lack of obvious connection between the faith statement of 2:14 and the preceding woe oracle has engendered much discussion, and it is often considered a gloss.[32] Andersen's alternative suggestion that it "could be a pious remark on the side"[33] comes close to understanding it from the point of view of a performance as a disembodied voice from the wings or an interjection by the prophet. A performance critical reading accepts such interjections as integral to the drama.

Shifts in verb tenses within Habakkuk and lack of precise identification of the characters, other than the prophet and Yahweh, provide openness for those attending to the drama to identify with the events, whether they are Israelite or Chaldean members of the audience or even audiences in the present time. Words of retribution for actions that lead to death can be heard by anyone at any time, the vision that leads to life can be accepted by anyone at any time, the bold statements of faith can be proclaimed by anyone at any time. There is an implicit expectation that the audience will engage in the process of self-reflexivity, considering their own position alongside that which is offered by the performance. Such emotional connection of audience with script and actor constitutes 'fusion' and evidences a successful performance.[34] When this occurs, the audience are able to use the performance for faithful re-enactment in their own time and setting.

---

29. Andersen, *Habakkuk*, 166.

30. Robertson, *The Books of Nahum, Habakkuk, and Zephaniah*, 137.

31. Anstey, "Habakkuk the Faithful Dissident," 53.

32. Széles, *Wrath and Mercy*, 40; Roberts, *Nahum, Habakkuk, and Zephaniah*, 123; Andersen, *Habakkuk*, 225.

33. Andersen, *Habakkuk*, 225.

34. Alexander, "Cultural Pragmatics," 54–55.

Silence as a motif is noticed more readily in performance of a text. In the book of Habakkuk silence is used effectively. The prophet complains of Yahweh's inattention to violence, injustice, and evil; accusing him of not seeing, hearing, or acting, culminating in the cry, "[Why do] you keep silence when wickedness swallows the more righteous?" (1:13). Yet the passages attributed to Yahweh are full of noisy action: Scene Two of Act One (1:5–11) describes the rushing, devastating army invasion as the work of Yahweh and Scene Five (2:6–19) is a verbal diatribe of condemnation understood to be the speech of Yahweh. The majority of Act Two is the theophany of Yahweh described in Chapter 7 as a 'sound and light show' or, to coin a more militant phrase, a performance characterized by 'shock and awe.' Experiencing such a performance has a profound physical effect on the prophet (3:16). But moments of silence are called for in the script between these descriptions. Twice the prophet is expected to wait (2:3; 3:16) and twice the script suggests a pause in the action (2:1, 20). With the possible exception of the words addressed to idols (2:19), the voice of the enemy is not heard in the script. At the end of Act One, arguably the 'peak' of the performance, "all the earth" is reduced to silence in the presence of Yahweh with the onomatopoeic הס ("Hush!" 2:20). Silence is effective as a contrast to what precedes and what follows, and its use in this script highlights the need for silence both as a response to crisis and a prelude to worship. Only in performance does silence come to the fore.

Actor in the Drama of Habakkuk

In Chapter 2 the role of actor as essential to performance was discussed. Two broad schools of thought govern any discussion of actor in theatre studies. The school of method acting (associated with its most celebrated proponent Stanislavski) encourages the actor to embody the character they are playing from the inside, while representational acting concentrates on 'presenting' the character from the outside so that the actor and audience are fully aware that the representation is a 'pretence' (famously taken to an extreme by Brechtian 'Epic theatre'). In performance studies the claim is often made that all communication and interaction is role-playing, especially when performance is taken beyond the limits of theatrical performance. Because embodiment is a recognizable theme in performance criticism, however, I have leant towards the first understanding of actor. Several studies of Biblical prophets as performance artists support this inclination.[35] The prophet acts more like a performance artist than a traditional actor, as there is a blurring between the individual and the role he/she presents.

A discussion of 'actor' is further complicated by the debate in prophetic studies over historical and literary representation in prophetic books. Do the books present actual historical characters and/or their words, or are they offered as *personae* fronting a theological statement made by a school or individual scribes of later periods? There has been a shift away from attempting to locate the historical character behind prophetic books to an understanding of the prophet as *persona*, an 'individual' presented by the compilers or editors of the prophetic book who is integral to the message. Reading the book of Habakkuk through the lens of performance theory renders such a debate irrelevant; rather, the prophet can be viewed as the character representing the drama of the book for both his own audience and later generations of faithful readers. Furthermore, reading the book as a performance allows Yahweh and any other actors presented in the script to be viewed as characters who also contribute to the drama.

Yahweh

Most faithful readers of a (prophetic) text located in the Hebrew Bible will be pre-conditioned to view Yahweh as the 'hero' of the text. As has been seen, however, Yahweh does not act very heroically in the first scenes of Habakkuk. He refuses to hear, see, and act on behalf of his suffering people. Yet in the midst of this portrayal is a scene that views him as decisive and authoritative, with the ability and determination to raise a powerful and destructive enemy against Israel. The character of Yahweh becomes less confusing as the performance continues in Act One. He acts as a powerful deity would be expected to, speaking decisively to and through the prophet in Scene Four (2:2–5) and authoritatively in relation to the enemy in Scene Five (2:6–19). At the end of Act One, Yahweh is in his remote "temple of holiness," a fitting location for Israel's god (Pss 5:7; 11:4; 65:4; 79:1; 138:2; Jonah 2:4, 27; Mic 1:2).

In Act Two Yahweh becomes actively involved again in the performance. The greater number of human characteristics attributed to him portray him as a powerful warrior with the ability to wreak havoc

---

35. See *The Bible and Critical Theory* 2.1 (2006), edited by Sherwood and devoted to "Prophetic Performance Art."

and destruction, but one committed to the salvation of his people. The repetition of significant vocabulary from earlier scenes gives continuity, but new characteristics are shown as well. A new gentleness is portrayed through the use of רחם (*compassion*). Despite this, יום צרה (*a day of distress*, 3:16), refers to the original crisis that has not yet been averted, showing that Yahweh is still understood as being responsible for the enemy invasion to come. Embodiment and role-playing can be characterized as opposing modes of acting in performance, but here Yahweh is an embodied character who nonetheless has the freedom to choose to act in or outside of character and so is not restricted to the audience's pre-understanding.[36] That is, in a performance reading the relationship of Yahweh to history and to the community's well-being is posed more as a question than as an answer.

The Prophet

Although a traditional reading of this book might assume Yahweh to be the star of the show, the prophet Habakkuk should arguably have equal billing. If the reading of Hab 2:14 as an interjection by the prophet is correct, then he alone appears in every scene. He goes beyond the traditional prophetic role of intermediary by challenging Yahweh in Scenes One (1:2–4) and Three (1:12–17).[37] These challenges are achieved through unusual use and improvisation of the genres of prayer of complaint and creation traditions and through repeated 'impudent' address to Yahweh pointing out inconsistency in his nature and message.

Glavin asserts that the skill of an actor is in the effect that is produced.[38] The prophet in this drama engages with other actors and his audience by challenging their presuppositions, surprising them with unexpected twists and drawing them into his own anguish and confu-

---

36. House's essay examining the character of God in the Book of the Twelve argues for a unity of character despite the diversity of images on two principles: first, the writers of the books were writing about the same God revealed through historical events and texts ("The Character of God," 128); and second, a single character can have many characteristics and yet remain consistent ("The Character of God," 145).

37. Ibid., 139, describes the characterization of Habakkuk as "an uncommon depiction of a prophet." He argues that this combined with the characterization of God as "revealer, judge, comforter, instructor, deliverer and sovereign Lord of history" provides "a strong theological statement about how God inspires faith in the faithful even as crisis unfolds."

38. Glavin, *After Dickens*, 31.

sion via his emotive language. As the performance evolves in Act One the prophet's character also develops, paradoxically both in confidence and in humility. The translation of Hab 2:1 is disputed but I read it as the prophet offering his own contribution ("what I will bring back concerning my rebuke"). By Scenes Four (2:2–5) and Five (2:6–19), the prophet's faith in Yahweh seems to have been largely restored, and he is prepared to state this publicly in a number of orthodox statements (2:4, 14, 20). Recurring themes and ideas in Act Two indicate further character development in the prophet on the basis of earlier events. A very personal description of physical and psychological symptoms frames the theophanic vision, indicating that the events affect him profoundly. The final confession of faith is conventional (and poetically beautiful) but reference by the prophet to a future enemy invasion (3:16) and potential environmental disaster (3:17) is a reminder that faith can and will continue to have meaning in situations of crisis. This confession puts into practice the statement already made in 2:4: "the righteous one in his faithfulness will live." The freedom of expression in the prophet that is affirmed in the script has been noted already. Anstey characterizes the prophet as a "faithful dissident," one ready to name a crisis honestly and allow questions to arise, one who critiques worldly power and one who offers visions for renewal.[39] The repeated personal pronoun in relation to Yahweh, "the God of my salvation . . . my Lord . . . my strength" (3:19a), indicates that for the prophet, he and Yahweh are inextricably bound. Yahweh's freedom is not absolute because his relationship with the prophet has given rise to faithful dependency. As the central character in this performance, the prophet becomes the model for faithful re-enactment. Even if not fully answered, his questions and complaints are not dismissed by Yahweh. His description of waiting for answers, offering his own suggestions (2:1), his interjection (2:14), his instructions to the audience (2:20), and his confessions of faith (2:1, 14; 3:1, 16–19) are all evidence of a thoughtful and committed public theologian.[40]

The Chaldean King

A third character introduced in the script is not explicitly identified and yet is depicted in such palpable terms that the image of a feared enemy is

---

39. Anstey, "Habakkuk the Faithful Dissident," 55.

40. This description of the prophet is used by Anstey, "Habakkuk the Faithful Dissident," 55.

portrayed. Mention of "the Chaldeans" (1:6) is quickly replaced by singular references so that the nation is represented by one man, presumably their king. This character is present throughout the performance but (in my reading) he speaks only once (2:19) where speech to idols is sarcastically quoted. Unlike the other characters he fulfills the expected role of the personified enemy, but as the performance continues his silence and the words spoken against him render him impotent. The lack of clear reference to him via a name forms a contrast to the other main characters and suggests that it is a *persona* that can be fulfilled by any one of a number of enemies perceived by the audience. This recognition is a key observation of a performance reading that pays attention to characters, their names, and their roles. A traditional historical-critical reading of the book would attempt an identification of the enemy, but a performance reading recognizes the potential for new performances in new circumstances to ensure that the message is relevant to each new audience. Indeed, the rendering of this enemy as "Kittim" by the Qumran *Pesher* is evidence of this freedom at work.[41]

Other Actors in Habakkuk

Analyzing the actors in each scene of the script of Habakkuk has yielded some surprising results. Several non-human objects or entities are given prominence by having a voice or embodied action in the script. Thus in Act One, Torah is "paralyzed" (1:4), a vision "breathes" (2:3), a stone "cries out" and a rafter "answers" (2:11). In Act Two, Deep "gives its voice" and Sun "lifts its hands" (3:10). Furthermore, in the theophany natural elements can be viewed as deities in their own right, with the ability to march alongside Yahweh (Pestilence and Fire-bolt in 3:5) or be attacked by him (Rivers and Sea in 3:8). Capitalizing these names in my translation highlight this possibility.

As mentioned earlier, a performance reading also notices when actors and entities are silenced or ignored, thus diminishing their importance in the drama. A significant factor in this script is the silence of the king of the Chaldeans: the only words he speaks are futile words addressed to mute idols (2:19). While the king is a fearsome presence in

---

41. A similar observation is made by Abrego, "Habakkuk," 1170, who claims: "An eschatological reading of the prophet blurs the historical features of any people and turns it into the vague shape of a mythical enemy. Although efforts to situate Habakkuk's message in a historical period are praiseworthy, the problem of evil, even at the international level, transcends particular historical moments."

Scenes Two (1:5–11) and Three (1:6–17) of Act One, his lack of effective voice in the remaining drama render him powerless and even ridiculous. His brief reappearance in Scene Two of Act Two (3:13) in effect demolishes him entirely so that he is no longer a threat. The king's strength is attributed to "his god" (1:11) but this "god" is a character who never speaks and so has little impact upon the whole performance (merely a 'celebrity appearance'?). Other actors marginalized in the script are the idols of Scene Five in Act One (2:18–19). Although a fairly lengthy description is dedicated to these characters, the use of words such as "dumb," "mute," and "worthless" highlight their lack of significance. Because they have "no wind (breath)" they are lifeless, forming an unfavorable contrast to the life-giving vision of the prophet that "breathes to the end" (2:3).

Audience in the Drama of Habakkuk

Performance demands an audience. While the role of the audience as participatory or purely spectatory is debated, it is undeniable that a definition of performance must include an audience. Fischer-Lichte states that performance arises as a result of "the bodily co-presence of those who perform and those who look on."[42] In this sense performance is public. Fischer-Lichte claims, "performances are particularly suitable as sites for different cultures to meet and negotiate their relationships through various processes of interweaving that result in something completely new and beyond the scope of any single participating culture."[43] Scripture also has a public nature in that texts have been preserved by a community of faith for ongoing authority and inspiration. It is clear that the revelations and visions of the prophet in the book of Habakkuk are intended to be heard. The public settings, the instruction to make the vision plain (2:2) and the frequent use of plural verbs, pronouns, and collective nouns (1:5; 2:6, 20; 3:13, 16) indicate that the book is no private conversation between the prophet and Yahweh. The woe oracles are introduced by gaining the attention of a gathered crowd (2:6), giving the impression that the taunts are publicly stated. While all Scripture is preserved and passed on via community, prophecy is particularly oriented beyond itself. Nonetheless, the cultural horizon of Scripture is

---

42. Fischer-Lichte, "Interweaving Cultures in Performance," 391.
43. Ibid., 400.

sufficiently removed from the present age to require new audiences to 'negotiate' meaning in the manner set out by Fischer-Lichte.

In reading the book of Habakkuk as a performance, the presence of an audience can be inferred on several levels. In Habakkuk an announcement of a revelation to a prophet is made (1:1). The understanding of a prophet as an intermediary between God and the community requires an understanding of original recipients. At any stage of redaction a new audience would receive the message, such that one might speak of an 'implied audience' as the group in the mind of the author or redactor. In this performance it is possible to speak both of an 'on-stage' audience and an implied audience although these groups overlap at times. In addition, attention to re-enactment in performance is a reminder that the ancient book of Habakkuk has continually had new audiences since its inception until the present day. The social location of the audience also has an impact on the performance, affecting interpretation. This is what makes improvisation such an important concept in performance, as will be discussed below.

In the ancient world, reading aloud to an audience was a more common practice than private reading. This recognition, coupled with the nature of Scripture as preserved text that is continually introduced to new audiences in the community of faith, compels an acknowledgement that the implied audience for this performance includes the contemporary reader. Unlike a reading that attempts to locate recipients of the text in its layers of redaction, a performance reading stresses the continuing impact of the text through to the present time.

An analysis of Habakkuk as a performance enables a discussion of the audience as a single entity. While their role is that of spectator or eavesdropper in Scenes One (1:2–4) and Three (1:12–17) of Act One, the plural second person verbs at the beginning of Scene Two (1:5–11) actively draw them into the action. The public setting of the rest of Act One (siege works and civic square) also implies an on-stage audience throughout.[44] Once again the audience is actively included in the action at the beginning of Scene Five (2:6) by the invitation to join in the taunting. This on-stage audience, referred to in the script as כל־הגוים (*all the nations*), may well have included the Chaldeans. The end of Act One states the expectation that "all the earth" will acknowledge Yahweh's presence (2:20) so that the audience is broadened to include later readers

---

44. Here I disagree with Andersen, *Habakkuk*, 195, who claims there is no identifiable audience at Hab 2:1.

and hearers. Act Two introduces aspects of communal liturgy including instructions for prayer or musical accompaniment and three *Selah* responses to the theophanic poem (3:3, 9, 13). The use of rhetorical questions (3:8), a collective noun (3:13), and a first person plural pronoun (3:16) all show ways in which the audience is invited into the prophet's contemplations.

The impact of the script on the audience can be demonstrated by attention to high iconicity in translation, particularly of verbs. Direct address to the audience ensures they do not remain impartial spectators, and the frequent use of present tense verbs means that this performance is not locked in the past but is intended to be re-imagined and re-lived. The shift in verb tenses in Habakkuk and lack of precise identification of the characters other than the prophet and Yahweh leave those attending to the performance open to identify with the events and enable them to use the performance for faithful re-enactment in their own time and setting.

The emphasis on seeing and hearing in this script that has already been noted is another way in which audience participation is invited throughout the performance. Graphic descriptions by the actors enhanced by wordplay and elements of surprise ensure that the audience is engaged and responsive. The liturgical nature of Act Two suggests that it is a performance that is to be re-appropriated by communities of faith.

Setting in the Drama of Habakkuk

The significance of the setting of the action is noticed when the book of Habakkuk is read as a performance. In particular, it is a book that begins and ends in crisis. The opening words of the prophet (1:2–4) suggest a situation of turmoil in which injustice reigns and no order is kept, giving rise to bitter complaint. The multitude of negative terms used in three brief verses paint an extremely negative picture: חמס (*violence*), און (*sorrow*), עמל (*trouble*), שד (*devastation*), ריב (*strife*), מדון (*contention*), רשע (*wickedness*), and מעקל משפט (*crooked justice*). The closing soliloquy in the performance (3:16–19a), while speaking of natural calamity rather than that made by human action, nonetheless continues to offer a description of crisis.[45]

45. The conditions pictured in these verses could, of course, be a result of the invading army as in Jeremiah 5:17 but whether it is viewed as a continuation of the same crisis or a crisis of another origin does not affect the drama.

As the scenes progress it is clear that for much of the book the crisis is of a military nature. The description of the invading army (1:5–11), the reference to being "on guard" at the "siege works" (2:1), the plunder (2:8), violence (2:8–9, 17), bloodshed mentioned in the woe oracles (2:8, 12, 17) and the mention of an imminent invasion (3:16) all evoke a situation of warfare in which Israel is in a vulnerable position.

The military imagery, however, is not limited to Israel's enemies. It is also used in the theophanic description of Yahweh as a warrior with weapons and chariot (3:3–15). Is the message of the performance therefore to be understood that violence is to be met with a greater violence, personified in the Warrior God?

Applying an inner-textual hermeneutic to this script helps to question this military setting as the normative and acceptable site for this particular revelation. There are at least three details of the performance that are relevant to this question. First, the prophet's elevated status (literal and figurative) expressed in Hab 2:1 and 3:19a puts him on a par with Yahweh and gives both his statements of complaint *and* his confessions of faithful trust an equal significance to triumphalist renderings of conquering warriors. Honestly expressed pain, bewilderment and quiet conviction are intended to be heard in this performance despite the 'shock and awe' of the forceful destructiveness of the invading army on the one hand and the thundering presence of Yahweh on the other.

Second, the woe oracles describe a paradoxical reversal of fortune for the tyrant, indicating that the seeds of destruction are contained within the system of tyranny rather than in retributive violence.[46] The Chaldean king is taunted by Yahweh and his people but the description of his downfall is presented as a consequence of his actions rather than as the result of a direct attack by Yahweh. Even the description of Yahweh's action as the conquering warrior in the theophany suggests that the Chaldeans collapse under self-destruction, shown in the phrase, "You have pierced with his spears the heads of his warriors" (3:14).[47]

The third nuance preventing this performance's domination by military triumphalism is the observation that natural and military im-

---

46. Hiebert, "The Book of Habakkuk," 647-48; see also Smith, *The Book of the Twelve Prophets*, 144.

47. My translation follows the MT here. G has rendered "You have pierced with *your* spears," an indication of the expectation that Yahweh would act decisively, but arguably missing the subtle point of the seeds of self-destruction seen in the woe oracles.

agery are merged in the theophany. The realm of human experience is explored to find appropriate metaphors for the presence of Yahweh, so that his blinding presence is akin to looking into the sun's light (3:4), thunderstorms become thundering horse-drawn chariots (3:8, 15) and lightning shafts become spears (3:11).Yahweh's presence, although described in words borrowed from warfare, is actually more pervasive than an invading army because it encompasses the entire natural world. The fact that the script moves on from this description and takes the audience back to the potential invasion of the human army (3:16) and the possibility of ecological disaster (3:17–18) shows an intentional focus on the community's experience of crisis as the predominant setting for the composition.

Recognition of Hab 2:20 as the 'peak' of the script suggests that despite the overall setting of crisis and the pervading, albeit qualified, military imagery, the vision of Yahweh in his temple of holiness is the central and dominant vision for the performance. When Yahweh is in his place, all human words, movement, and power are ultimately silenced before him. The flow in the script from an announcement of Yahweh in his temple at the end of Act One to prayer as the opening scenario for Act Two suggests that the appropriate response by the prophet and the audience to Yahweh's presence in the temple is worship. Worship becomes the context for the rest of the performance. Throughout the script, linguistic and geographical allusions to the Exodus event (mention of "a work" in 1:5 and 3:2; the "tablets" in Hab 2:2; significant geographical locations in 3:3, 7; and the four-fold reference to Yahweh as a "saving" God in 3:8, 3:13 [x2], 3:18) reiterate the context of faith and trust introduced by reference to the temple and the implied context of worship.

The priority of worship is already seen in Act One in the mention of Sheol (2:5) and the related references to life and death. Such allusions lift the performance from a specific time and place and offer relevance for all times and places. The community of Yahweh's followers will continue to experience crisis and yet will be led by its prophets to continue to respond in worship.

Improvisation in the Drama of Habakkuk

Improvisation in performance is understood as respecting and building on a tradition but allowing a new situation to create new possibilities (see Chapter 2). Schechner, who uses the language of the theatre in his anthropological studies, argues that improvisation is inevitable in performance because performance is always characterized by "restored behavior,"[48] where the performer draws on stored "strips" of behavior from past experience to re-use in new circumstances. The conditions of those new circumstances will influence the choices made by the performer. In improvised performance on the stage, actors work together to pick up cues from each other that will build or block the theme of the performance.

The author of the book of Habakkuk draws on a number of Hebrew Bible conventions but modifies them for the new setting presented, sometimes building and sometimes blocking the accepted meaning in support of the message of the book. From the outset, the presentation of a prophetic oracle is challenged. Even though the book of Habakkuk is introduced as המשא (*the revelation*), the term has been broadened from its common usage as an oracle against a foreign nation to include prayers of complaint, visions, taunts, and songs of praise. Some of these forms themselves have been modified. For example, the prayers of complaint (1:2–4 and 12–18) include no "voice of tradition" in an expression of trust or vow of praise and the taunts of Habakkuk 2 make use of wisdom terminology and the funereal הוי (*woe*) rather than legal terminology, despite the impression that the setting is a public hearing.

Other well-known conventions are also innovatively modified. The prophetic concept of a "day of distress" (3:16) is used in relation to the enemy rather than to Yahweh's own people. Creation imagery is turned on its head (1:14) by presenting humankind as the equivalent of the lowlife of creation rather than the pinnacle. Terminology from the liturgical tradition is inserted in Habakkuk 3, which may itself be viewed as a psalm except that the placement of the *Selah* instruction and the colophon at the end rather than the beginning depart from the norm. It can be difficult to discover the full significance of these changes when a clear understanding of the convention that is being modified is not known. In the book of Habakkuk the terms "Shigionoth" and "Niginoth" seem to have significance for knowing how to perform the text, but their meaning is unclear and could lead to very different renderings (lament or passionate song? stringed music or mocking verse?). Despite the uncertainty, the recognition that liturgical terminology is used in the book reiterates the notion that the material is to be performed in new settings.

48. Schechner, *Performance Studies*, 34.

Improvisations made by an author give an insight into how the author's circumstances influenced the presentation or how the author wanted to modify convention to present a particular message. When one expects a prophetic word (1:1) but hears a prayer of complaint instead (1:2–4), the complaint becomes an integral part of the prophetic word. When one expects judgment (2:20) but is led into worship instead (3:1), there is an implied priority of worship over judgment. When there are several references to "waiting" (2:1, 3; 3:16) but the script ends in movement (ידרכני [*he makes me walk*], Hab 3:19a), an impression is given that faithfulness cannot be static but involves dynamic re-enactment.

As noted in Chapter 2, improvised performance commonly makes use of ready-mades. These are stock patterns or phrases that are known to both performer and audience. They represent a body of tradition that is familiar to those involved in the performance, but by using them in a new setting a new meaning may be invested in them. A number of words and phrases act as ready-mades in this script. Their innovative use has a shock value that might cause the audience to re-assess their understanding of the concepts. For example, תורה (*Torah*), is mentioned in Hab 1:4 but is described as "paralyzed"—an unusual and arresting description. משפט (*justice*), another term familiar to a Biblical audience, is used twice to highlight the lack of justice perceived in the presentation of Yahweh at this point in the book. In Hab 1:4 justice is described as "crooked" and in 1:7 "justice" and "dignity" are qualities attributed to the enemy. The re-use of the term חמס (*violence*), in Scene One (1:2) and Scene Two (1:9) would also be surprising: the very "violence" that the prophet had complained about was being brought about by a new set of actors, engineered by Yahweh!

Using the ready-made הלחות (*the tablets*), in Scene Four (2:2–5) would have evoked memories of the reception of the law by Moses but surprised the audience by summing up "the law" in one phrase (2:4). That this improvisation had a lasting effect on the meaning of the law can be seen in the way the Midrash and New Testament writers have adopted this phrase as a summation of the law. Towards the end of the script the ready-mades drawn on by the author such as רחם (*compassion*) and ישע (*to save*) retain their conventional meaning in order to emphasize the ability of Yahweh to care for and save his faithful ones.

It is clear that choices that have been made by the author of Habakkuk in the re-presentation of older material relates to the circum-

Reading Habakkuk through a Performance Lens 189

stances of his audience as a people in the midst of crisis and serves his message of the necessity for faithfulness under such circumstances. This insight is not dissimilar to that of redaction criticism, which views redactional additions as adaptations of an old text in relation to changed historical circumstances. Viewing such changes as 'improvisation' emphasizes the inevitability of adaptation in every new performance. It is also a reminder that the original 'script' of Habakkuk was already improvising inherited and established traditions, making use of ready-mades to surprise and challenge the audience's expectations. The openness that characterizes improvised performance suggests that no text can be viewed as fixed in time. This freedom may serve as a model for later interpreters. The characteristic of performance that impels it to be re-enacted implies that new settings will continue to result in improvisation as faithful communities persist in using this ancient text as a source for faith and behavior.[49] Indeed, the performative potential of Habakkuk has been realized in many varied contexts.

HABAKKUK 'RE-ENACTED'

The following ten examples could be characterized as improvisations of Habakkuk in the history of its interpretation and performance. Some re-enactments of the book have only minor, albeit significant, changes; others use the message of Habakkuk as a major source of inspiration for new literary, artistic or multi-media works. The selection is not exhaustive, but samples a variety of works from across a wide time-span. In each instance, it will be argued that a new setting has influenced the way the ancient text has been understood and re-presented.

Septuagint (c. 225 BCE)

The Septuagint (LXX) version of Habakkuk has several significant variations but two examples stand out as the most interesting in relation to improvisation. The first is the rendering of Hab 1:11 as *then he shall change his spirit, he shall pass through, and make an atonement [saying] this strength belongs to my god* (Brenton's Edition, 1851). The Hebrew is admittedly difficult and has given rise to a number of variations, but

---

49. Of interest there is the PhD dissertation of Cleaver-Bartholomew that analyzes the Old Greek version of Habakkuk, noting both continuity and differences between it and MT due to what he calls 'actualization' or 'updating' due to a new historical context (*An Analysis of the Old Greek Version of Habakkuk*, 322).

the LXX seems to understand the verse as referring to the spirit of the Chaldean king and relates it to the account of the conversion of King Nebuchadnezzar in Daniel 4, suggesting that the Chaldean king will similarly be converted. Such a change could reflect an interest in attracting Gentile proselytes in the Diaspora.

The second example is the much discussed Hab 2:4, rendered by the LXX as *the just shall live by my faith* (Brenton's Edition, 1851). By attributing faithfulness to Yahweh rather than to the individual believer, the text came to inform much subsequent discussion in apocalyptic and New Testament literature of "the problem of the delay in the appearance of God's eschatological justice."[50] Apocalyptic concerns of later generations resulted in small but significant improvisations to the script.

The idea that the LXX was 'updated' for new generations is widely accepted, as shown by Levinson's comment: "The translators sought to explain difficult words, to reconcile inconsistent laws, and to make the ancient text of the Pentateuch 'present' and relevant to their situation . . . In many cases, the Septuagint preserves a witness to earlier religious ideas in the biblical text that were subsequently 'corrected' to bring it into conformity with later Jewish monotheism."[51]

Qumran (c. 50 CE)

The writer of the Qumran *pesher* on Habakkuk clearly 'updated' the enemy from *Kasdim* (Chaldeans) to *Kittim* (Romans) in his commentary on Hab 1:6a: "This refers to the Kittim, w[ho are] swift and mighty in war, annihilating [many people]" (1QpHab 2.12–13).[52] The *pesher* must be understood in the light of the rise of apocalypticism in the post-exilic period and the belief that the Righteous Teacher was able to reveal the prophecies made in the book of Habakkuk.[53] Nonetheless, it is significant that the circumstance of the Qumran community was also one of military crisis that compelled them to hide their writings in nearby caves. It is this crisis that results in the change to the original script. Archaeological evidence of Roman arrowheads and coins suggest that

---

50. Hays, *Echoes of Scripture in the Letters of Paul*, 40. This "delay" is the context for the quotation of the LXX version of Hab 2:4 in Heb 10:38.

51. Levinson, *Legal Revision*, 160.

52. Translation from Wise et al, *The Dead Sea Scrolls*, 116.

53. Brownlee, *The Midrash Pesher of Habakkuk*, 28-30.

Paul (Mid-First Century CE)

Paul uses Hab 2:4 in his letters to the Galatians and to the Romans (Gal 3:11; Rom 1:17). Beker claims that 2:4 is "*the* crucial Old Testament text for Paul."[55] Hays makes explicit the new "crisis" facing Paul: "not the occupation of Israel by a Gentile military power but the apparent usurpation of Israel's favored covenant status by congregations of uncircumcised Gentile Christians."[56] In this crisis Paul affirms the justice of God's ways by drawing on Scripture, including the prophetic book of Habakkuk. Nonetheless, his writing evidences "small but significant revisions of familiar scripts."[57] When quoting Hab 2:4 Paul writes, Ὁ δὲ δίκαιος ἐκ πίστεως ζήσεται (*the one who is righteous shall live by faith*), following neither the Hebrew text ("[the] righteous one in *his* faithfulness will live") nor the Greek version ("the just shall live by *my* faith") but instead eliding the personal pronoun and leaving the meaning ambiguous. Through this ambiguity the quotation now serves the dual claims of Paul that the gospel reveals God's own righteousness and is salvation to everyone who believes.

Masoretes (c. 750 CE)

Habakkuk 1:12 is an example of a *tiqqun* made by the Masoretic scribes and evidence of another small but significant improvisation. The alteration of the original text לא תמות (*you shall not die*) to that which is found in the MT לא נמות (*we shall not die*), could reflect an uneasiness on the part of the translators to express the possibility of the death of Yahweh[58] or uneasiness due to the implied sarcasm on the part of the prophet.[59]

---

54. Murphy-O'Connor, "Qumran, Khirbet," 593. Robertson, *The Books of Nahum, Habakkuk, and Zephaniah*, 144, writes rather disparagingly of the Qumran scribes' "zeal to contemporize the message of Habakkuk" resulting in significant departures in the commentary from the original text. I would characterize this instead as creative improvisation, keeping the message relevant for its new audience.

55. Beker, "Echoes and Intertextuality," 68, author's italics.

56. Hays, *Echoes of Scripture in the Letters of Paul*, 40.

57. Alexander and Mast, "Introduction," 15.

58. Ginsburg, *Introduction to the Massoretico-Critical Edition*, 348-63.

59. Floyd, *Minor Prophets Part 2*, 108.

Either way, a new sensitivity to speaking to or about Yahweh is shown that was not part of the original script with its bold and derisive questioning of Yahweh.

Old English Exodus (c. Ninth Century CE)

This epic poem composed in medieval English retells the story of the Israelites' exodus from Egypt, crossing of the Red Sea and wanderings in the wilderness.[60] Much discussion has revolved around possible sources for the poem outside of relevant chapters in the Biblical book of Exodus, but only recently has the book of Habakkuk been cited as a possible source of inspiration. Breeze[61] points out the similarity of language between passages in Habakkuk and the Old English *Exodus*, specifically the power of Yahweh over the sea and reference to Ethiopians (lines 68–71), which may be compared to the Vulgate translation of Hab 3:7 (*vidi tentoria Aethiopiae*); possible influence of Hab 1:9 on the description of "beasts of battle" in lines 161–69 of *Exodus* and "nets of death" (lines 200–2) which corresponds to Hab 1:14–17. Breeze notes that the location of the canticle "Song of Habakkuk" (Habakkuk 3) immediately after Moses' song in ninth-century Anglian canticles suggests an ancient connection between the stories.[62] In Old English *Exodus* the sea crossing is understood as an allegory for Christian baptism. Even if the author of Habakkuk had drawn on the Exodus tradition in rendering his psalm, the author of Old English *Exodus* has introduced a new Christian element to update Habakkuk for his own rendition.

William Cowper (1779 CE)

The poetry of Habakkuk 3 inspired a well-known hymn written by William Cowper, an English poet and hymnodist (1731–1800). Originally titled "Joy and Peace in Believing," it has been preserved under the title "Sometimes a Light Surprises." The final verse of the hymn has an explicit reference to Hab 3:17:

> Though vine, nor fig-tree neither,
> Their wonted fruit should bear,

---

60. A translation, commentary and notes for this Anglo-Saxon poem can be found in Lucas, *Exodus (Anglo-Saxon Poem)*.

61. Breeze, "The Book of Habakkuk and Old English Exodus," 210-14.

62. Ibid., 210.

> Tho' all the fields should wither,
> Nor flocks, nor herds, be there:
> Yet God the same abiding,
> His praise shall tune my voice;
> For while in him confiding,
> I cannot but rejoice.

A brief survey of Cowper's life indicates that this hymn was written during or shortly after a period of manic-depression, although not published until some years later in the Olney Hymnbook co-authored by John Newton.[63] Cowper, too, was a victim of crisis—this time of a more personal nature—and his words paraphrasing Hab 3:17 give another example of faithful re-enactment in the midst of such.

Charles Tompson (1825 CE)

Tompson is of historical interest as Australia's first native-born published poet. His father was a transported convict, but Tompson himself was educated in a Christian seminary and later worked as a public servant. In 1826 at 20 years of age he published *Wild Notes, from the Lyre of a Native Minstrel* that included a poem based on Habakkuk 3.[64] The poem that lyrically paraphrases Habakkuk 3 is his only composition in *Wild Notes* with direct Biblical allusion. Widespread drought is a regular phenomenon in Australia and could have occasioned this reflection. The poet seems to reflect the visionary experience of the prophet when he yearns for the same inspiration that was given to the prophet who was able to "paint" God with vivid descriptions:

> O, for a beam, from Sion's sacred hill,
> Of inspiration! Then my soaring muse
> Would wake, with hope, her bold aspiring lyre
> To notes of rapture! Such the seer inspired,
> Whose holy strains essayed to paint his God!

The three lines that close the poem depart from paraphrase with a reference to heaven, described by Tompson as "the conclusion I have naturally drawn in order to amplify the piece":

---

63. Routley, *I'll Praise my Maker*, 65.

64. Tompson, *Wild Notes*. A digital copy of Tompson's poem is held by the University of Sydney Library's Electronic Text and Image Service (SETIS). http://setis.library.usyd.edu.au/ozlit/pdf/v00007.pdf.

And dwell, with hope, on joys that bloom in heaven,
The pilgrim's goal—the sinner's home of peace,
Where all is bright, and Love Eternal reigns!

This augmentation to the original script indicates the influence of a Christian interpretation of the book of Habakkuk.

Max Ernst (1934 CE)

A large sculpture entitled *Habakuk* by German sculptor Max Ernst is part of the permanent collection in the National Gallery of Australia, currently on display in the main entry foyer. Although this abstract artwork is not intended to be a re-enactment of the entire book of Habakkuk, it does serve to illustrate creative improvisation of the relevant subjects of idolatry and prophetic vision. The 4.5m high sculpture has a bird-like appearance with a large beak and protruding eyes. Ernst pays an ironic tribute to Hab 2:18, a verse that condemns the makers of idols (sculptors), but is probably also equating art with the visionary powers of a prophet, suggested by the large eyes on the sculpture and a third eye at the base. Despite its static form, this sculpture reflects performance themes that have been identified, particularly the themes of self-reflexivity (as described above), and process, the latter well illustrated by the description of the artwork as "casts of flowerpots [with] stacked and turning forms, the openings between them, and the lack of stable horizontal planes suggesting impending movement."[65]

Paul Hasluck (1969 CE)

Sir Paul Hasluck was an important political figure in Australia in the mid-twentieth century, appointed sequentially as Minister for Territories, Minister for Defense, and Foreign Minister before resigning from Parliament to take up the office of Governor General in 1969, a post he held until 1974. Political rivalries marked his last few years in the political arena, with reported animosity between Hasluck and Prime Ministers Gorton, McMahon, and Whitlam.[66] He was also a poet, writer, and historian. A book of poetry published in 1969 includes a "recitation for wireless broadcast" titled "The Burden of Habakkuk and

---

65. Radford, *Collection Highlights*, 215. An image of this sculpture may be found at www.nga.gov.au.

66. Hasluck, *The Chance of Politics*.

the Sword of Gideon." As far as I can ascertain, this play was never put to air. Hasluck's introduction to the book gives a telling description of the issues weighing on his mind at the time of publication, although the poem had been written around the time of the Second World War: "I also use dialogue as a device because there is argument and contention, but this is composed as a monologue—the tumult of many voices playing around inside a man's mind, the man's mind itself, like that of a troubled prophet in a wilderness, being full of echoes of his own age as well as of all he has inherited from the past."[67]

Though evidencing a significant departure from the original script of Habakkuk, the repeated refrain, "How long, O Lord, how long," and the recurring imagery of drought re-enacts Habakkuk's complaining, questioning voice in the midst of crisis. Interestingly, the first two lines of the concluding stanza in the composition begin, "we shall stop talking now for we have come/Into the presence of the Lord,"[68] an echo of the concluding peak to Act One in Habakkuk (2:20).

"Habakkuk" InterVarsity 2100 Multi-media Production (1980)

"Habakkuk" was one of the first multi-media presentations developed and used for evangelistic purposes by InterVarsity Christian Fellowship's Twentyonehundred Productions.[69] A central concern of the organization is to communicate the gospel through contemporary media in ways that are understandable to people in modern society. The production was shown on a sixty-five foot screen with twenty-six slide projectors and other special effects projectors. A soundtrack including a recitation of the book of Habakkuk was interspersed with original music and songs written by David Maddox, statements representing contemporary attitudes such as, "If there's a god, he has really let this world get all messed up . . . I don't see any evidence that he is doing anything," and reference to significant twentieth-century events such as the Watergate scandal.

---

67. Hasluck, "The Burden of Habakkuk," 117.

68. Ibid., 140.

69. http://www.intervarsity.org/2100/history.php. The name 2100 Productions was adopted when the producers noted the acronym for multi-media communication (MMC) was the Roman numerals for the number 2100. Information about the production was gathered from Dan Pinka, Associate Producer at InterVarsity's Twentyonehundred Productions (personal communication, 17 December 2009) and Steve Falk, Senior Editor in the same organization (personal communication, 15 January 2010).

It was introduced with the statement, "Habakkuk is asking in his whole book 'how do I make sense out of the world I live in?'" and concluded with an allusion to Mark 8:35: "the very one who would try to save his life will lose it . . . to live by faith is to live by the strength of God." The presentation toured college campuses in the USA for about five years, and was presented with a gold medal at the International Multi-Image Festival in Colorado in 1980. This is a fascinating example of a performance of Habakkuk that has maintained the original script yet 'updated' its message and re-interpreted it with an explicitly Christian evangelical intention.

Summary

These performative re-enactments of the book of Habakkuk could be described as examples of how the Scriptures are a 'rolling corpus,' a phrase coined by McKane in his commentary on Jeremiah where he speaks of the prophetic book evidencing "ongoing development over several generations, with many voices, interests, and advocacies contributing to its emerging shape."[70] Such a 'rolling corpus' moves beyond the canonical boundaries to speak to new audiences in new ways. Brueggemann speaks of "rereading" in a similar fashion to what has been here characterized 're-enactment.' For him, the text itself is always pushing forward for reinterpretation, giving the Biblical text a future with "paradigmatic power."[71]

FAITHFUL PERFORMANCE OF HABAKKUK

As the book of Habakkuk opens, the audience is thrust into the midst of a crisis, ostensibly the Neo-Babylonian invasion of Judah in the sixth century BCE. As has been noted, however, it is unlikely that the book was fully compiled prior to the Persian era. The original audience of the book of Habakkuk, or more probably their forebears, had already lived through and survived the crisis of the Neo-Babylonian invasion, the exile, and return to a devastated land. The lack of specific identification of actors and events in the book of Habakkuk ensures that it is a text applicable to any crisis facing communities of faith.

70. Brueggemann, *A Commentary on Jeremiah*, ix; see also McKane, *A Critical and Exegetical Commentary on Jeremiah*, l–liii.

71. Brueggemann, *Like Fire in the Bones*, 115.

In a study of the book of Jeremiah, O'Connor speaks of the importance of lament as response to crisis and as a way to rebuild community and restore life.[72] She argues that the power of lament is its ability to cling to God while expressing "overwhelming discontent with God's treatment of the world."[73] She describes how the expressions of lament by Jeremiah give words to the pain of the surviving community and provide a model for survival. There is a performative nature to Jeremiah's personal prayers: "Rather than ignoring the community's shattered faith, Jeremiah's personal prayers enact it, dramatize it, and put it into the public sphere as a work of liturgy."[74] The articulation of pain, even in the context of liturgy, enables emergence from victimhood and gives new meaning to the experience.

The prayer of the prophet that opens the book of Habakkuk is a complaint rather than a lament. Although it includes an address to the deity and a detailed description of the situation, it does not include the formal elements of a confession of trust, petition or vow of praise. On the other hand, the structure of the book as a whole does include these elements, beginning with a description of the problem, followed by a confession of confidence in the intervention of Yahweh, and finally a vow of praise. By recognizing lament in the macro-structure of the book of Habakkuk, the whole book can be seen as a model for faith in the midst of crisis. Reading the script as a unified performance has shown a movement from confusion and complaint to faith and worship and a return to an expectation of renewed crisis but with a faith that will "rejoice" despite the crisis.

In Chapter 2 the intention was stated to read the book of Habakkuk as a performance following the schema of Conquergood, who argues that performance studies should encompass three dimensions: artistry, analysis, and activism.[75] Conquergood describes the third dimension as any of the following possibilities: "activism, outreach, connection to community; applications and interventions; action research; projects that reach outside the academy and are rooted in an ethic of reciprocity and exchange; knowledge that is tested by practice within a community; social commitment, collaboration, and contribution/intervention as a

---

72. O'Connor, "Lamenting Back to Life."
73. Ibid., 36.
74. Ibid., 39.
75. Conquergood, "Performance Studies," 318.

way of knowing: praxis."[76] Conquergood is concerned to show that performance studies do not remain a purely academic exercise, but have an impact within the community. This emphasis makes performance studies a particularly apt method of reading Biblical books. When performing Scripture, a goal is shared with modern theatre that the audience be transformed. The audience should become the actor, embodying the script and re-enacting it in their own setting. A careful reading of the text as a 'script' helps to draw out performative aspects already embedded in the text and the inherent hermeneutical possibilities that allow for a variety of faithful re-enactments. The open-endedness of the text of Habakkuk with its final verb "to walk" and its colophon inviting re-performance ensures that it will continue to be relevant to communities of faith as they face new situations of crisis.

CONCLUSION

In this study performance critical methodology has been applied to the book of Habakkuk. Going further than those who have simply applied the metaphor of performance to the interpretation of Scripture or who have applied a select few aspects of performance theory to Biblical texts, this study has engaged in a close reading of Habakkuk as a performance in its entirety. It has also taken seriously Conquergood's challenge that for performance studies to reach beyond the academy there must be a threefold emphasis on artistry, analysis, and activism.

The artistry of the book of Habakkuk has been accentuated through a highly iconic translation that paid particular attention to rhetorical devices, verbal forms that fluctuated between singular and plural references as well as past and non-past forms. The artistry is enhanced by the presence and absence of grammatical features that draw attention to or marginalize actors and events, evocative images offered by the text, extra-verbal features implicit in the text, the use of ready-mades, the ambiguity of unidentified voices, and the use of silence.

The analysis of the book of Habakkuk sought to 'marry' the methodologies of historical-critical and literary readings in order to pay attention to both the historical and theological issues underlying the original composition of the book and to notice the impact of the book in its canonical form. The context of crisis that forms the setting to the

---

76. Ibid., 319.

book is of crucial importance, but the lack of specificity ensures that the book can continue to be relevant in new settings where cultural trauma is a reality. The historical and theological role of Habakkuk in the Book of the Twelve was noted, but its contribution as an individual composition that continues to live on imaginatively and sensitively in a variety of settings has also been appreciated. Analysis of the book via performance characteristics of script, actor, audience, setting, and improvisation suggests that the book was compiled of older traditions modified to suit its new setting. But at the same time, historical details of its setting and characters were deliberately blurred to keep the script open for re-enactment by an attentive audience.

Re-enactment is the focus of activism, the third of Conquergood's categories for successful appropriation of performance methodology. A performance reading of the book of Habakkuk has shown that Scripture is particularly suited as a script for faithful re-enactment in the public arena. Scripture, like all performance, is aware of its audience and aims for transformation of its readers/hearers. Reconfiguring Scripture as a performance places a greater emphasis on embodiment because the script is not fully realized until it is performed. A script such as Habakkuk that includes the dissonant voices of complaint, lament, woe, and taunt reminds us that both complaint and praise are legitimate in faithful re-enactment of Scripture. Despite the resolution towards worship in this script, that the journey includes trauma is recognized and validated through the prophet's exemplary utterances and the script's open-ended nature, typified by its final verb of movement and its colophon inviting new performance. Interpreting the book of Habakkuk as a script in two Acts reveals just how much it conveys the drama of faithfulness in the midst of crisis—a faithfulness that is to be re-enacted in new settings characterized by cultural trauma and public crises.

Stepping back from a specific focus on the book of Habakkuk, the implications of this method of reading the canon of Judeo-Christian Scripture through the lens of performance criticism has a profound impact on the discussion of the nature and authority of Scripture. The question that arises in performance studies over whether authority lies with the script or the performance is given an added layer of complexity when the "script" is viewed by a faithful reader as "Scripture"—no less than the word of God. I have argued for re-interpretation and re-enactment brought about by new situations and new communities such that Scripture cannot remain relevant *unless* it is performed, re-enacted, and improvised continually. Seeing the Biblical text through the lens of performance criticism makes explicit the re-interpretive process that is continually undertaken by faithful readers who read with a presumption that the Scriptures are relevant today. Approaching Scripture as a script that cannot be fully realized until performed requires both respect for the script *and* preparedness for the dynamism of performance driven by ever-changing settings, actors, and audiences. The co-investigative nature of a performance approach (and the dialogical nature of drama) requires interaction between script and performer that will very likely result in change: in the interpreter, the script, and the world they both inhabit. It is in 'performing' Habakkuk (or any other Biblical script) that Scripture remains relevant and alive in today's world. Reading Scripture through the lens of performance studies ensures that these ancient texts are not locked away as historical artifacts but instead continue to have an impact on communities of faith and the surrounding world.

APPENDIX ONE

Glossary of Key Terms

BIBLICAL PERFORMANCE CRITICISM IS a relatively new field with a still evolving set of terms and vocabulary, some of which may be foreign to students of Biblical studies. The table below is intended to provide short definitions for the key terms used in this book, and show how other authors use different terms for the same concepts. The glossary is not exhaustive.

Term as used in this Study	Definition as used in this Study	Comparable Terms (Author Reference)
Actor	Characters presented in the script: a combination of *personae* and performance artists	*Persona* (Pelias)
Audience	Those attending to and participating in the performance when invited	Audience formation (Giles and Doan)
Author	The creative force behind the script, with recognition that more than one hand may be involved	Creator (Pelias)
Carnivalization (Bahktin)	Revisions of usual behaviour due to 'in-between' places or times where rules are suspended or relaxed	Liminal spaces (Turner)
Dialogism/Heteroglossia (Bakhtin)	A diversity of voices within a text	Intertextuality (Tull)

APPENDIX ONE

Term as used in this Study	Definition as used in this Study	Comparable Terms (Author Reference)
Drama	A performative term for "message" in relation to a biblical book: irrespective of whether or not a performance was ever staged	Tragedy/Comedy Closet Drama (House) Untheatrical Drama (Shelton) Act-scheme (Giles and Doan)
Embodiment	Knowledge is participatory (experienced in a body) rather than propositional (experienced from outside of oneself)	'Iconic' mode of presentation (Giles and Doan)
Frame	That which sets the performance apart from the ordinary and highlights it (see discussion of 'setting,' ch 2)	*mise-en-scène*
Improvisation	The way in which established traditions are re-used and modified in new settings	Intertextuality Inner-Biblical exegesis Transposition
Performance	An ongoing event involving actor(s) and audience	
Performance Art	The actors' own bodies are the artwork and the lines between artist and audience are blurred	
Performance Studies	Cultural discourse that focuses on the material body	
Performative	An adjective describing the quality of performance in everyday activity	In Linguistics the term refers to words that perform an action as distinct from 'constative' words that state something (Austin)

Glossary of Key Terms

Term as used in this Study	Definition as used in this Study	Comparable Terms (Author Reference)
Process	The description of the ongoing activity of the performance that is as important as the completed event	
Re-enactment	All performance is based on a pre-existing model, script or pattern	Restored behaviour (Schechner) Pre-formance (MacAloon) Dialectic mode of presentation (Giles and Doan)
Script	In relation to Biblical texts: the canonical form of the text	
Self-reflexivity	Awareness on the part of a performer of the separation between self and role	
Setting	The 'frame' of the performance, including physical, cultural, and social factors	*mise-en-scène*
Universality	Performance is a holistic means of communication and therefore relevant to a broad range of experiences	Medium transferability (Giles and Doan)

APPENDIX TWO

Detailed Translation of Habakkuk

A NOTE ON TRANSLATION OF VERB FORMS

ALL THREE CHAPTERS OF Habakkuk are preserved in the MT as poetry. Hebrew grammarians warn that translators of Hebrew poetry should be aware of a less regular verbal system than that found in prose. Buth states: "In Hebrew poetry, the author will sometimes play with the tenses for poetic effect and leave the reader unsure of exactly what is being referred to."[1]

Because poetry is characterized by segmented communication, it switches from one temporal axis to another very freely, resulting in abrupt transitions from one verb form to another. Niccacci observes: "Given the difficulty of understanding the verb system in poetry, most scholars simply disregard the verb forms appearing in the texts and translate according to their own taste. However, as a norm one should assign to the various verb forms their usual function(s) and interpret the text accordingly, rather than to make the analysis of the various verb forms dependent on one's own interpretation. It is only reasonable to assume that if a writer uses different verb forms, he has in mind different temporal or aspectual references."[2] Buth concurs: "The tense-aspects mean exactly what they say, but the application of the poetic embellishment is not necessarily clear . . . Let the Hebrew poet speak with his multiple layers."[3]

---

1. Buth, *Living Biblical Hebrew*, 162.
2. Niccacci, "Poetic Syntax," 59.
3. Buth, *Living Biblical Hebrew*, 162–64.

A relevant example is the characteristic interaction of *qatal* and *yiqtol* verbs in Hebrew poetry,[4] seen several times in Habakkuk (1:2; 3:6, 16). Andersen argues that such cases are examples of the use of archaic verb forms, where *yiqtol* and *wayyiqtol* forms should both be understood as having a past-tense meaning and translates accordingly.[5] Tatu, by contrast, claims such sequences are primarily for aesthetic reasons, with no reference to time or aspect.[6] Buth simply notes that the poetry deliberately tolerates the ambiguity resulting from such mixed verbal forms.[7]

This translation assumes a tense-prominent approach and adopts the position that the *qatal* verb is past in its core meaning.[8] Hebrew verb-forms are generally followed as they are set out in the MT, i.e. *wayyiqtol* is translated as past tense, *qatal* as past or perfect, *yiqtol* as non-past (or jussive if found in the first position in the clause), participles as progressive present (but could be past or future depending on the context), and *weqatal* follows the tense of the preceding clause.

---

4. For example, ibid., 163; Tatu, "Rhetorical Interpretation," 17; Tatu, *The Qatal// Yiqtol (Yiqtol//Qatal) Verbal Sequence*.
5. Andersen, *Habakkuk*, 103.
6. Tatu, *The Qatal//Yiqtol (Yiqtol//Qatal) Verbal Sequence*, 22.
7. Buth, *Living Biblical Hebrew*, 164.
8. Revell, "The System of the Verb," 1–3; Niccacci. "Poetic Syntax," 55.

Translation

Prelude (1:1)

¹ The revelation that Habakkuk the prophet saw.

הַמַּשָּׂא אֲשֶׁר חָזָה חֲבַקּוּק הַנָּבִיא: ¹

Translation Notes

VERSE 1:

מַשָּׂא (*revelation*) is a debated term that probably derives from the verb נשׂא (*to lift up, carry*). In other prophetic contexts it is paired with a word designating a spoken message (for example, נשׂא קינה [*to lift up a lamentation*], Amos 5:1; משׁל נשׂא [*to lift up a taunt*], Hab 2:6). In a more general sense the word מַשָּׂא means *burden*, either in the literal sense of carrying something heavy or in the figurative sense of bearing a responsibility. G, T, and S thus translate מַשָּׂא as *burden* in this verse, as do several modern commentaries and translations.

מַשָּׂא has been understood as a term relating to oracles against the nations[9] but the term can also be used in contexts of the prophet speaking to his own community (Ezek 12:10; Zech 12:1; Mal 1:1; Jer 23:33; 2 Chr 24:27). It is, without doubt, a technical term for a message given to a prophet (Isa 13:1; Ezek 12:10; Nah 1:1; Zech 9:1; 12:1; Mal 1:1; Lam 2:14). Other occasions where מַשָּׂא introduces or describes prophetic speech are 2 Kings 9:25; Isa 14:28; 15:1; 17:1; 19:1; 21:1, 11, 13; 22:1; 23:1; 30:6; and Jer 23:33, 34, 35, 38. The English word used to translate מַשָּׂא in most modern translations is *oracle*, although this word can be used to translate other Hebrew words also.[10]

The verb חזה (*he saw*), is commonly associated with prophetic revelation (Isa 1:1; Amos 1:1; Mic 1:1). Indeed, prophets were sometimes called חזים (*seers*) (Isa 29:10; Mic 3:7). The combination of מַשָּׂא with the verb חזה (*to see*), gives justification for translating the term *revelation* rather than *oracle*. The book emphasizes visionary perception and this term enhances the performative reading of Habakkuk.

---

9. Stolz, "נשׂא," 774.

10. For example, the following words are translated *oracle* in a variety of versions: נאם, Num 24:3 (ESV, NIV, RSV); דבר, 2 Sam 16:23 (ASV, KJV, RSV); דביר, Ps 28:2 (ASV, KJV).

Act One—Scene One (1:2–4)

² How long, Yahweh, shall I call	² עַד־אָנָה יְהוָה שִׁוַּעְתִּי
and you not hear?	וְלֹא תִשְׁמָע
I cry out to you 'violence!'	אֶזְעַק אֵלֶיךָ חָמָס
and you do not save?	וְלֹא תוֹשִׁיעַ׃
³ Why do you make me look at sorrow	³ לָמָּה תַרְאֵנִי אָוֶן
and to trouble you pay attention?	וְעָמָל תַּבִּיט
And devastation and violence are before me	וְשֹׁד וְחָמָס לְנֶגְדִּי
and there is strife, and contention carries on.	וַיְהִי רִיב וּמָדוֹן יִשָּׂא׃
⁴ Therefore [the] Torah is paralyzed	⁴ עַל־כֵּן תָּפוּג תּוֹרָה
and justice never goes forth.	וְלֹא־יֵצֵא לָנֶצַח מִשְׁפָּט
For wickedness surrounds the righteous one.	כִּי רָשָׁע מַכְתִּיר אֶת־הַצַּדִּיק
Therefore crooked justice goes forth.	עַל־כֵּן יֵצֵא מִשְׁפָּט מְעֻקָּל׃

Translation Notes

VERSE 2

The parallelism in this verse allows for the second phrase to be translated as a question although there is no repetition of the interrogative particle. The verbs שׁוע and זעק are often both translated *call for help* but as they have different roots and have the sense of escalating in intensity, this translation has tried to capture that.

VERSE 3

The term ריב (*strife*), is often understood as a formal legal complaint or lawsuit, leading Andersen to suggest that a covenant lawsuit is being brought against Yahweh, since the dispute is neither conducted in human courts nor against the wicked.[11] The legal term could alternatively emphasize the prophet's frustration with the breakdown of justice in human

---

11. Andersen, *Habakkuk*, 116–18.

courts. 1QpHab 1:9 replaces ריב with מריבה, taking the emphasis away from a juridical reference and referring to the wilderness experience of Israel at Meribah (Exod 17:7; Num 20:13, 24) where complaining and rebellion were typical but considered unjustified. The pairing of ריב and מדון (*contention*), occurs in wisdom literature where strife is presented as the antithesis of the ideal of self-control (Prov 15:18; 17:14), and ריב and חמס (*violence*), occur together in Ps 55:10. Such occurrences also show that ריב is used outside of juridical settings. In the poetry of this verse שד וחמס (*devastation and violence*) and ריב ומדון (*strife and contention*), function as parallel pairs and so the more general term *strife* is justified.

VERSE 4

תפוג (*is paralyzed*)—the verb פוג is rare (only three or four other occurrences in the Hebrew Bible: Gen 45:26; Pss 38:9; 77:3; and perhaps 88:16) and here only is applied to a non-human subject. 1QpHab 1:11 attributes the ineffectiveness of the Torah to those of the community who had rejected it, not allowing any accountability for its failure to God.

תורה (*[the] Torah*)—as in most Biblical poetry, the prose particles are sparsely used, but it is probable that a seventh century audience and definitely a post-exilic audience would have a particular understanding of the word as the written form of the will of Yahweh for the community.[12] Hence a definite article has been included in this translation, taking a cue from Andersen: "When reading Hebrew poetry or poetic prophecy, one must deliberately search for the implicit signals from the context that a noun, formally indefinite, might have a definite reference."[13]

הצדיק (*the righteous one*)—the use of a definite article stands in contrast to רשע in the same verse. The identity of רשע (*wicked*), and צדיק (*righteous*), in Hab 1:4 and 1:13 generates much discussion in scholarly literature.[14] The inclusion of both object marker and definite article in conjunction with צדיק in v. 4 suggests that the righteous one is a specific group or a specific individual. 1QpHab (1:13) identifies הצדיק as *the Teacher of Righteousness* and although the rest of the line is lost, the implication is that רשע is the Wicked Priest. But in its original context in the book of Habakkuk הצדיק may well have been a reference to the prophet himself as a representative of the innocent righteous. Taking

12. Crüsemann, *The Torah*, 26.
13. Andersen, *Habakkuk*, 98.
14. Dangl, "Habakkuk in Recent Research," 139–44.

cognizance of the contrast between the use of the definite article for צדיק and the lack of article for רשע, this translation removes the need for precise identification of רשע by translating צדיק (as *the righteous one*) and רשע with the generic term *wickedness* in both Hab 1:4 and 1:13.

משפט (*justice*) is often paired with צדק (*righteous*), where משפט is the objective norm of justice and צדק the subjective sense of righteousness.[15] This pairing can also be seen in Hab 1:4 where הצדיק (*the righteous one*), is unable to practice משפט (*justice*), due to רשע (*wickedness*). The term משפט is often used in reference to a God-given norm for a well ordered society and Achtemeier understands this meaning behind its use in Hab 1:4. משפט in Hab 1:7 is used in reference to the Chaldean king (in contrast to God's order) and so is understood by Achtemeier as God's righteous punishment: "The punishment fits the sin."[16] For this reason the fourth use of the term in Hab 1:12 is often translated *judgment* rather than *justice*. On the other hand, משפט (*justice*), can have either a retributive or a restorative meaning, whereas *judgment* is clearly negative; hence the term has been translated consistently in vv. 4, 7, and 12 to convey the uncertainty of its connotation.

Act One—Scene Two (1:5–11)

[5] All of you, look at the nations and pay attention!	רְאוּ בַגּוֹיִם וְהַבִּיטוּ [5]
And be profoundly astounded!	וְהִתַּמְּהוּ תְמָהוּ
For a work is being worked in your days	כִּי־פֹעַל פֹּעֵל בִּימֵיכֶם
— you would not believe it if it was recounted!	לֹא תַאֲמִינוּ כִּי יְסֻפָּר׃
[6] For behold, I am raising the Chaldeans,	כִּי־הִנְנִי מֵקִים אֶת־הַכַּשְׂדִּים [6]
that nation hurtful and hasty,	הַגּוֹי הַמַּר וְהַנִּמְהָר
the man who marches across expanses of earth	הַהוֹלֵךְ לְמֶרְחֲבֵי־אֶרֶץ

---

15. Weber, quoted in Johnson, "משפט," 91.
16. Achtemeier, *Nahum—Malachi*, 38.

to possess dwelling places not his own.	לָרֶשֶׁת מִשְׁכָּנוֹת לֹא־לוֹ׃
⁷ Terrible and fearful is he,	אָיֹם וְנוֹרָא הוּא
from himself his justice and his dignity go forth.	מִמֶּנּוּ מִשְׁפָּטוֹ וּשְׂאֵתוֹ יֵצֵא׃
⁸ And swifter than leopards are his horses,	וְקַלּוּ מִנְּמֵרִים סוּסָיו
and keener than wolves of the evening.	וְחַדּוּ מִזְּאֵבֵי עֶרֶב
And they gallop his gallopers and his gallopers.	וּפָשׁוּ פָּרָשָׁיו וּפָרָשָׁיו
From far they come, they fly,	מֵרָחוֹק יָבֹאוּ יָעֻפוּ
like a vulture he hastens to eat.	כְּנֶשֶׁר חָשׁ לֶאֱכוֹל׃
⁹ Every one comes for violence.	כֻּלֹּה לְחָמָס יָבוֹא
The eagerness of their faces goes forward.	מְגַמַּת פְּנֵיהֶם קָדִימָה
And he gathered captives like sand.	וַיֶּאֱסֹף כַּחוֹל שֶׁבִי׃
¹⁰ And as for him, at the kings he scoffs	וְהוּא בַּמְּלָכִים יִתְקַלָּס
and rulers are an object of derision to him.	וְרֹזְנִים מִשְׂחָק לוֹ
As for him, at every fortress he laughs.	הוּא לְכָל־מִבְצָר יִשְׂחָק
And he heaped up dust and he captured her.	וַיִּצְבֹּר עָפָר וַיִּלְכְּדָהּ׃
¹¹ Then he swept through [as] wind,	אָז חָלַף רוּחַ
and he passed by and was guilty.	וַיַּעֲבֹר וְאָשֵׁם
This is his strength for his god.	זוּ כֹחוֹ לֵאלֹהוֹ׃

Translation Notes

Verse 5

Plural imperative forms are used throughout this verse. This is an important performative feature but difficult to convey in English translation where no difference exists between second person singular and plural forms. Thus the addition of the phrase "all of you" at the beginning of the verse.

והתמהו תמהו (*and be profoundly astounded*)—the combination of a hithpael and qal infinitive absolute of the same root occurs for emphasis, highlighted by assonance in Hebrew and imitated in this translation.

פֹּעַל פֹּעֵל (*a work is being worked*)—the difficulties in translating this phrase can be seen in the versions: G adds ἐγώ, S also supplies a subject and T and V emend the participle to make it passive. Contemporary translators also often add the subject "I" in reference to Yahweh although the pronoun is absent in the MT. While the plural imperative verbs signal the beginning of a new section and suggest a new speaker, the verses do not constitute a ready answer to the prophet's complaint. As well as the change in address (plural verbs when an individual has asked questions) there is no direct reference to the questions that have been asked. A literal translation, although not smooth, is important for the performative analysis of this book.

Verse 6

המר והנמהר (*hurtful and hasty*)—this translation tries to mirror the alliteration present in the Hebrew text.

Verse 8

זאבי ערב (*wolves of the evening*)—G translates τοὺς λύκους τῆς Ἀραβίας (*wolves of Arabia*), presupposing the MT but indicating a dissatisfaction with *wolves of the evening*. Roberts suggests emending the word to עֲרָבָה (*steppes*) both here and in Zeph 3:3 in line with Jer 5:6.[17] The phrase makes perfect sense as it is found in MT, however, where the fierce enemy is likened to wolves ready to devour their prey in the evening—their usual hunting time.

ופשו פרשיו ופרשיו (*And they gallop his gallopers and his gallopers*)— against the MT that divides the verses before the second ופרשיו, I trans-

---

17. Roberts, *Nahum, Habakkuk, and Zephaniah*, 92.

late literally with the poetic word *gallopers* for onomatopoeic effect. In the Book of the Twelve there are only eleven other examples of adjacent identical nouns (Hos 12:13; Joel 1:6; 2:2; 4:14, 20; Mic 7:12; Nah 3:8; Zeph 3:5; Zech 12:12, 14; 14:16) and most examples express either plural or totality. Only Joel 4:14 (המונים המונים [*multitudes, multitudes*]) has a similar repetition of a plural noun that functions as repetitive parallelism for emphasis, although in the example from Joel the accents indicate the words belong together unlike the placement of the *athnach* on פרשיו in Hab 1:8.

Verse 9

מגמת פניהם קדימה (*the eagerness of their faces goes forward*)—the variety in the versions and in translations indicates the difficulty in determining the meaning of these three Hebrew words. While the normal translation of קדים is *eastward*, most translations read *forward*. *Eastward* gives rise to speculation about the identity of the invading army (the Chaldeans would be expected to come facing westward). Q renders קדים as *east wind*, consistent with its interpretation of the invaders as the Romans. Despite the uncertainty of translation, *eagerness* appropriately conveys the haste and urgency engendered by the invasion.

Verses 9–10

ויאסף (*and he gathered*), ויצבר (*and he heaped up*), וילכדה (*and he captured her*)—the narrative verb form *wayyiqtol* is rare in Hebrew poetry. Maintaining the recurring *waw* forms in translation provide a sense of movement and therefore are indicative of the theme of process in performance.

Verse 10

הוא (*him*)—the singular masculine pronoun is used to refer to the invading nation rather than the plural as one might expect, although it is probable the king of the invading nation is referred to as representative of the enemy.

וילכדה (*and he captured her*)—the feminine suffix does not fit with the masculine מבצר (*fortress*). Both G and Q translate as masculine but another suggestion is that the antecedent is elliptical for the feminine phrase עיר מבצר (*fortified city*).[18] I have retained the feminine suffix as it adds emphasis to an invasion personified in an individual male.

Verse 11

רוח (*wind*)—this feminine noun is problematically associated with masculine verbs here. Andersen, however, argues that the noun רוח is sometimes masculine and therefore could be the subject of the verbs. His translation of v. 11 reads: *Then the Spirit swept on and passed by.*[19] The ancient translations (G, V, S, T) also took רוח as the subject, but assumed it refers to the spirit of the Chaldean king. They seem to be dependent upon the account of the 'conversion' of King Nebuchadnezzar in Daniel 4. Here I have followed the many translations that assume רוח is a simile (also known as accusative of specification).[20] In support of this translation are the other comparisons in the scene (leopards, wolves, vultures, sand) as well as the appropriateness of the depiction of the Chaldeans as a destructive force.

וְאָשֵׁם (*and was guilty*)—Roberts suggests reading this verb as וָאֶשֹּׁם—qal *wayyiqtol* 1cs of שמם (*to be astonished*), on the basis that "almost all exegetes regard the form וְאָשֵׁם [*and he will become guilty*] as corrupt."[21] However, few other translations follow this suggestion. G translates this verb as a future: διελεύσεται (*and he will make propiation*). Despite the difficulties in the MT, the *weqatal* verb should be translated in the past tense as it follows a *wayyiqtol* verb.

Act One—Scene Three (1:12–17)

[12] Are you not from old, Yahweh?	[12] הֲלוֹא אַתָּה מִקֶּדֶם יְהוָה
My God of holiness, you will not die!	אֱלֹהַי קְדֹשִׁי לֹא נָמוּת
Yahweh, for justice you set him;	יְהוָה לְמִשְׁפָּט שַׂמְתּוֹ
and Rock, for rebuke you established him.	וְצוּר לְהוֹכִיחַ יְסַדְתּוֹ:

---

18. Roberts, *Nahum, Habakkuk, and Zephaniah*, 93.
19. Andersen, *Habakkuk*, 135; 160–65.
20. *IBHS*, 10.2.2e.
21. Roberts, *Nahum, Habakkuk, and Zephaniah*, 93; 97.

¹³ Your eyes are too pure to look at evil.	¹³ טְהוֹר עֵינַיִם מֵרְאוֹת רָע
And you are not able to pay attention to trouble.	וְהַבִּיט אֶל־עָמָל לֹא תוּכָל
Why do you pay attention to those who act treacherously?	לָמָּה תַבִּיט בּוֹגְדִים
[Why do] you keep silence when wickedness	תַּחֲרִישׁ בְּבַלַּע רָשָׁע
Swallows [the] righteous one?	צַדִּיק מִמֶּנּוּ׃
¹⁴And you made humankind like the fish of the sea,	¹⁴ וַתַּעֲשֶׂה אָדָם כִּדְגֵי הַיָּם
like a lowly sea-creature with no-one ruling over it.	כְּרֶמֶשׂ לֹא־מֹשֵׁל בּוֹ׃
¹⁵ Every one he brought up with a fishing hook,	¹⁵ כֻּלֹּה בְּחַכָּה הֵעֲלָה
he drags him away with his net,	יְגֹרֵהוּ בְחֶרְמוֹ
and gathers him with his fish-trap.	וְיַאַסְפֵהוּ בְּמִכְמַרְתּוֹ
Therefore he is glad and rejoices.	עַל־כֵּן יִשְׂמַח וְיָגִיל׃
¹⁶ Therefore he sacrifices to his net,	¹⁶ עַל־כֵּן יְזַבֵּחַ לְחֶרְמוֹ
and offers smoke to his fish-trap.	וִיקַטֵּר לְמִכְמַרְתּוֹ
For with them his portion grew rich,	כִּי בָהֵמָּה שָׁמֵן חֶלְקוֹ
and his food was fat.	וּמַאֲכָלוֹ בְּרִאָה׃
¹⁷ Shall he therefore empty his net and continue	¹⁷ הַעַל כֵּן יָרִיק חֶרְמוֹ וְתָמִיד
to slay nations without mercy?	לַהֲרֹג גּוֹיִם לֹא יַחְמוֹל׃

Translation Notes

Verse 12

נמות—rendered here as in MT: נמות (*we will not die*), but translated *you will not die*. Traditional rabbinic sources recognize it as a *tiqqun*—one of the eighteen 'corrections of the scribes' made for dogmatic reasons: a pious scribe altered the text because the idea that Yahweh could be spoken of as dying was abhorrent.²² This emended reading is supported by the parallelism one would expect following v. 12a, *Are you not from old, Yahweh?*

Verse 16

בראה (*fat*)—a feminine adjective that does not agree with the masculine noun. Note that Q has the masculine form ברי. Roberts suggests that dittography may explain the *hê*.²³

Verse 17

העל כן יריק חרמו ותמיד (*shall he therefore empty his net*)—Q reads quite differently: על כן יריק חרבו תמיד (*He therefore unsheathes his sword continually*). My translation accepts the MT due to the prominence of the net metaphor in this scene.

Act One—Introduction to Scene Four (2:1)

¹ On my guard let me stand,	עַל־מִשְׁמַרְתִּי אֶעֱמֹדָה ¹
and let me set myself on siege works,	עַל־מָצוֹר וְאֶתְיַצְּבָה
and let me keep watch to see what he says to me,	וַאֲצַפֶּה לִרְאוֹת מַה־יְדַבֶּר־בִּי
and what I will bring back concerning my rebuke.	וּמָה אָשִׁיב עַל־תּוֹכַחְתִּי:

Translation Notes

Verse 1

עַל־מִשְׁמַרְתִּי (*on my guard*)—this term is used in the priestly tradition for periods of service in the temple, often translated *duty, service,* or *watch* (for example, Neh 13:30; 2 Chr 7:6; 8:14; 35:2). I have translated *on my guard* in recognition of the context of the Neo-Babylonian invasion and accompanying warfare metaphors.

מצור (*siege works*)—similarly, the context presupposes warfare so the translation *siege works* is appropriate.

---

22. Ginsburg, *Introduction to the Massoretico-Critical Edition*, 348–63.
23. Roberts, *Nahum, Habakkuk, and Zephaniah*, 101.

אשיב (*what I will bring back*)—discomfort with this verb is evidenced in the versions: S reads ישיב (*what he returns*), G reads τί ἀποκριθῶ (*what I will answer*), in T the verb is passive and תוכח is translated as *prayer*, and this section is missing in Q. The *hiphil* form of the verb suggests a deliberate intention on the prophet's part.

Act One—Scene Four (2:2–5)

² And Yahweh answered me and said:	² וַיַּעֲנֵנִי יְהוָה וַיֹּאמֶר
Write [the] vision	כְּתוֹב חָזוֹן
and make plain on the tablets	וּבָאֵר עַל־הַלֻּחוֹת
so that [the] reader will run with it.	לְמַעַן יָרוּץ קוֹרֵא בוֹ׃
³ For [the] vision is yet for the appointed time,	³ כִּי עוֹד חָזוֹן לַמּוֹעֵד
and it breathes to the end and does not lie.	וְיָפֵחַ לַקֵּץ וְלֹא יְכַזֵּב
If it tarries, wait for it,	אִם־יִתְמַהְמָהּ חַכֵּה־לוֹ
for it surely comes, it will not delay.	כִּי־בֹא יָבֹא לֹא יְאַחֵר׃
⁴ Behold, it is swollen:	⁴ הִנֵּה עֻפְּלָה
his soul is not upright in him,	לֹא־יָשְׁרָה נַפְשׁוֹ בּוֹ
but [the] righteous one in his faithfulness will live.	וְצַדִּיק בֶּאֱמוּנָתוֹ יִחְיֶה׃
⁵ And moreover the wine is treacherous!	⁵ וְאַף כִּי־הַיַּיִן בּוֹגֵד
A mighty man is haughty and does not abide,	גֶּבֶר יָהִיר וְלֹא יִנְוֶה
who widens his soul like Sheol,	אֲשֶׁר הִרְחִיב כִּשְׁאוֹל נַפְשׁוֹ
and he is like death and is not sated.	וְהוּא כַמָּוֶת וְלֹא יִשְׂבָּע
And he gathered to himself all the nations,	וַיֶּאֱסֹף אֵלָיו כָּל־הַגּוֹיִם

and collected to himself all the peoples.	וַיִּקְבֹּץ אֵלָיו כָּל־הָעַמִּים׃

Translation Notes

Verse 2

חזון (*[the] vision*)—There is no definite article in the MT but the association to the previous scene suggests a definite article should be applied to the vision (vv. 2 and 3). The prophet has waited for an answer, has expected a dialogue with Yahweh and so what is given is significant, warranting the definite designation.

קורא (*[the] reader*)—Q (הקורא) adds the definite article to the participle suggesting it could be read as a noun: that is, *the one who reads*.

Verse 3

ויפח (*and it breathes*)—much attention is paid to this word because the meaning *to breathe, blow* does not seem to fit in this context. An Ugaritic noun *yph* meaning *witness* seems to fit the context better and may be translated *testifier* or *it will testify*.[24] Although not as obvious, *breathes* could also be a parallel term for *testify*.

Verse 4

עפלה (*it is swollen*)—many suggestions have also been made to emend this form including reading the final *hê* as a reference to place so that it is read as a toponym, *the Ophel*.[25] Roberts[26] states that the parallelism with צדיק in the next line would suggest a noun with a negative connotation is expected and some versions evidence this: T paraphrases *the wicked*; S uses an abstract noun *wickedness* and V translates *qui incredulous est* (*the one who is unbelieving*). The plain meaning seems to relate to the contrast between הצדיק (*the righteous one*), referred to in Hab 1:4, 13, possibly synonymous with the prophet; and the one who is לא־ישרה (*not upright*), probably synonymous with the Chaldean king. The feminine term עפלה relates to the feminine word נפש (*soul*), in the next colon, ἡ ψυχή μου.

---

24. See Roberts, *Nahum, Habakkuk, and Zephaniah*; Andersen, *Habakkuk*.

25. Scott, "A New Approach," 335–40; Pinker, "Habakkuk 2:4," 102–3; Boyle, *The Rhetoric of Taunt Language*, 202.

26. Roberts, *Nahum, Habakkuk, and Zephaniah*, 107.

נפשו (*his soul*)—this word appears many times in the Hebrew Bible with a variety of meanings. Here it speaks of the whole person. G reads ἡ ψυχή μου (*my soul*), understanding it as a reference to Yahweh, similarly באמונתו (*in his faithfulness*) in the same verse is read by G as, ἐκ πίστεώς μου (*in my faith*). G clearly has a theological motivation for translating this way since the MT is supported by 8HevXIIgr.

Following my translation principle to translate the same word consistently, נפש has been translated *soul* in both Hab 2:4 and 2:5 where צדיק (*[the] righteous one*), is contrasted with גבר (*a mighty man*).

וצדיק (*[the] righteous one*)—my translation adds the definite article in order to link it with the references in Hab 1:4 and 1:13.

באמונתו (*in his faithfulness*)—Andersen points out connections between Habakkuk 2 and Psalm 89 where "the author of Psalm 89 is grappling with a problem similar to Habakkuk's ... and reaffirms, after agonizing spiritual struggles, Yahweh's ḥesed sworn in his 'ĕmûnâ^h."[27] Interestingly, אמונה occurs as a hendiadys with צדק in Ps 96:13 and the two words are also paired in Hab 2:4. Therefore אמונה in this context could refer to the steadfastness of the righteous person, or to the reliability of the vision, or to the fidelity of God. As noted, G comes down in support of the latter. Andersen believes the subject of Hab 2:2–4 is the vision and translates *the righteous person by its trustworthiness will survive*[28] but my translation reads אמונה as a characteristic of the righteous one, forming a connection with 1:4 and 1:13.

Verse 5

ואף (*moreover*)—BDB has in the entry on אף: "with ref. to a preceding sentence (which is often introduced by הן or הנה), *yea, that* ... ! i.e., *how much more* (or *less*)!"[29] On this basis and noting the initial *waw*, I view ואף as a link that secures continuity between vv. 4 and 5, against those who see a major break at this point of the book.

היין בוגד (*wine is treacherous*)—Q reads הון יבגוד (*wealth deceives*). Other Hebrew manuscripts read הוי בוגד (*woe to the treacherous one*). The translation here is in view of the later woe oracle against drunkenness (v. 15).

27. Andersen, *Habakkuk*, 213.
28. Ibid., 198.
29. *BDB*, 65.

Act One—Scene Five, Part One (2:6–13)

⁶ Are not all these	⁶ הֲלוֹא־אֵלֶּה כֻלָּם
lifting up a taunt against him?	עָלָיו מָשָׁל יִשָּׂאוּ
And satirical riddles about him?	וּמְלִיצָה חִידוֹת לוֹ
And he says:	וְיֹאמַר
Woe to him who piles up what is not his own	הוֹי הַמַּרְבֶּה לֹּא־לוֹ
— How long?	עַד־מָתַי
And the one making heavy debts upon himself.	וּמַכְבִּיד עָלָיו עַבְטִיט׃
⁷ Will not the ones biting you suddenly arise?	⁷ הֲלוֹא פֶתַע יָקוּמוּ נֹשְׁכֶיךָ
And will not the ones violently shaking you wake?	וְיִקְצוּ מְזַעְזְעֶיךָ
And you will be their spoil.	וְהָיִיתָ לִמְשִׁסּוֹת לָמוֹ׃
⁸ Because you plundered many nations	⁸ כִּי אַתָּה שַׁלּוֹתָ גּוֹיִם רַבִּים
let the remaining peoples plunder you —	יְשָׁלּוּךָ כָּל־יֶתֶר עַמִּים
On account of blood of man and violence of earth,	מִדְּמֵי אָדָם וַחֲמַס־אֶרֶץ
a town and all who live in it.	קִרְיָה וְכָל־יֹשְׁבֵי בָהּ׃ פ
⁹ Woe to him who violently gains unjust gain!	⁹ הוֹי בֹּצֵעַ בֶּצַע
Evil belongs to his house	רָע לְבֵיתוֹ
who has set his nest in the heights	לָשׂוּם בַּמָּרוֹם קִנּוֹ
to be delivered from the grasp of evil.	לְהִנָּצֵל מִכַּף־רָע׃
¹⁰ You counseled shame for your house,	¹⁰ יָעַצְתָּ בֹּשֶׁת לְבֵיתֶךָ
to cut off many people,	קְצוֹת־עַמִּים רַבִּים
and your soul is sinning.	וְחוֹטֵא נַפְשֶׁךָ׃

¹¹ For a stone from a wall will cry out,	כִּי־אֶבֶן מִקִּיר תִּזְעָק ¹¹
and a rafter from the woodwork will answer it.	וְכָפִיס מֵעֵץ יַעֲנֶנָּה: פ
¹² Woe to him who builds a city with bloodshed	הוֹי בֹּנֶה עִיר בְּדָמִים ¹²
and establishes a town with iniquity!	וְכוֹנֵן קִרְיָה בְּעַוְלָה:
¹³ Behold! Is it not from Yahweh of Hosts?	הֲלוֹא הִנֵּה מֵאֵת ¹³ יְהוָה צְבָאוֹת
And peoples labor for fire	וְיִיגְעוּ עַמִּים בְּדֵי־אֵשׁ
and nations grow faint for nothing.	וּלְאֻמִּים בְּדֵי־רִיק יִעָפוּ:

Translation Notes

Verse 6

מָשָׁל (*taunt*)—this term is used in both positive and negative contexts. In wisdom and prophetic literature מָשָׁל can appear as proverbs, maxims, riddles, parables, or the content of a vision (Num 23:7, 18; Prov 1:1; Ezek 17:2). The negative idea is taken up in the historical books and prophets in relation to Israel, but also to mock the misfortunes of others (Isa 14:4; Ezek 14:8). The use of the term in Hab 2:6 is to be understood in the negative sense of a taunt song.

הוֹי (*woe*)—an interjection that cannot be traced to a verbal root. It occurs fifty-one times in the Hebrew Bible, almost exclusively in the prophetic literature, usually found in series and directed against foreign nations or Yahweh's own people. In the majority of cases הוֹי introduces a prophetic woe oracle, followed by a participle describing the conduct of the person or country to whom it is addressed.³⁰ Jenni claims that the prophetic woe is an adaptation of the funeral lament, whereby "the seed of death is already inherent in a particular human behavior."³¹ It thus functions as a warning against the behavior described. The switch from third-person forms to second-person forms occurs elsewhere in הוֹי oracles (Isa 1:4–5, 30:1; Jer 22:13–15; 23:1–2; Ezek 34:2–3; Amos 6:1–2;

---

30. Jenni, "הוֹי," 360.
31. Ibid., 358.

Detailed Translation of Habakkuk

Mic 2:1–3). I have maintained the verb forms as they appear in MT for their possible significance for a performance analysis.

עד־מתי (*how long?*)—Andersen states it is not surprising that these words are often deleted, as they spoil the rhythm of the poetry and have no grammatical or thematic connection with the context, but acknowledges: "As an interjection, they echo the concern expressed in the opening prayer"[32] (see the phrase עד־אנה in Hab 1:2). The phrase has an important performative function as a 'ready-made' as noted in Chapter 6.

Verse 7

נשביך (*the ones biting you*)—this verb is connected to the noun נשך (*interest*), and may have the meaning *debtors* (*the ones paying interest*) or *creditors* (*the ones taking interest from you*). My more literal translation of the verb, however, fits the context of retribution for a violent enemy.

Verse 8

ישלוך/אתה שלות (*you plundered/let [them] plunder you*)—in my translation the *yiqtol* form of the second use of the verb שלל occurring in first position in the clause is translated as jussive.

Verse 9

בצע בצע (*violently gains unjust gain*)—repetition of the word "gain" attempts to mirror the Hebrew use of a verb and noun from the same root.

רע (*evil*)—following Roberts[33] who argues that because the noun בצע carries the connotation of "profits obtained illegally or unjustly" it is difficult to take רע (*evil*), as an adjective modifying בצע. Here רע is translated it as a noun relating to the greedy man's house.

מכף־רע (*from the grasp of evil*)—although כף is often understood as a synonym of יד (*hand*), Andersen points out that in Hebrew anatomical terminology יד refers to the hand and forearm, used to deliver a blow, while כף is used for clutching, translated by Andersen as *fist*.[34]

---

32. Andersen, *Habakkuk*, 236.
33. Roberts, *Nahum, Habakkuk, and Zephaniah*, 114.
34. Andersen, *Habakkuk*, 241.

Verse 10

יעצת בשת לביתך (*you counseled shame for your house*)—in a participial clause the personal pronoun would be expected but is not infrequently omitted as here.[35]

Verse 11

כפיס (*rafter*)—a *hapax legomenon* in the Hebrew Bible that has resulted in different translations: some versions of G understood it as an insect in the woodwork, other ancient translations took it to be a knot or bond in the woodwork. A word related to wood is likely, given the parallel term אבן (*stone*), in the previous line.

יעננה (*will answer it*)—my translation maintains *answer* for consistency with Hab 2:2.

Verse 13

הנה (*Behold!*)—G, V, and S all read הֵנָּה, *these*, but the feminine plural pronoun does not have an obvious referent. Note the synchronicity with Hab 1:6, 2:4, and 2:19.

הלוא הנה מאת יהוה צבאות (*Behold! Is it not from Yahweh of Hosts?*)—although this phrase is often considered a marginal gloss it plays a significant role in a performance reading of this book.

Interjection (2:14)

[14] But the earth will be filled with the knowledge of the glory of Yahweh	כִּי תִּמָּלֵא הָאָרֶץ [14] לָדַעַת אֶת־כְּבוֹד יְהוָה
as the waters cover the sea!	כַּמַּיִם יְכַסּוּ עַל־יָם: ס

Translation Notes

Verse 14

Variations of this verse exist in Num 14:21 and Isa 11:9 and so it is often considered a gloss. Its significance from the point of view of performance is discussed in chapter 6.

---

35. *GKC*, §116s.

Act One—Scene Five, Part Two (2:15–19)

¹⁵ Woe to him making his neighbor drink;	¹⁵ הוֹי מַשְׁקֵה רֵעֵהוּ
Who clings to your rage and even drunkenness	מְסַפֵּחַ חֲמָתְךָ וְאַף שַׁכֵּר
in order to gaze upon their nakedness!	לְמַעַן הַבִּיט עַל־מְעוֹרֵיהֶם:
¹⁶ You are sated with shame rather than glory.	¹⁶ שָׂבַעְתָּ קָלוֹן מִכָּבוֹד
Drink, you also, and be counted as uncircumcised!	שְׁתֵה גַם־אַתָּה וְהֵעָרֵל
A cup in the right hand of Yahweh will turn around upon you,	תִּסּוֹב עָלֶיךָ כּוֹס יְמִין יְהוָה
and shameful shame will be upon your glory.	וְקִיקָלוֹן עַל־כְּבוֹדֶךָ:
¹⁷ For the violence of Lebanon covers you,	¹⁷ כִּי חֲמַס לְבָנוֹן יְכַסֶּךָּ
and the devastation of beasts causes them to be terrified —	וְשֹׁד בְּהֵמוֹת יְחִיתַן
On account of blood of man and violence of earth,	מִדְּמֵי אָדָם וַחֲמַס־אֶרֶץ
a town and all who live in it.	קִרְיָה וְכָל־יֹשְׁבֵי בָהּ: ס
¹⁸ Of what benefit is an idol	¹⁸ מָה־הוֹעִיל פֶּסֶל
when he who hewed it made it?	כִּי פְסָלוֹ יֹצְרוֹ
— an image and a teacher of deception?	מַסֵּכָה וּמוֹרֶה שָּׁקֶר
For the maker who makes it trusted on it,	כִּי בָטַח יֹצֵר יִצְרוֹ עָלָיו
To make dumb worthless idols.	לַעֲשׂוֹת אֱלִילִים אִלְּמִים: ס
¹⁹ Woe to him who says to a tree 'wake up!'	¹⁹ הוֹי אֹמֵר לָעֵץ הָקִיצָה
'awake!' to the mute stone.	עוּרִי לְאֶבֶן דּוּמָם

'It is teaching!'	הוּא יוֹרֶה
Behold it, overlaid with gold and silver	הִנֵּה־הוּא תָּפוּשׂ זָהָב וָכֶסֶף
and full of wind? There is nothing in it!	וְכָל־רוּחַ אֵין בְּקִרְבּוֹ׃

Translation Notes

Verse 15

מספח (*who clings to*)—BHS suggests that the participle should be read *from the goblet* [מִסַּף] *of your fury,* understanding the final *hê* to be the result of dittography.[36] The verse may then be compared with Isa 51:17, 22; Jer 25:15–17, 28; 49:12; 51:7; and Ezek 23:30–34, where this imagery is used. However, each of these references uses כוס (*cup*), the same word used in Hab 2:16. Andersen points out that each woe oracle has two participles, and if מספח were changed here the pattern would be altered.[37]

חמתך (*your rage*)—Q reads חמתו (*his rage*). The NRSV translates the verse as second person address, thus harmonizing the verbs and pronouns. Here the grammar of the MT has been preserved in order to highlight performative implications that arise from a more literal translation.

מעוריהם, (*their nakedness*)—Q reads מועדיהם (*their festivals*), and G reads τὰ σπήλαια αὐτῶν (*their caves*). Neither of these variations makes sense in context. The metaphor of nakedness for the treatment of conquered nations, in the sense of stripping away their dignity, has its roots in the actual practice of leading prisoners of war away naked.[38] Thematically the MT reading fits within the woe oracle as can be seen by the next verse.

Verse 16

והערל (*and be counted as uncircumcised*)—G reads σείσθητι (*quake*), and Q reads רעל (*shake, tremble, stagger*), evidencing some discomfort with this phrase. Support for MT can be found in a phrase in Lam 4:21, ותתערי תשכרי (*you shall become drunk and strip yourself bare*), which shares the

---

36. *BHS*, 706.
37. Andersen, *Habakkuk*, 248.
38. Roberts, *Nahum, Habakkuk, and Zephaniah*, 124.

idea of the uncircumcised member being exposed as an act of shame. It is interesting to note that the Qumran *pesher* refers to circumcision in the commentary with reference to the priest (1QpHab 11:13), indicating a familiarity with ערל in the original Hebrew text.

תסוב (*will turn around*)—the *niphal* verb is usually translated with middle or passive voice, but can be translated as active in English for inanimate entities acting as subject of the verb.[39]

קיקלון, (*shameful shame*)—this *hapax legomenon* is translated to indicate the word play with קלון earlier in the verse where the word is intensified by repetition of the first syllable.

Verse 19

וכל־רוח אין בקרבו, (*and full of wind? There is nothing in it!*)—the combination of the particles כל and אין express an absolute negation.[40] This woe is addressed to the enemy and has been translated quite literally to capture its sarcastic tone, implying that the speaker is "standing mockingly before an idol exclaiming: 'It teaches! Look! It is gold and silver! And full of breath! Oh, there isn't any in it.'"[41]

Interlude (2:20)

20 And Yahweh is in his temple of holiness.	20 וַיהוָה בְּהֵיכַל קָדְשׁוֹ
Hush before him all the earth.	הַס מִפָּנָיו כָּל־הָאָרֶץ: פ

Translation Notes

Verse 20

הס (*hush*)—the serendipity of the onomatopoeic nature of the Hebrew word and a similar sounding English colloquialism allows for this highly iconic translation. This word appears once in a narrative (Judg 3:19) and in four other prophetic texts, all of which are in the context of expected judgment (Amos 6:10, 8:3; Zeph 1:7; Zech 2:17). There are two verbal forms of the word, found in Num 13:30 (*hiphil*) and Neh 8:11 (*qal*). The most significant inter-textual connection is with Zephaniah, the book

---

39. Seow, *A Grammar*, 289.
40. *GKC*, §152p.
41. Bruckner, *Jonah, Nahum, Habakkuk, Zephaniah*, 233.

following Habakkuk. Zephaniah 1:7 echoes Hab 2:20 in its exhortation הס מפני אדני יהוה כי קרוב יום יהוה (*Hush before the Lord Yahweh, for the day of Yahweh is near*). The expression הס links the two books together and Zephaniah's mention of the *day of Yahweh* links with Hab 3:16 where יום צרה (*day of distress*), is anticipated by the prophet. This in turn links Habakkuk to the preceding book in the Book of the Twelve where יום צרה is mentioned in Nah 1:7.

Act Two—Prelude (3:1)

¹ A prayer of Habakkuk the prophet ¹ תְּפִלָּה לַחֲבַקּוּק הַנָּבִיא

according to Shigionoth. עַל שִׁגְיֹנוֹת׃

Translation Notes

VERSE 1

שגינות (*Shigionoth*)—thought to be the plural of שגיון that occurs in Ps 7:1, the content of which suggests שגיון is a technical name for a sung lament.[42] Apart from the similar annotation, however, there is not much in common between Psalm 7 and Habakkuk 3. Other suggestions include a relationship to נגינות in Hab 3:19, sometimes translated *music*,[43] a connection to the Akkadian word *sigu* meaning *lamentation*, or the Hebrew root שגה (*to stagger*), describing the song of an ecstatic: "a song which provoked great excitement by its performance,"[44] or reference to a situation of distress in which Yahweh is being petitioned for relief from enemies.[45] Due to the uncertainty of translation and potential for multiple interpretations I have chosen to leave this term along with Niginoth in 3:19b in transliterated form.

---

42. Roberts, *Nahum, Habakkuk, and Zephaniah*, 130.
43. *BDB*, 993.
44. *HALOT*, 1414.
45. Sweeney, *The Twelve Prophets*, 480.

Act Two—Scene One (3:2)

² Yahweh, I have heard of your reputation,	יְהוָה שָׁמַעְתִּי שִׁמְעֲךָ ²
I am in awe, Yahweh, of your work.	יָרֵאתִי יְהוָה פָּעָלְךָ
In the midst of years you will make it live.	בְּקֶרֶב שָׁנִים חַיֵּיהוּ
In the midst of years you will make yourself known.	בְּקֶרֶב שָׁנִים תּוֹדִיעַ
In turmoil, you will remember compassion.	בְּרֹגֶז רַחֵם תִּזְכּוֹר׃

Translation Notes

Verse 2

שמעתי (*I have heard*)—an echo of the prophet's earlier accusation of Yahweh לא תשמע (*you do not hear*, Hab 1:2).

פעל (*work*)—in combination with יראתי (*I am in awe*), this reference serves as a reminder of the earlier "work" of Yahweh (Hab 1:5).

ברגז (*in turmoil*)—I have chosen to translate the root רגז consistently throughout Habakkuk 3 and *turmoil* was the best fit for the different contexts.

Act Two—Scene Two (3:3–15)

³ God comes from Teman	אֱלוֹהַּ מִתֵּימָן יָבוֹא ³
and [the] Holy One from Mount Paran. *Selah.*	וְקָדוֹשׁ מֵהַר־פָּארָן סֶלָה
His splendour has clothed the heavens	כִּסָּה שָׁמַיִם הוֹדוֹ
and his praise has filled the earth.	וּתְהִלָּתוֹ מָלְאָה הָאָרֶץ׃
⁴ And bright as the light it is,	וְנֹגַהּ כָּאוֹר תִּהְיֶה ⁴
rays from his hand has he.	קַרְנַיִם מִיָּדוֹ לוֹ

And there is a hiding place for his strength.	וְשָׁם חֶבְיוֹן עֻזֹּה:
⁵ Before him Pestilence marches	⁵ לְפָנָיו יֵלֶךְ דָּבֶר
and Fire-bolt goes forth before his feet.	וְיֵצֵא רֶשֶׁף לְרַגְלָיו:
⁶ He has taken his stand and he measures earth.	⁶ עָמַד וַיְמֹדֶד אֶרֶץ
He has looked, and he makes nations free.	רָאָה וַיַּתֵּר גּוֹיִם
And has shattered the mountains of old,	וַיִּתְפֹּצְצוּ הַרְרֵי־עַד
bent down are the ancient hills.	שַׁחוּ גִּבְעוֹת עוֹלָם
The ways of old are his.	הֲלִיכוֹת עוֹלָם לוֹ:
⁷ Below I saw trouble at the tents of Cushan.	⁷ תַּחַת אָוֶן רָאִיתִי אָהֳלֵי כוּשָׁן
Let curtains be in turmoil in the earth of Midian.	יִרְגְּזוּן יְרִיעוֹת אֶרֶץ מִדְיָן: ס
⁸ Has Yahweh burned against the Rivers?	⁸ הֲבִנְהָרִים חָרָה יְהוָה
Is your face against the Rivers?	אִם בַּנְּהָרִים אַפֶּךָ
Is your fury against the Sea?	אִם־בַּיָּם עֶבְרָתֶךָ
For you ride on your horses,	כִּי תִרְכַּב עַל־סוּסֶיךָ
on your chariots of salvation.	מַרְכְּבֹתֶיךָ יְשׁוּעָה:
⁹ Indeed laid bare is your bow.	⁹ עֶרְיָה תֵעוֹר קַשְׁתֶּךָ
Sworn are the spears of your word. *Selah*.	שְׁבֻעוֹת מַטּוֹת אֹמֶר סֶלָה
With streams you cleave the earth.	נְהָרוֹת תְּבַקַּע־אָרֶץ:
¹⁰ Having looked at you, mountains shake.	¹⁰ רָאוּךָ יָחִילוּ הָרִים
A downpour of waters has passed by.	זֶרֶם מַיִם עָבָר

Deep has given its voice,	נָתַן תְּהוֹם קוֹלוֹ
Sun has lifted its hands on high.	רוֹם יָדֵיהוּ נָשָׂא:
¹¹ Moon has stood in its lofty abode.	¹¹ שֶׁמֶשׁ יָרֵחַ עָמַד זְבֻלָה
As light your arrows dart,	לְאוֹר חִצֶּיךָ יְהַלֵּכוּ
as brightness, your glittering spear.	לְנֹגַהּ בְּרַק חֲנִיתֶךָ:
¹² In indignation you stride through the earth.	¹² בְּזַעַם תִּצְעַד־אָרֶץ
In anger you tread down nations.	בְּאַף תָּדוּשׁ גּוֹיִם:
¹³ You go forth to save your people,	¹³ יָצָאתָ לְיֵשַׁע עַמֶּךָ
to save your anointed one.	לְיֵשַׁע אֶת־מְשִׁיחֶךָ
You have smitten the head of the house of wickedness,	מָחַצְתָּ רֹּאשׁ מִבֵּית רָשָׁע
to lay bare foundation to neck. Selah.	עָרוֹת יְסוֹד עַד־צַוָּאר סֶלָה:פ
¹⁴ You have pierced with his spears the head of his warriors	¹⁴ בְמַטָּיו רֹאשׁ פְּרָזוֹ נָקַבְתָּ [פְּרָזָיו]
They storm out to scatter me.	יִסְעֲרוּ לַהֲפִיצֵנִי
Their exaltation was like he who devours the poor in secret.	עֲלִיצֻתָם כְּמוֹ־לֶאֱכֹל עָנִי בַּמִּסְתָּר:
¹⁵ You have walked through the Sea (with) your horses,	¹⁵ דָּרַכְתָּ בַיָּם סוּסֶיךָ
a heap of great waters.	חֹמֶר מַיִם רַבִּים:

Translation Notes

Verse 3

סלה (*Selah*)—this word (also in vv. 9 and 13), usually thought of as musical annotation, occurs seventy times in Psalms but nowhere else in the prophetic literature. Plausible translations include *Amen* or *Shalom*[46] and *HALOT* gives four possible senses of the term: raising the voice;

---

46. BDB, 700.

always; a pause sign; and siglum.⁴⁷ Along with שגינות (*Shigionoth*) and נגינות (*Niginoth*), the uncertainty of meaning led to merely transliterating the terms, while noting that their presence in the script provides a clear impulse for performance.

מלאה (*has filled*)—following Hiebert,⁴⁸ I have translated מלאה as the predicate of תהלתו (*his praise*), in order to maintain parallelism with the previous colon.

Verse 4

קרנים מידו לו (*rays from his hand has he*)—this seems to be a corrupt text, evidenced by problems in the MT and the variety of readings in the versions. Prior to Hiebert's monograph, *rays of light* was the usual translation but Hiebert points out the noun קרן is not translated this way elsewhere in the Hebrew literature, but always in reference to the literal horn of an ox or ram or to the figurative horns of a human being suggesting strength or power.⁴⁹ Roberts relates this image to ancient near-eastern iconography of the storm god portrayed with lightning bolts coming from his hand⁵⁰ and Shupak finds connections to a residue of the Egyptian solar religion so that קרנים reflects the imagery of the sun disc with radiating arms.⁵¹ Tsumura solves the issue by understanding the tricolon as an example of Janus parallelism in which the term קרנים "corresponds to 'brightness' in the first line with the meaning of 'rays' and to 'his power' in the third line with the meaning of 'horns.'"⁵² It seems that both *horns* and *rays* are credible alternatives. I have translated *rays* in order to emphasize the imagery associated with light in these verses.

Verse 5

דבר (*Pestilence*) and רשף (*Fire-bolt*)—these have been capitalized to indicate they may be proper names. Hiebert states: "All translators except the translator of the OG understood this as part of the retinue accompanying Yahweh in his theophanic march."⁵³ Day finds further support

---

47. *HALOT*, 756.
48. Hiebert, *God of My Victory*, 16.
49. Ibid., 18. See also Széles, *Wrath and Mercy*, 47; and Andersen, *Habakkuk*, 283.
50. Roberts, *Nahum, Habakkuk, and Zephaniah*, 128.
51. Shupak, "The God from Teman," 113.
52. Tsumura, "Janus Parallelism," 126.
53. Hiebert, *God of My Victory*, 19.

for the Canaanite imagery in this verse in an Ugaritic text that mentions the Canaanite plague god Resheph alongside Baal in the conflict with the dragon.[54] Andersen explores the probable mythological background to the text but concludes the biblical lists generally demythologize the 'destroyers' by listing them as sword, famine, wild animals, and plague (see Jer 14:12; Ezek 5:17; 14:21).[55] Despite the probable mythological background, any deities are subordinated to Yahweh and become instruments of his judgment as suggested by my translation in which the capitalization of Pestilence and Fire-bolt suggest independent actors, but their role is described in relation to Yahweh.

Verse 6

וימדד (*he measures*)—this verb is supported by V and *Barb* but G and T read *he shakes*, understanding the original verb to be נוד. Translating *he measures* provides a reasonable parallel to *set free* (hiphil form of נתר).

The end of v. 6 and the beginning of v. 7 cause problems for translators, evidenced by the editorial suggestions in *BHS* and variations in the earliest Greek translations. In support of the MT, the prophet is describing a vision that he saw. Understanding תחת as a preposition places the speaker in the midst of the vision.

Verse 7

כושן (*Cushan*)—this name appears only here in the Hebrew Bible, usually thought to be a derivative of כוש (*Cush*) that refers to Ethiopia or upper Egypt throughout the Hebrew Bible. Hence G renders Αἰθιόπων (*Ethiopians*). Notably, Cush and Midian are associated in the Moses tradition in that Moses' wife is identified as Midianite and Cushite (Exod 2:15–22; Num 12:1).

ירגזון יריעות (*let curtains be in turmoil*)—a grammatical problem occurs here where a masculine verb (ירגזון) is followed by a feminine noun (יריעות). Hiebert suggests resolving the problem by identifying the masculine term אהל that precedes the verb as the subject of the verb, thus he translates *Tents of Kushan shook, / Tent curtains of the earth of Midian*.[56] The *athnach* accent divides the verse into two parts, however,

---

54. Day, "New Light on the Mythological Background," 354.
55. Andersen, *Habakkuk*, 305.
56. Hiebert, *God of My Victory*, 4, 22.

suggesting a parallelism whereby tents and curtains are paired so that the verb רגז is to be read with יריעות.

Verse 8

הבנהרים (*the Rivers*)—the plural of נהר is more frequently rendered with the feminine form נהרות. The final *mem* could mark the dual form of the noun as in Ugaritic literature[57] or it could be a locative ending.[58]

The NJPS translation prefers to leave the words for "Rivers" (*Neharim*) and "Sea" (*Yam*) in this verse untranslated, in reference to the marine monsters vanquished by Yahweh in other examples of ancient poetry (see Ps 74:13; Job 7:12). Early Canaanite literature refers to Yam and Nahar as deities.[59] Similarly, the NRSV gives an alternative reading as *against River* and *against Sea*. I have also chosen to capitalize the names but have left the plural translation of "Rivers" to render the MT more faithfully.

Verse 9

קשתך is generally agreed to refer to Yahweh's bow, although of the many uses of the term in the Hebrew Bible, only a few references are specifically to a bow used by Yahweh (Gen 9:13–14, 16; Ezek 39:9; Lam 2:4, 3:12). In relation to the bow, the phrase שבעות מטות אמר (*sworn are the spears of your word*), does not make much sense as it stands. The variety of translations supports the assertion that this is one of the most difficult lines in Habakkuk 3.[60] Hiebert reads *his quivers* with *Barb*, although replaces the pronoun with the second person form. He agrees with the suggestion in *BHS* that שבעות be read שִׂבַּעְתָּ (*piel qatal* 2ms of שבע [*to be satisfied*]), supported by *Barb*. Thus the phrase would read *Sated are the rods [shafts] of your quiver*. Smith tries to maintain MT: *The stave is charged by a word*;[61] Roberts also follows *Barb*: *You sate the shafts of the bowstring*;[62] Bailey derives *You called for many arrows* from a literal translation of the three words in the MT: *sworn – arrows – decree*;[63] and

---

57. Ibid., 23.
58. *BDB*, 626.
59. Day, "New Light on the Mythological Background," 353.
60. Hiebert, *God of My Victory*, 26.
61. Smith, *Micah—Malachi*, 113.
62. Roberts, *Nahum, Habakkuk, and Zephaniah*, 129.
63. Bailey, "Habakkuk," 357.

Andersen follows G in reading שבעות as *seven*: *Seven clubs thou didst bring to view.*[64] Pinker agrees שבעות should be understood as *seven*, linking the meaning to the interpretation of bow as the seven layered rainbow, reading: *Naked bare is your bow of seven strips!*[65]

I use the suggested *spears* for מטות found in *BDB*[66] to maintain the MT but keep the weaponry imagery, while the translation of אמר as *word* relates to the participle of בעש (*the ones sworn*).

נהרות תבקע־ארץ (*with streams you cleave the earth*)—my translation reflects an adverbial use of a noun and may be compared with Hab 1:11—*then he swept through as wind*.

Verse 10

ראוך יחילו (*having looked at you, they shake*)—according to Ewald, when a *qatal* verb with a preposition precedes a *yiqtol* verb in poetry, the action must precede the following action as its condition.[67] Hiebert sees this as an example of archaic poetry where a preterit form (an old form of prefixed verbs) is juxtaposed to a *qatal* to convey past narrative.[68]

ידיהו (*its hands*)—a rare form of a plural noun with a suffix. Gesenius calls this a "wholly abnormal" form,[69] and *BHS* understands it as a corrupt text, giving several suggestions for emending it.

Verse 11

שמש (*sun*)—a text critical note in *BHS* suggests that this word belongs to the previous verse, a suggestion that I have followed. OG and *Barb* translate in this way, as do many modern translators. The re-division solves a number of grammatical and stylistic problems: removing a second subject from the first line of v. 11 where no conjunction is present and only a singular verb follows, and providing a subject for the last line of v. 10. The image of the sun raising its hands is a common one in ancient Near Eastern iconography.

לאור חציך יהלכו (*as light your arrows dart*)—this translation reads חציך as the subject of the verb יהלכו, supported by Ps 77:18, a parallel

64. Andersen, *Habakkuk*, 312.
65. Pinker, "The Lord's Bow," 420.
66. *BDB*, 641.
67. Ewald, *Syntax of the Hebrew*, §357b.
68. Hiebert, *God of My Victory*, 29.
69. *GKC*, §91*l*.

reading to this text, in which the verb הלך describes the movement of divine arrows. An alternate reading that takes חציך as the subject of לאור (*at the light of your arrows they dart*) assumes the sun and moon are the subjects that dart, an assumption that does not make sense as the previous phrase describes them as 'standing.' The translation *as light* follows one of the meanings of ל in *BDB*: "denoting the principle with regard to which an act is done."[70] Thus the translation לאור (*as light*), and לנגה (*as brightness*), in the following line.

Verse 13

משיחך (*your anointed one*)—the Greek versions change this noun to a plural form, but the singular form is attested in most other versions and is always found in the singular in the Hebrew Bible with the exception of Ps 105:15 and 1 Chr 16:22.

The many variations in translation of the second half of v. 13 indicate "disturbance of the text from very early times."[71] The modern translations NEB and JB take a building metaphor, understanding ראש to mean *roof*, בית to mean *house* (leaving out the *mem* as suggested in *BHS*), and יסוד to mean *foundation* so that it reads *Thou dost shatter the wicked man's house from the roof down, uncovering its foundations to the bare rock*. This verse has also been translated with reference to a mythological god/monster. Albright understands a reference to Mot ('Death'),[72] Stephens proposes that a reference to Behemot lies behind the corrupted text,[73] and Hiebert, who argues that the terms in vv. 13b and 14a are more readily translated as body parts: head, neck, buttocks and back, suggests the reference to *the wicked one* is a reference to Tiamat, the dragon of chaos.[74] Such interpretations fit with a mythological reading of the poem that understands references to ancient deities in vv. 8, 14 and 15. This translation mixes the metaphors, maintaining *the house of wickedness* as an echo of Hab 2:9 but allowing the head of the house to be the one attacked, so that the structural imagery (*house* and *foundation*) combines with anatomical imagery (*neck* and *head*), connecting with *head* in the following verse.

70. *BDB*, 516.
71. Hiebert, *God of My Victory*, 36.
72. Albright, "The Psalm of Habakkuk," 11, 13, 17.
73. Stephens, "The Babylonian Dragon Myth," 290–93.
74. Hiebert, *God of My Victory*, 36, 40.

ערות (*to lay bare*)—although the form of the verb ערה in MT is *piel* infinitive absolute, all versions read it as *piel qatal* 2ms. Despite the *qatal* form providing a better parallel to מחצת in the previous colon, translating as an infinitive also makes sense in the context so I have maintained the MT form.

Verse 14

Hiebert states that the last eight words of v. 14 "is the lengthiest textual puzzle of the chapter . . . [indicating] an ancient disruption in the text which may no longer be possible to correct."[75] While there is greater unanimity in reading the text of the final four word phrase, its meaning is unclear. מטות (*spears*) was used in v. 9, there identified as belonging to Yahweh. The 3ms suffix in MT (also attested by V and T) suggests the spears belong to the enemy. There may be an implication in MT that Yahweh will turn the enemy's weapons against itself. Many commentaries opt to read with Barb "*Your shafts.*" There is also disagreement among the versions as to whether ראש (*head*) is singular (MT, V) or plural (G, T). Plural readings may be accounted for by seeing the word in construct with the plural noun following. If singular, it may refer to the monster being killed, an idea similar to that in the *Enuma Elish*.[76] [פרזיו] פרזו (*his warriors*) is a *hapax legomenon*, the meaning of which is dubious. Versions translate this word variously as *warriors* (V), *rulers* (G), *sinners* (*Barb*), *open places* (8HevXIIgr). The bewildering variety of translations of this verse nonetheless attest to the metaphor of Yahweh as warrior who is able to vanquish his foes and vindicate his people, reflected in this translation where מטיו is translated *his spears* as in Hab 3:9, showing that Yahweh is even stronger than the foe who had attacked the prophet and his community, turning the enemy's weapons on himself.

---

75. Ibid., 43.
76. Ibid.

Act Two—Scene Three (3:16–19a)

¹⁶ I heard and my belly is in turmoil,	שָׁמַעְתִּי וַתִּרְגַּז בִּטְנִי ¹⁶
at a voice my lips tingled.	לְקוֹל צָלֲלוּ שְׂפָתַי
Decay comes into my bones,	יָבוֹא רָקָב בַּעֲצָמַי
and in my place I am in turmoil,	וְתַחְתַּי אֶרְגָּז
where I wait for a day of distress	אֲשֶׁר אָנוּחַ לְיוֹם צָרָה
to come up to a people who will invade us.	לַעֲלוֹת לְעַם יְגוּדֶנּוּ׃
¹⁷ If the fig tree does not sprout,	כִּי־תְאֵנָה לֹא־תִפְרָח ¹⁷
and no produce is on the vines,	וְאֵין יְבוּל בַּגְּפָנִים
if the yield of the olive tree has failed	כִּחֵשׁ מַעֲשֵׂה־זַיִת
and fields have not produced food,	וּשְׁדֵמוֹת לֹא־עָשָׂה אֹכֶל
the flock has been cut off from the fold	גָּזַר מִמִּכְלָה צֹאן
and no cattle are in the stalls,	וְאֵין בָּקָר בָּרְפָתִים׃
¹⁸ yet I will exult in Yahweh,	וַאֲנִי בַּיהוָה אֶעְלוֹזָה ¹⁸
I will rejoice in the God of my salvation.	אָגִילָה בֵּאלֹהֵי יִשְׁעִי׃
¹⁹ᵃ Yahweh my Lord is my strength.	יְהוִה אֲדֹנָי חֵילִי ¹⁹ᵃ
He places my feet like the hinds'	וַיָּשֶׂם רַגְלַי כָּאַיָּלוֹת
and on my high places he makes me walk.	וְעַל בָּמוֹתַי יַדְרִכֵנִי

Translation Notes

VERSE 16

אשר—BHS suggests reading אֲשֻׁרָי (dual form of the noun אֲשֻׁר [*step*] with the first singular suffix). The term is used frequently in poetic writing to denote a mode of life (Pss 17:5; 37:31; 40:3; 44:19; 73:2; Job 23:11;

Prov 14:15). As already noted, however, prose particles are sometimes found in Hebrew poetry and a relative particle is not out of place here.

ליום—Greek versions read the preposition בּ- rather than לְ-. As Roberts points out, however, the use of ליום may be compared to other prophetic texts such as Isa 30:8; Jer 12:3; and Zeph 3:8, where a future time is awaited.[77]

Verse 17

ושדמות (*field*)—plural in the MT but the following predicate does not agree in number. Ewald includes this verse amongst several cases where noun and verb do not agree in gender and/or number because of "a later and more special meaning attached to the word as actually employed in living language."[78] שְׁדֵמוֹת is a poetic word not found in the singular, but as it is almost synonymous with the more common שדה it is construed with the masculine singular. The disagreement is explained in *GKC* as due to "the collective character of שדמות,"[79] while Andersen notes that the plural term is due to the artistry of the poetry, alternating singular and plural forms in the colon.[80]

ברפתים (*in the stalls*)—a *hapax legomenon* but all versions agree that it is a term parallel to *sheepfold* in the previous phrase.

Verse 19a

במותי (*on my high places*)—the 1cs suffix is omitted in G. It may have been omitted as dittography (a suggestion in *BHS*). Hiebert translates במת as *back* here as in v. 13b,[81] understanding that the victor treads on the back of his foe. This would provide a parallel between Yahweh's victory and that of the poet. The suffix has been retained, however, as it is not unusual in this section where the prophet's speech multiplies the personal pronouns.

---

77. Roberts, *Nahum, Habakkuk, and Zephaniah*, 146.
78. Ewald, *Syntax of the Hebrew*, §318a.
79. *GKC*, §145u.
80. Andersen, *Habakkuk*, 346.
81. Hiebert, *God of My Victory*, 57.

Postlude (3:19b)

19b To the Director, according to my Niginoth.   לַמְנַצֵּחַ בִּנְגִינוֹתָי: 19b

Translation Notes

The final two terms of the book of Habakkuk are obscure. מנצח occurs frequently as a heading in the Psalter and is often translated *leader*. The term also occurs three times in 2 Chronicles with a meaning of overseer or director (2:1, 17; 34:13), always in the plural and only in the third instance in relation to music. The underlying verb נצח is translated *lasting, successful* in *HALOT*[82] and may be related to the Aramaic root *nsh*, *to conquer*, as T renders *to whom belongs victories and mighty deeds* and G reads με τοῦ νικῆσαι ἐν τῇ ᾠδῇ αὐτοῦ (*that I may conquer by his song*).

The 1cs suffix on נגינות is retained in T and V but read as 3ms by G and V. The term seems to be a technical term, perhaps denoting music played on strings (Isa 38:20; Lam 5:14) or a mocking song (Ps 69:13; Job 30:9; Lam 3:14).

---

82. *HALOT*, 716.

Bibliography

Abrego, José María. "Habakkuk." In *The International Bible Commentary*, edited by William R. Farmer, 1168–74. Collegeville, MN: Liturgical, 1998.

Achtemeier, E. *Nahum—Malachi*. Interpretation. Atlanta: John Knox, 1986.

Ackermann, Denise M. "Lamenting Tragedy from 'the Other Side.'" *Sameness and Difference: Problems and Potentials in South African Society*, 2000. No pages. Online: http://www.crvp.org/book/Serieso2/II-6/chapter_viii.htm.

Ahlström, Gösta W. *The History of Ancient Palestine*. 2nd ed. Minneapolis: Fortress, 1994.

Albright, W. F. "The Psalm of Habakkuk." In *Studies in Old Testament Prophecy*, edited by H. H. Rowley, 1–18. Edinburgh: T. & T. Clark, 1950.

Alexander, Jeffrey C. "Cultural Pragmatics: Social Performance between Ritual and Strategy." In *Social Performance: Symbolic Action, Cultural Pragmatics and Ritual*, edited by Jeffrey C. Alexander, et al, 29–90. Cambridge: Cambridge University Press, 2006.

Alexander, Jeffrey C., and Jason L Mast. "Introduction to *Social Performance: Symbolic Action, Cultural Pragmatics and Ritual*." In *Social Performance: Symbolic Action, Cultural Pragmatics and Ritual*, edited by Jeffrey C. Alexander, et al, 1–28. Cambridge: Cambridge University Press, 2006.

Alonso Schökel, L. *A Manual of Hebrew Poetics*. Translated by Adrian Graffy. Subsidia Biblica. Rome: Biblical Institute Press, 1988.

Alter, Robert. *The Art of Biblical Narrative*. New York: Basic Books, 1981.

———. *The Art of Biblical Poetry*. New York: Basic Books, 1985.

Amit, Yairah. *Reading Biblical Narratives: Literary Criticism and the Hebrew Bible*. Translated by Yael Lotan. Minneapolis: Fortress, 2001.

———. "The Role of Prophecy and Prophets in the Chronicler's World." In *Prophets, Prophecy and Prophetic Texts in Second Temple Judaism*, edited by Michael H. Floyd and Robert D. Haak, 80–101. London: T. & T. Clark, 2006.

Andersen, Francis I. *Habakkuk: A New Translation with Introduction and Commentary*. Anchor Bible 25. New York: Doubleday, 2001.

Anstey, Matthew. "Habakkuk the Faithful Dissident: A Performative Hermeneutic for Anglicans in Australia." *St Mark's Review* 203.2 (2007) 47–60.

Ararat, Nisan. *Drama in the Bible*. Jerusalem: World Centre for Bible, 1997.

Arrandale, Rick. "Artaud and the Concept of Drama in Theology." *New Blackfriars* 88.1013 (2007) 100–112.

Aschkenasy, Nehama. "Reading Ruth through a Bakhtinian Lens: The Carnivalesque in a Biblical Tale." *Journal of Biblical Literature* 126 (2007) 437–53.

Auerbach, Erich. *Mimesis: The Representation of Reality in Western Literature*. Translated by William R. Trask. Princeton: Princeton University Press, 1953.

Austin, J. L. *How to Do Things with Words.* Edited by J. O. Urmson and Marina Sbisà. 2nd ed. Cambridge: Harvard University Press, 1975.

Avishur, Y. *Studies in Hebrew and Ugaritic Psalms.* Jerusalem: Magnes, 1994.

Bailey, W. "Habakkuk." In *Micah, Nahum, Habakkuk, Zephaniah,* edited by K. Barker and W. Bailey, 245-378. Nashville: Broadman & Holman, 1999.

Baker, David W. *Nahum, Habakkuk and Zephaniah.* London: Inter-Varsity, 1988.

Bakhtin, Mikhail. *The Dialogic Imagination: Four Essays.* Translated by Caryl Emerson and Michael Holquist. Austin: University of Texas Press, 1981.

―――. *Rabelais and His World.* Translated by Helene Iswolsky. 1st Midland book ed. Bloomington: Indiana University Press, 1984.

Balthasar, Hans Urs von. *Theo-Drama: Theological Dramatic Theory.* 5 vols. Translated by Graham Harrison. San Francisco: Ignatius, 1988-1998.

Baltzer, Klaus *Deutero-Isaiah: A Commentary on Isaiah 40–55.* Translated by Margaret Kohl. Hermeneia. Minneapolis: Fortress, 1999.

Barthes, Roland. "The Death of the Author." In *Image–Music–Text,* 142–48. London: Fontana, 1977.

Barton, John. *Oracles of God: Perceptions of Ancient Prophecy in Israel after the Exile.* London: Darton, Longman & Todd, 1986.

Bauman, Richard. "Performance." In *International Encyclopedia of Communications,* edited by E. Barnouw, et al., 262–66. New York: Oxford University Press, 1989.

Beker, J. Christiaan. "Echoes and Intertextuality." In *Paul and the Scriptures of Israel,* edited by Craig A. Evans and James A. Sanders, 64–69. Sheffield: JSOT Press, 1993.

Ben Zvi, E. "Introduction: Writing, Speeches, and Prophetic Books—Setting an Agenda." In *Writings and Speech in Israelite and Ancient Near Eastern Prophecy,* edited by Ehud Ben Zvi and Michael H. Floyd, 1–29. SBL Symposium Series 10. Atlanta: Society for Biblical Literature, 2000.

―――. "Twelve Prophetic Books or 'the Twelve': A Few Preliminary Considerations." In *Forming Prophetic Literature: Essays on Isaiah and the Twelve in Honor of John D. W. Watts,* edited by J. D. W. Watts and Paul R. House, 125–56. JSOT Supplements 235. Sheffield: Sheffield Academic, 1996.

Ben Zvi, E., and Michael H. Floyd, editors. *Writings and Speech in Israelite and Ancient Near Eastern Prophecy.* SBL Symposium 10. Atlanta: Society of Biblical Literature, 2000.

Bennet, Mark. "On Reading the Whole of Ecclesiastes out Loud in Public." *Practical Theology* 1.3 (2009) 309–11.

Berlin, Adele. "Introduction to Hebrew Poetry." In *NIB,* 4:301–15.

―――. *Poetics and Interpretation of Biblical Narrative.* Bible and Literature Series 9. Sheffield: Almond, 1983.

Berquist, Jon L. *Approaching Yehud: New Approaches to the Study of the Persian Period.* Semeia Studies 50. Atlanta: Society for Biblical Literature, 2007.

Beyse, K.-M. "משל." In *TDOT,* 9:64–67.

Bial, Henry. *The Performance Studies Reader.* London: Routledge, 2004.

Blenkinsopp, Joseph. *A History of Prophecy in Israel.* Rev. ed. Louisville: Westminster John Knox, 1996.

Boal, Augusto. "The Theatre as Discourse." In *The Twentieth Century Performance Reader.* edited by M. Huxley and N. Witts, 80–92. London: Routledge, 2002.

Boda, M. J., and Michael H. Floyd. *Bringing out the Treasure: Inner Biblical Allusion in Zechariah 9-14.* JSOT Supplements 370. London: Sheffield Academic, 2003.

Boogaart, Thomas A. "Drama and the Sacred: Recovering the Dramatic Tradition in Scripture and Worship." In *Touching the Altar: The Old Testament for Christian Worship*, edited by Carol M. Bechtel, 35–61. Grand Rapids: Eerdmanns, 2008.

Boyle, Terence. "The Rhetoric of Taunt Language in Isaiah, Micah and Habakkuk." PhD diss., Dallas Theological Seminary, 2010.

Brant, Jo-Ann A. *Dialogue and Drama: Elements of Greek Tragedy in the Fourth Gospel*. Peabody, MA: Hendrickson, 2004.

Brawley, Robert L. "Resistance to the Carnivalization of Jesus: Scripture in the Lucan Passion Narrative." *Semeia* 69/70 (1995) 33–60.

Brecht, Bertolt. "Short Description of a New Technique in Acting Which Produces an Alienation Effect." In *The Twentieth Century Performance Reader*, edited by Michael Huxley and Noel Witts, 93–104. London: Routledge, 2002.

Breeze, Andrew. "The Book of Habakkuk and Old English Exodus." *English Studies* 75.3 (1994) 210–14.

Briggs, Richard S. "The Use of Speech-Act Theory in Biblical Interpretation." *Currents in Research* 9 (2001) 229–76.

Brownlee, William H. *The Midrash Pesher of Habakkuk*. SBL Monograph Series 24. Missoula, MT: Scholars, 1977.

Bruch, Debra. "The Prejudice against Theatre." *The Journal of Religion and Theatre* 3.1 (2004). No pages. Online: http://www.rtjournal.org/vol_3/no_1/bruch.html.

Bruckner, James. *Jonah, Nahum, Habakkuk, Zephaniah*. NIV Application Commentary. Grand Rapids: Zondervan, 2004.

Brueggemann, Walter. *A Commentary on Jeremiah: Exile and Homecoming*. Grand Rapids: Eerdmans, 1998.

———. *Like Fire in the Bones: Listening for the Prophetic Word in Jeremiah*. Edited by Patrick D. Miller. Minneapolis: Fortress, 2006.

———. *Theology of the Old Testament: Testimony, Dispute, Advocacy*. Minneapolis: Fortress, 1997.

Brummitt, Mark. "Of Broken Pots and Dirty Laundry: The Jeremiah *Lehrstücke*." *The Bible and Critical Theory* 1 (2006) 3.1—3.10.

Bruno, Franklin. "Representation and the Work–Performance Relation." *The Journal of Aesthetics and Art Criticism* 64 (2006) 355–65.

Budde, K. "Die Bücher Habakuk und Zephanja." *Theologische Studien und Kritiken* 66 (1898) 383–93.

———. "Habakuk." *Zeitschrift der deutschen morgenländischen Gesellschaft* 84 (1930) 139–47.

Burke, Kenneth. *A Grammar of Motives*. New York: Prentice-Hall, 1945.

Buth, Randall. *Living Biblical Hebrew: Selected Readings with 500 Friends*. Zeeland: Biblical Language Center, 2006.

Calvin, Jean. *Commentaries on the Twelve Minor Prophets. Volume IV: Habakkuk, Zephaniah, Haggai*. Translated by John Owen. Grand Rapids: Eerdmans, 1950.

Carlson, Marvin. *Performance: A Critical Introduction*. 2nd ed. New York: Routledge, 2004.

Childs, Brevard S. *Introduction to the Old Testament as Scripture*. Philadelphia: Fortress, 1979.

Clark, David J., and Howard A. Hatton. *A Handbook on the Books of Nahum, Habakkuk, and Zephaniah*. UBS Handbook Series. New York: United Bible Societies, 1989.

Cleaver-Bartholomew, David. "An Alternative Approach to Hab 1,2—2,20." *Scandinavian Journal of the Old Testament* 17 (2003) 206–25.

———. *An Analysis of the Old Greek Version of Habakkuk*. PhD diss., Claremont Graduate University, 1998.

Collins, John J. "Dead Sea Scrolls." In *ABD*, 2:85–101.

Conquergood, Dwight. "Performance Studies: Interventions and Radical Research." In *The Performance Studies Reader*, edited by Henry Bial, 311–22. London: Routledge, 2004.

Cook, Steve. "Habakkuk 3, Gender, and War." *Lectio Difficilior* (2009). No pages. Online: http://www.lectio.unibe.ch.

Cotterell, Peter. "Linguistics, Meaning, Semantics and Discourse Analysis." In *NIDOTTE* 1: 134–60.

Courtenay, Bryce. *April Fool's Day*. Port Melbourne: Mandarin, 1993.

Craigo-Snell, Shannon. "Command Performance: Rethinking Performance Interpretation in the Context of *Divine Discourse*." *Modern Theology* 16 (2000) 475–94.

Crüsemann, Frank. *The Torah: Theology and Social History of Old Testament Law*. Translated by Allan W. Mahnke. Minneapolis: Fortress, 1996.

Culley, Robert C. "Orality and Writtenness in the Prophetic Texts." In *Writings and Speech in Israelite and Ancient Near Eastern Prophecy*, edited by Ehud Ben Zvi and Michael H. Floyd, 45–64. SBL Symposium Series 10. Atlanta: Society for Biblical Literature, 2000.

Dangl, Oskar. "Habakkuk in Recent Research." *Currents in Research: Biblical Studies* 9 (2001) 131–68.

Davies, Andrew. "Oratorio as Exegesis: The Use of the Book of Isaiah in Handel's Messiah." *Biblical Interpretation* 15 (2007) 464–84.

Davies, P. R. "'Pot of Iron, Point of Diamond' (Jer 17:1): Prophecy as Writing." In *Writings and Speech in Israelite and Ancient Near Eastern Prophecy*, edited by Ehud Ben Zvi and Michael H. Floyd, 65–81. SBL Symposium Series 10. Atlanta: Society for Biblical Literature, 2000.

Davis, Tracy C. *The Cambridge Companion to Performance Studies*. Cambridge: Cambridge University Press, 2008.

Day, John. "New Light on the Mythological Background of the Allusion to Resheph in Habakkuk 3:5." *Vetus Testamentum* 29 (1979) 353–55.

De Marinis, Marco, "Dramaturgy of the Spectator." Translated by Paul Dwyer. *Drama Review* 31.2 (1987) 100–14.

De Vries, Simon J. "The Book of Habakkuk." In *The Interpreter's One-Volume Commentary on the Bible*, edited by C. M. Laymon, 494–95. Nashville: Abingdon, 1971.

Derrida, Jacques. *Writing and Difference*. Translated by Alan Bass. Chicago: University of Chicago Press, 1978.

Doan, William, and Terry Giles. *Prophets, Performance, and Power: Performance Criticism of the Hebrew Bible*. New York: T. & T. Clark, 2005.

———. "The Song of Asaph: A Performance-Critical Analysis of 1 Chronicles 16:8–36." *Catholic Biblical Quarterly* 70 (2008) 29–43.

———. *Twice Used Songs: Performance Criticism of the Songs of Ancient Israel*. Peabody, MA: Hendrickson, 2008.

Downer, Alan S. *The Art of the Play: An Anthology of Nine Plays*. New York: Holt, Rinehart & Winston, 1955.

Driver, S. R. *The Minor Prophets: Nahum, Habakkuk, Zephaniah, Haggai, Zechariah, Malachi*. Century Bible. Edinburgh: T. C. & E. C. Jack, 1906.

Duhm, Bernhard. *Das Buch Habakuk: Text, Übersetzung und Erklärung.* Tübingen: Mohr/Siebeck, 1906.

Eaton, John H. *Festal Drama in Deutero-Isaiah.* London: SPCK, 1979.

———. *Obadiah, Nahum, Habakkuk, Zephaniah.* London: SCM, 1961.

———. "Origin and Meaning of Habakkuk 3." *Zeitschrift fur die alttestamentliche Wissenschaft* 76 (1964) 144–71.

Engels, Frederick. *Ludwig Feuerbach and the Outcome of Classical German Philosophy.* 1845. Reprinted, New York: International Publishers, 1941.

Engnell, Ivan. *A Rigid Scrutiny: Critical Essays on the Old Testament.* Translated by John T. Willis. Nashville: Vanderbilt University Press, 1969.

Everson, J. "The Canonical Location of Habakkuk." In *Thematic Threads in the Book of the Twelve*, edited by Paul L. Reddit and Aaron Schart, 165–73. Berlin: de Gruyter, 2003.

Ewald, G. H. A. *Commentary on the Prophets of the Old Testament.* Vol. 3. Translated by J. F. Smith. London: Williams & Norgate, 1878.

Ewald, Heinrich. *Syntax of the Hebrew Language of the Old Testament.* Translated by James Kennedy. 1881. Reprinted, Piscataway, NJ: Gorgias, 2005.

Fiddes, Paul S. "Story and Possibility: Reflections on the Last Scenes of the Fourth Gospel and Shakespeare's *The Tempest*." In *Revelation and Story: Narrative Theology and the Centrality of Story*, edited by Gerhard Sauter and John Barton, 29–51. Aldershot, UK: Ashgate, 2000.

Fischer-Lichte, Erika. "Interweaving Cultures in Performance: Different States of Being in-Between." *New Theatre Quarterly* 25 (2009) 391–401.

Floyd, Michael H. *Minor Prophets Part 2.* Forms of Old Testament Literature 22. Grand Rapids: Eerdmans, 2000.

———. "Prophecy and Writing in Habakkuk 2:1–5." *Zeitschrift fur die alttestamentliche Wissenschaft* 105 (1993) 462–81.

———. "'Write the Revelation!' (Hab 2:2): Re-Imagining the Cultural History of Prophecy." In *Writings and Speech in Israelite and Ancient Near Eastern Prophecy*, edited by Ehud Ben Zvi and Michael H. Floyd, 103–43. SBL Symposium Series 10. Atlanta: Society for Biblical Literature, 2000.

Friedman, Michael D. "In Defense of Authenticity." *Studies in Philology* 90 (2002) 33–56.

Gafney, Wilda. *Daughters of Miriam: Women Prophets in Ancient Israel.* Minneapolis: Fortress, 2008.

Garcia-Treto, Francisco O. "The Fall of the House: A Carnivalesque Reading of 2 Kings 9 and 10." *Journal for the Study of the Old Testament* 46 (1990) 47–65.

Giles, Terry and William Doan. "Performance Criticism of the Hebrew Bible." *Religion Compass* 2 (2008) 237–86.

Ginsburg, C. D. *Introduction to the Massoretico-Critical Edition of the Hebrew Bible.* 1897. Reprinted, New York: Ktav, 1966.

Girard, Rene. *The Girard Reader.* Edited by James G. Williams. New York: Crossroad, 1996.

Glavin, John. *After Dickens: Reading, Adaptation and Performance.* Cambridge Studies in Nineteenth-Century Literature and Culture 20. Cambridge: Cambridge University Press, 1999.

Goffman, Erving. *The Presentation of Self in Everyday Life.* 1959. New York: Overlook, 1973.

Gottwald, Norman K. "Tragedy and Comedy in the Latter Prophets." *Semeia* 32 (1984) 83–96.

Gowan, Donald E. "Habakkuk and Wisdom." *Perspective* 9 (1968) 157–66.

———. *The Triumph of Faith in Habakkuk*. 1976. Reprinted, Eugene, OR: Wipf & Stock, 2009.

Green, Barbara. *Mikhail Bakhtin and Biblical Scholarship: An Introduction*. SBL Semeia Studies 38. Atlanta: Society of Biblical Literature, 2000.

Grimes, Ronald L. "Ritual Studies." In *ER* 12:422–25.

Haak, Robert D. *Habakkuk*. Vetus Testamentum Supplements 44. Leiden: Brill, 1992.

———. "'Poetry' in Habakkuk 1:1—2:4." *Journal of the American Oriental Society* 108 (1988) 437–44.

Habel, Norman. *The Book of Job*. Old Testament Library. London: SCM, 1985.

Hasluck, Paul. "The Burden of Habakkuk and the Sword of Gideon: A Recitation for Wireless Broadcasting. Several Voices and a Chorus." In *Collected Verse*, 115–40. Melbourne: Hawthorn, 1969.

Hasluck, Nicholas. *The Chance of Politics*. Melbourne: Text Publishing, 1997.

Hassan, Ihab. "The Question of Postmodernism." *Bucknell Review* 25 (1980) 117–26.

Hayes, Katherine M. *'The Earth Mourns': Prophetic Metaphor and Oral Aesthetic*. Academia Biblia 8. Atlanta: Society of Biblical Literature, 2002.

Hays, Richard B. *Echoes of Scripture in the Letters of Paul*. New Haven: Yale University Press, 1989.

Heschel, Abraham J. *The Prophets: An Introduction*. Vol. 1. New York: Harper & Row, 1962.

Hiebert, Theodore. "The Book of Habakkuk: Introduction, Commentary and Reflections." In *NIB* 7:621–55.

———. *God of My Victory: The Ancient Hymn in Habakkuk 3*. Atlanta: Scholars, 1986.

Hill, Andrew E. "רמש." In *NIDOTTE* 3:1127–28.

Holladay, William L. "Plausible Circumstances for the Prophecy of Habakkuk." *Journal of Biblical Literature* 120 (2001) 123–30.

Hornsby, Teresa. "Ezekiel Off-Broadway." *The Bible and Critical Theory* 1 (2006) 2.1—2.8.

House, Paul R. "The Character of God in the Book of the Twelve." In *Reading and Hearing the Book of the Twelve*, edited by James D. Nogalski and Marvin A. Sweeney, 125–45. Atlanta: Society of Biblical Literature, 2000.

———. *The Unity of the Twelve*, JSOT Supplements 97. Sheffield: Almond, 1990.

———. *Zephaniah: A Prophetic Drama*. JSOT Supplements 69. Sheffield: Almond, 1989.

Hurwitz, M. S. "Ezekiel the Poet." In *EJ* 6:649.

Iacoboni, Marco. *Mirroring People: The New Science of How We Connect with Others*. New York: Farrar, Straus & Giroux, 2008.

Iser, Wolfgang. *The Act of Reading: A Theory of Aesthetic Response*. Baltimore: John Hopkins University Press, 1978.

Iverson, Kelly R. "Orality and the Gospels: A Survey of Recent Research." *Currents in Biblical Research* 8 (2009) 71–106.

Jackson, Shannon. *Professing Performance: Theatre in the Academy from Philology to Performativity*. Theory and Performance Theory. Cambridge: Cambridge University Press, 2004.

Janzen, J. Gerald. "Eschatological Symbol and Existence in Habakkuk." *Catholic Biblical Quarterly* 44 (1982) 394–414.

Jenni, Ernst. "הוי." In *TLOT* 1:357–58.

Jeremias, Jörg. *Kultprophetie und Gerichtsverkündigung in der späten Königszeit Israels*. Wissenschaftliche Monographien zum Alten und Neuen Testament 35. Neukirchen-Vluyn: Neukirchener Verlag, 1970.

Jöcken, Peter. "War Habakuk ein Kultprophet?" In *Bausteine Biblischer Theologie*, edited by Heinz-Josef Fabry, 319–32. Cologne: Hanstein, 1977.

Johnson, B. "משפט." In *TDOT* 9:86–98.

Johnson, Marshall D. "The Paralysis of Torah in Habakkuk 1:4." *Vetus Testamentum* 35 (1985) 257–66.

Kalimi, Isaac. "Was the Chronicler a Historian?" In *The Chronicler as Historian*, edited by M. Patrick Graham, et al. 73–89. JSOT Supplements 238. Sheffield: Sheffield Academic, 1997.

Kelle, Brad E. "Ancient Israelite Prophets and Greek Political Orators: Analogies for the Prophets and Their Implications for Historical Reconstruction." In *Israel's Prophets and Israel's Past: Essays on the Relationship of Prophetic Texts and Israelite History in Honor of John H. Hayes*, edited by Brad E. Kelle and Megan Bishop Moore, 57–82. Library of Hebrew Bible/Old Testament Studies 446. New York: T. & T. Clark, 2006.

Keller, Carl-A. "Nahoum, Habacuc, Sophonie." In *Micheé, Nahoum, Habacuc, Sophonie*, edited by René Vuilleumier and Carl-A. Keller, 93–222. Neuchâtel: Delachaux & Niestlé, 1971.

Kershaw, Baz. "Performance as Research: Live Events and Documents." In *The Cambridge Companion to Performance Studies*, edited by Tracy C. Davis, 23–45. Cambridge Companions to Literature. Cambridge: Cambridge University Press, 2008.

Khovacs, Ivan Patricio. "A Cautionary Note on the Use of Theatre for Theology." In *Faithful Performances: Enacting Christian Tradition*, edited by Trevor A. Hart and Steven R. Guthrie, 33–50. Ashgate Studies in Theology, Imagination, and the Arts. Aldershot, UK: Ashgate, 2007.

Kirshenblatt-Gimblett, Barbara. "Performance Studies." In *The Performance Studies Reader*, edited by Henry Bial, 43–55. London: Routledge, 2004.

Kivy, Peter. *The Performance of Reading: An Essay in the Philosophy of Literature*. Malden, MA: Blackwell, 2006.

Koch, Klaus. *The Prophets*. Vol. 1: *The Assyrian Period*. Translated by Margaret Kohl. London: SCM, 1982.

Kugel, James L. *The Idea of Biblical Poetry: Parallelism and Its History*. New Haven: Yale University Press, 1981.

Kuntz, J. Kenneth. "Biblical Hebrew Poetry in Recent Research, Part 1." *Currents in Research: Biblical Studies* 6 (1998) 31–64.

LaCocque, André. *Esther Regina: A Bakhtinian Reading*. Evanston, IL: Northwestern University Press, 2008.

Langacker, Ronald. *The Cognitive Basis of Grammar*. Berlin: Mouton de Gruyter, 2002.

Lash, Nicholas. *Theology on the Way to Emmaus*. London: SCM, 1986.

Levinson, Bernard M. *Legal Revision and Religious Renewal in Ancient Israel*. Cambridge: Cambridge University Press, 2008.

Levy, Shimon. *The Bible as Theatre*. Brighton, UK: Sussex Academic, 2000.

———. "The Performance of Creation, Creation in Performance." In *The Creation of Man and Woman: Interpretations of the Biblical Narratives in Jewish and Christian Traditions*, edited by G. Luttikhuizen, 187–205. Themes in Biblical Narrative 3. Leiden: Brill, 2000.

Lindblom, Johannes. *Prophecy in Ancient Israel*. Philadelphia: Muhlenberg, 1962.

Lischer, Richard. "Martin Luther King, Jr.: 'Performing' The Scriptures." *Anglican Theological Review* 77 (1995) 160–72.

Lucas, Peter J. *Exodus (Anglo-Saxon Poem)*. London: Methuen, 1977.

MacAloon, John J. *Rite, Drama, Festival, Spectacle: Rehearsals toward a Theory of Cultural Performance*. Philadelphia: Institute for the Study of Human Issues, 1984.

Mackenzie, Ian. "Improvisation, Creativity, and Formulaic Language." *The Journal of Aesthetics and Art Criticism* 58 (2000) 173–79.

Mandolfo, Carleen. *Daughter Zion Talks Back to the Prophets*. SBL Semeia 58. Atlanta: Society of Biblical Literature, 2007.

———. *God in the Dock: Dialogic Tension in the Psalms of Lament*. JSOT Supplements 357. London: Sheffield Academic, 2002.

———. "Talking Back: The Perseverance of Justice in Lamentation." In *Lamentations in Ancient and Contemporary Cultural Contexts*, edited by Nancy C. Lee and Carleen Mandolfo, 47–56. SBL Symposium Series 43. Atlanta: Society of Biblical Literature, 2008.

Matthews, Victor H. *Social World of the Hebrew Prophets*. Peabody, MA: Hendrickson, 2001.

Maxey, James L. "Performance Criticism and Its Implications for Bible Translation. Part 1: Oral Performance and New Testament Studies." *The Bible Translator* 60 (2009) 37–49.

———. "Performance Criticism and Its Implications for Bible Translation. Part 2: Challenges and Experiences." *The Bible Translator* 60 (2009) 165–82.

Maxey, James, and Ernest R. Wendland, editors. *Translating Scripture for Sound and Performance*. Biblical Performance Criticism Series. Eugene, OR: Wipf & Stock, forthcoming.

McAuley, Gay. "State of the Art: Performance Studies." *SemiotiX*, (November 2007), No pages. Online: http://www.semioticon.com/semiotix/semiotix10/sem-10-05.html.

McFague, Sallie. *Super, Natural Christians: How Should We Love Nature*. Minneapolis: Fortress, 1997.

McKane, William. *A Critical and Exegetical Commentary on Jeremiah*. Vol. 1. International Critical Commentary. Edinburgh: T. & T. Clark, 1986.

Meyers, Carol L., and Eric M. Meyers. *Zechariah 9–14: A New Translation with Introduction and Commentary*. Anchor Bible 25C. New York: Doubleday, 1993.

Miller, Geoffrey D. "Intertextuality in Old Testament Research." *Currents in Biblical Research* 9 (2011) 283–309.

Miller, J. Maxwell, and John H. Hayes. *A History of Ancient Israel and Judah*. 2nd ed. Louisville: Westminster John Knox, 2006.

Miller, Patrick D. "The Theological Significance of Biblical Poetry." In *Language, Theology and the Bible: Essays in Honour of James Barr*, edited by Sam E. Balentine and John Barton, 213–30. Oxford: Clarendon, 1994.

Monaco, James. *How to Read a Film*. New York: Oxford University Press, 1977.

Mowinckel, Sigmund. *The Psalms in Israel's Worship*. Translated by D. R. Ap-Thomas. 1962. Reprint, Grand Rapids: Eerdmans, 2004.

———. *The Spirit and the Word: Prophecy and Tradition in Ancient Israel*. Edited by K. C. Hanson. Fortress Classics in Biblical Studies. Minneapolis: Fortress, 2002.

Murphy-O'Connor, J. "Qumran, Khirbet." In *ABD* 5:590–94.

Naudé, Jackie A. "חרן." In *NIDOTTE* 2:56–61.

Neusner, Jacob. *Habakkuk, Jonah, Nahum and Obadiah in Talmud and Midrash: A Source Book.* Studies in Judaism. Lanham: University Press of America, 2007.

Newsom, Carol. "The Book of Job as Polyphonic Text." *Journal for the Study of the Old Testament* 97 (2002) 87–108.

New York Times. "War in the Gulf: Commander's Briefing; Excerpts from Schwarzkopf News Conference on Gulf War." 1991. No pages. Online: http://www.nytimes.com/1991/02/28/world/war-gulf-commander-s-briefing-excerpts-schwarzkopf-conference-gulf-war.html

Niccacci, Alviero. "Analysing Biblical Hebrew Poetry." *Journal for the Study of the Old Testament* 74 (1997) 77–93.

———. "Poetic Syntax and Interpretation of Malachi." *Liber Annus* 51 (2001) 55–107.

Nichols, Aidan. *No Bloodless Myth: A Guide through Balthasar's Dramatics.* Edinburgh: T. & T. Clark, 2000.

Niditch, Susan. *Oral World and Written Word: Orality and Literacy in Ancient Israel.* Library of Ancient Israel. Louisville: Westminster John Knox, 1996.

Nissinen, Martti. *Prophets and Prophecy in the Ancient Near East.* Edited by Peter Machinist. Writings from the Ancient World 12. Atlanta: Society for Biblical Literature, 2003.

———. "What Is Prophecy? An Ancient Near Eastern Perspective." In *Inspired Speech: Prophecy in the Ancient Near East—Essays in Honor of Herbert B. Huffmon*, edited by John Kaltner and Louis Stulman, 17–37. JSOT Supplements 378. London: T. & T. Clark, 2008.

Nogalski, James. *Literary Precursors to the Book of the Twelve.* Beihefte zur Zeitschrift für die alttestamentliche Wissenschaft 217. Berlin: de Gruyter, 1993.

———. *Redactional Processes in the Book of the Twelve.* Beihefte zur Zeitschrift für die alttestamentliche Wissenschaft 218. Berlin: de Gruyter, 1993.

Nogalski, James D, and Marvin A. Sweeney, editor. *Reading and Hearing the Book of the Twelve.* SBL Symposium 15. Atlanta: Society of Biblical Literature, 2000.

O'Brien, Julia M. "From Exile to Empire: A Response." In *Approaching Yehud: New Approaches to the Study of the Persian Period*, edited by Jon L. Berquist, 209–14. SBL Semeia Studies 50. Atlanta: Society for Biblical Literature, 2007.

———. *Nahum, Habakkuk, Zephaniah, Haggai, Zachariah, Malachi.* Abingdon Old Testament Commentaries. Nashville: Abingdon, 2004.

O'Connor, Kathleen. "Lamenting Back to Life." *Interpretation* 62 (2008) 34–47.

Osipovich, David. "What Is Theatrical Performance?" *The Journal of Aesthetics and Art Criticism* 64, no. 4 (2006) 461–70.

Otto, Eckart. "Die Stellung der Wehe-Worte in der Verkündigung des Propheten Habakuk." *Zeitschrift für die alttestamentliche Wissenschaft* 89 (1977) 73–107.

Page, Hugh. "Performance as Interpretive Metaphor: The Bible as *Libretto* for Research, Translation, Preaching and Spirituality in the 21st Century—Prolegomenon." *Memphis Theological Seminary Journal* 41 (2005) 11–33.

———. "Performance as Interpretive Metaphor: The Bible as *Libretto* for Research, Translation, Preaching and Spirituality in the 21st Century—Moving from Theory to Praxis." *Memphis Theological Seminary Journal* 41 (2005) 34–56.

Park, Robert Ezra. *Race and Culture.* Glencoe: Free Press, 1950.

Patterson, Richard D. "Habakkuk." In *Habakkuk, Nahum, Zephaniah*, edited by Kenneth L. Barker, 115–272. Chicago: Moody, 1991.

———. "The Psalm of Habakkuk." *Grace Theological Journal* 8 (1987) 163–94.

Peckham, Brian. "The Vision of Habakkuk." *Catholic Biblical Quarterly* 48 (1986) 617–36.

Pelias, Ronald J. *Performance Studies: The Interpretation of Aesthetic Texts*. Dubuque: Kendall/Hunt, 1992.

Person, Raymond. "The Ancient Israelite Scribe as Performer." *Journal of Biblical Literature* 117 (1998) 601–9.

Petersen, David L. *The Prophetic Literature: An Introduction*. Louisville: Westminster John Knox, 2002.

———. *Zechariah 9–12 and Malachi: A Commentary*. Old Testament Library. Louisville: Westminster John Knox, 1995.

Pinker, Aron. "Habakkuk 2.4: An Ethical Paradigm or a Political Observation?" *JSOT* 32 (2007) 91–112.

———. "The Lord's Bow in Habakkuk 3:9a." *Biblica* 84 (2003) 417–20.

———. "Was Habakkuk Presumptuous?" *Jewish Bible Quarterly* 32 (2004) 27–34.

Polk, Timothy. *The Prophetic Persona: Jeremiah and the Language of the Self*. JSOT Supplements 32. Sheffield: JSOT Press, 1984.

Radford, Ron. *Collection Highlights: National Gallery of Australia, Canberra*. Canberra: National Gallery of Australia, 2008.

Redditt, Paul L. *Introduction to the Prophets*. Grand Rapids: Eerdmans, 2008.

Redditt, Paul L., and Aaron Schart, editors. *Thematic Threads in the Book of the Twelve*. Berlin/New York: Walter de Gruyter, 2003.

Regt, Lénart de. "Person Shifts in Prophetic Texts: Its Function and Its Rendering in Ancient and Modern Translations." In *The Elusive Prophet: The Prophet as Historical Person, Literary Character and Anonymous Artist*, edited by Johannes C. de Moor, 214–31. Oudtestamentische Studiën 45. Leiden: Brill, 2001.

Revell, E. J. "The System of the Verb in Standard Biblical Prose." *Hebrew Union College Annual* 160 (1989) 1–37.

Rhoads, David. "Performance Criticism: An Emerging Methodology in Second Testament Studies—Part 1." *Biblical Theology Bulletin* 36 (2006) 118–33.

———. "Performance Criticism: An Emerging Methodology in Second Testament Studies—Part 2." *Biblical Theology Bulletin* 36 (2006) 164–84.

Roberts, J. J. M. *Nahum, Habakkuk, and Zephaniah: A Commentary*. Old Testmanet Library. Louisville: Westminster John Knox, 1991.

Robertson, O. Palmer. *The Books of Nahum, Habakkuk, and Zephaniah*. New International Commentary on the Old Testament. Grand Rapids: Eerdmans, 1990.

Routley, Erik. *I'll Praise My Maker: A Study of the Hymns of Certain Authors Who Stand in or near the Tradition of English Calvinism 1700–1850*. London: Independent Press, 1951.

Rudolph, W. *Micha—Nahum—Habakuk—Zephanja*. Gutersloh: Mohn, 1975.

Sakenfeld, Katharine Doob. "Love (OT)." In *ABD* 4:375–81.

Sawyer, R. Keith. "Improvisation and the Creative Process: Dewey, Collingwood, and the Aesthetics of Spontaneity." *Journal of Aesthetics and Art Criticism* 58 (2000) 149–61.

Schechner, Richard. "Invasions Friendly and Unfriendly: The Dramaturgy of Direct Theater." In *Critical Theory and Performance*, edited by Janelle Reinelt and Joseph Roach, 88–106. Ann Arbor: University of Michigan Press, 1992.

———. *Performance Studies: An Introduction*. 2nd ed. New York: Routledge, 2006.

Schechner, Richard, and W. Appel. *By Means of Performance: Intercultural Studies of Theatre and Ritual.* Cambridge: Cambridge University Press, 1990.

Schoneveld, Jacobus. "Torah in the Flesh: A New Reading of the Prologue of the Gospel of John as a Contribution to a Christology without Anti-Judaism." *Immanuel* 24/25 (1990) 77–94.

Scott, James M. "A New Approach to Habakkuk 2:4–5a." *Vetus Testamentum* 35 (1985) 330–40.

Seitz, Christopher R. *Prophecy and Hermeneutics: Toward a New Introduction to the Prophets.* Grand Rapids: Baker Academic, 2007.

Seow, C. L. *A Grammar for Biblical Hebrew.* Rev. ed. Nashville: Abingdon, 1995.

Shelton, Pauline. "Making a Drama out of a Crisis? A Consideration of the Book of Job as a Drama." *Journal for the Study of the Old Testament* 83 (1999) 69–82.

Shemesh, Yael "The Elisha Stories as Saints' Legends." *The Journal of Hebrew Scriptures* Article 5 (2008). No pages. Online: http://www.arts.ualberta.ca/JHS/Articles/article_82.pdf.

Shepherd, Michael B. "Compositional Analysis of the Twelve." *Zeitschrift für die alttestamentliche Wissenschaft* 120 (2008) 184–93.

Sherwood, Yvonne. "Editorial to Prophetic Performance Art." *The Bible and Critical Theory* 2 (2006) 1.1–1.4.

———. *The Prostitute and the Prophet: Hosea's Marriage in Literary-Theoretical Perspective.* JSOT Supplements 212. Sheffield: Sheffield Academic, 1996.

Shupak, Nili. "The God from Teman and the Egyptian Sun God: A Reconsideration of Habakkuk 3:3–7." *Journal of the Ancient Near Eastern Society* 28 (2001) 97–116.

Shusterman, Richard. "Art as Dramatization." *The Journal of Aesthetics and Art Criticism* 59 (2001) 363–72.

Smith, Amy L. "Performing Marriage with a Difference: Wooing, Wedding and Bedding in *the Taming of the Shrew*." *Comparative Drama* 36 (2002/2003) 289–320.

Smith, George A. *The Book of the Twelve Prophets, Vol. 2, Zephaniah, Nahum, Habakkuk, etc.* 8th ed. London: Hodder & Stoughton, 1905.

Smith, Ralph L. *Micah—Malachi*, Word Biblical Commentary. Waco: Word Books, 1984.

Snyman, S. D. "Non-Violent Prophet and Violent God in the Book of Habakkuk." *Old Testament Essays* 16, no. 2 (2003) 422–34.

Spronk, Klaas. "Deborah, a Prophetess: The Meaning and Background of Judges 4.4–5." In *The Elusive Prophet: The Prophet as a Historical Person, Literary Character and Anonymous Artist*, edited by Johannes C. de Moor, 232–42. Oudtestamentische Studiën 45. Leiden: Brill, 2001.

Stacey, David. *Prophetic Drama in the Old Testament.* London: Epworth, 1990.

Stanislavski, Konstantin. "Intonations and Pauses." In *The Twentieth Century Performance Reader*, edited by M. Huxley and N. Witts, 386–91. London: Routledge, 2002.

Steck, Odil Hannes. *The Prophetic Books and Their Theological Witness.* Translated by James D. Nogalski. St Louis: Chalice, 2000.

Stephens, Ferris J. "The Babylonian Dragon Myth in Habakkuk 3." *Journal of Biblical Literature* 43 (1924) 290–93.

Stolz, F. "גשׂא." In *TLOT* 2:769–74.

Stordalen, T. "Dialogue and Dialogism in the Book of Job." *Scandinavian Journal of the Old Testament* 20 (2006) 18–37.

Sullivan, Lawrence E. "Sound and Senses: Toward a Hermeneutic of Performance." *History of Religions* 26 (1986) 1–33.

Sweeney, Marvin A. "Habakkuk, Book of." In *ABD* 3:1–6.

———. *The Prophetic Literature*. Nashville: Abingdon, 2005.

———. "Structure, Genre, and Intent in the Book of Habakkuk." *Vetus Testamentum* 41 (1991) 63–83.

———. *The Twelve Prophets*. Vol. 2. Berit Olam. Collegeville, MN: Liturgical, 2000.

Széles, Mária Eszenyei. *Wrath and Mercy: A Commentary on the Books of Habakkuk and Zephaniah*. International Theological Commentary. Grand Rapids: Eerdmans, 1987.

Tatu, Silviu. *The Qatal//Yiqtol (Yiqtol//Qatal) Verbal Sequence in Semitic Couplets: A Case Study in Systemic Functional Grammar with Applications on the Hebrew Psalter and Ugaritic Poetry*. Gorgias Ugaritic Studies. Piscataway, NJ: Gorgias, 2008.

Tatu, Silviu. "The Rhetorical Interpretation of the *Yiqtol//Qatal (Qatal/Yiqtol)* Verbal Sequence in Classical Hebrew Poetry and Its Research History." *Transformation* 23 (2006) 17–23.

Thomas, Kenneth J., and Margaret Orr Thomas. *Structure and Orality in 1 Peter: A Guide for Translators*. New York: United Bible Societies, 2006.

Thomas, Michael D. "The World Turned Upside-Down: Carnivalesque and Satiric Elements in Acts." *Perspectives in Religious Studies* 31 (2004) 453–65.

Thompson, Michael E. W. "Prayer, Oracle and Theophany: The Book of Habakkuk." *Tyndale Bulletin* 44 (1993) 33–53.

Tiemeyer, Lena-Sofia. "Recent Currents in Research on the Prophetic Literature." *The Expository Times* 119 (2008) 161–69.

Tomasello, Michael. *Constructing a Language*. Cambridge: Harvard University Press, 2003.

Tompson, Charles. *Wild Notes, from the Lyre of a Native Minstrel*. Facsimile reprint with an introduction by G. A. Wilkes & G. A. Turnbull. Sydney: Robert Howse, 1826.

Tsumura, David Toshio. "Janus Parallelism in Hab. iii 4." *Vetus Testamentum* 54 (1983) 124–28.

Tull, Patricia. "Intertextuality and the Hebrew Scriptures." *Currents in Research: Biblical Studies* 8 (2000) 59–90.

Turner, Victor. "Are There Universals of Performance in Myth, Ritual, and Drama?" In *By Means of Performance*, edited by Richard Schechner and W. Appel, 8–19. Cambridge: Cambridge University Press, 1990.

———. *From Ritual to Theatre*. New York: Performing Arts Journal Publications, 1982.

Vanhoozer, Kevin J. *The Drama of Doctrine: A Canonical-Linguistic Approach to Christian Theology*. Louisville: Westminster John Knox, 2005.

von Rad, G. *The Message of the Prophets*. London: SCM, 1968.

Wade, G. W. *The Book of the Prophet Habakkuk with Introduction and Notes*. London: Methuen, 1929.

Walker, Julia A. "Why Performance? Why Now? Textuality and the Rearticulation of Human Presence." *The Yale Journal of Criticism* 16 (2003) 149–75.

Ward, William Hayes. *A Critical and Exegetical Commentary on Micah, Zephaniah, Nahum, Habakkuk, Obadiah and Joel*. Edinburgh: T. & T. Clark, 1911.

Watts, John D. W. *Books of Joel, Obadiah, Jonah, Nahum, Habakkuk and Zephaniah*. Cambridge Bible Commentary. Cambridge: Cambridge University Press, 1975.

———. *Isaiah 1–33*. Word Biblical Commentary 24. Waco, TX: Word, 1985.

———. *Isaiah 34–66*. Word Biblical Commentary 25. Waco, TX: Word, 1987.

———. "Superscriptions and Incipits in the Book of the Twelve." In *Reading and Hearing the Book of the Twelve*, edited by James D. Nogalski and Marvin A. Sweeney, 110–24. Atlanta: Society of Biblical Literature, 2000.

Watts, James W. "Psalmody in Prophecy: Habakkuk 3 in Context." In *Forming Prophetic Literature: Essays on Isaiah and the Twelve in Honor of John D. W. Watts*, edited by James W. Watts and Paul R. House, 209–23. JSOT Supplements 235. Sheffield: Sheffield Academic, 1996.

Watts, James W., and Paul R. House, editors. *Forming Prophetic Literature: Essays on Isaiah and the Twelve in Honor of John D. W. Watts*. JSOT Supplements 235. Sheffield: Sheffield Academic, 1996.

Weber, Samuel. *Theatricality as Medium*. New York: Fordham University Press, 2004.

Wells, Samuel. "The Drama of Liturgy and the Liturgy of Drama." *Performance Research* 13, no. 3 (2008) 176–83.

———. *Improvisation: The Drama of Christian Ethics*. Grand Rapids: Brazos, 2005.

Wendland, Ernest R. "Performance Criticism: Assumptions, Applications, and Assessment." *Translation Information Clearinghouse Talk* 65 (2008) 1–11.

Wilks, John G. F. "The Prophet as Incompetent Dramatist." *Vetus Testamentum* 53 (2003) 530–43.

Williamson, David. "Retire? Just a Mitty Fantasy." *The Age*, June 7, 2008, 19.

Wilson, Ame. "Literary Theory and Dramaturgy: Interpreting the Dust." *Theatre Studies* 45 (2001) 4–15.

Wise, Michael, et al. *The Dead Sea Scrolls: A New Translation*. San Francisco: HarperSanFrancisco, 1996.

Wiseman, D. J. *Chronicles of Chaldean Kings (626-556 B.C.) in the British Museum*. London: British Museum, 1956.

Wollheim, Richard. *Art and Its Objects*. 2nd ed. Cambridge: Cambridge University Press, 1980.

Worthen, W. B. "Disciplines of the Text." In *The Performance Studies Reader*, edited by Henry Bial, 10–25. London/New York: Routledge, 2004.

Wright, N. T. "How Can the Bible Be Authoritative?" *Vox Evangelica* 21 (1991) 7–32.

Yadin, Yigael. *The Art of Warfare in Biblical Lands: In the Light of Archaeological Discovery*. Translated by M. Pearman. London: Weidenfeld & Nicolson, 1963.

Young, Frances *The Art of Performance: Towards a Theology of Holy Scripture*. London: Darton, Longman & Todd, 1990.

Zarilli, Phillip. "For Whom Is the King a King? Issues of Intercultural Production, Perception and Reception in a Kathikali *King Lear*." In *Critical Theory and Performance*, edited by Janelle Reinelt and Joseph Roach, 16–40. Ann Arbor: University of Michigan Press, 1992.

www.ingramcontent.com/pod-product-compliance
Lightning Source LLC
Chambersburg PA
CBHW050438240426

43661CB00055B/2430